Double Takes

Other books by Alexander Walker

The Celluloid Sacrifice
Stardom
Stanley Kubrick Directs
Hollywood/England
Rudolph Valentino

DOUBLE TAKES

NOTES AND AFTERTHOUGHTS ON THE MOVIES 1956-76
ALEXANDER WALKER

ELM TREE BOOKS   Hamish Hamilton/London

FOR PAUL DEHN and RICHARD SCHICKEL

First published in Great Britain, 1977
by Elm Tree Books Ltd
90 Great Russell Street, London WC1B 3PT

Copyright © 1977, Alexander Walker

SBN 241 89395 x

Printed in Great Britain by
Western Printing Services Ltd, Bristol

Contents

vi

Acknowledgements

The author wishes to thank the editors and proprietors of the following newspapers and periodicals in which the review sections of this book originally appeared: Mr Charles Wintour, editor, *Evening Standard*, and Sir Max Aitken, chairman, Beaverbrook Newspapers Ltd; Miss Beatrix Miller, editor, *Vogue*, and Condé Nast Publications; Mr Melvyn J. Lasky and Mr Anthony Thwaite, editors *Encounter*; Mr N. J. Reedy, editor, *The Birmingham Post*, and The Birmingham Post and Mail Ltd.

Preface

One of the principles that guided me in making the selection of pieces for this book was pleasure. I don't claim that all of them originally gave me pleasure to write; but for a variety of reasons, I experienced pleasure again when I re-read them. I hope they will have some kind of entertainment value for people reading them for the first time, or remembering them from the first, often cursory reading in the news-papers or magazines where they appeared over the last twenty years. Most of them were not written against any very pressing deadline: certainly there was nothing like the guillotine that customarily operates on, say, theatre critics who have to rush from curtain-to-column in maybe no more than an hour. But part of criticism is communication; the need to connect with a reader, to claim attention among a myriad distractions that compete for a newspaper reader's eye and mind, dictates a style that has its own exacting opportunities—and limits. This is especially true where 'an experience' is being communicated, the pleasure or pain, or, more frequently, the mixed blessings that a new film offers. Composure in such cases is a luxury, as rare in journal-ism as 'space'. Emotions have to be tuned up, prose kept running smoothly, corners cut without jeopardising judgments, in short, the need to take the reader along with one on the ride is an obligation few newspaper critics dare forget. Whatever cohesion a critic's opinions possess in such circumstances usually comes from the passion with which they're expressed. If there's any quality I'd like this book to possess it is this—passion. Passion for actors, personalities and talent; for cult figures and film trends; for occasions to celebrate and examples to deplore; for surprises, eccentricities, pop phenomena, great or unpredictable performances and rank, bad, silly ones; for directors who change the cinema and movies which reflect society; for producers in love with the medium and, yes, for those who rape it. . . . In short, passion for a job of work that, to me, has never seemed like one thanks to a limitless capacity for pleasure and punishment. Passion is a great preservative, even of the unworthy work on which it may have to be expended. I think this is probably why even bad films—correction, bad films especially—evoke a quicker sense of gratification on turning back through the files. It may not be easier to write badly of a film that deserves it than it is to write well of a film one has enjoyed—though some critics say it is—but the target area is easier to define, the aim more deadly, the satisfactions more passionately engaged. One should resist doing this too often, for the capacity for admiration and enjoyment of what's best is in the long run more important to the critic and the cinema that gives him his living. I've tried to hold a judicious balance in this anthology. But because it is a book, I have two advantages that most weekly columnists are denied: hindsight and afterthought. I haven't scrupled to make the most use of them. Generally, a critic can only do this in his year's round-up column: even then the reflections are generalised and not tied to the particular reviews that suggested them. A book is different. I don't claim that the title *Double Takes* extracts any tighter logic from the amazing variety of movies this collection contains; but it has enabled me to formulate a few tentative opinions about the changes that time, popularity, taste, conviction or personal preference—no, hang it, call it *prejudice*—have wrought in my original opinions. I see that some movies I overpraised, others I scanted; a few reviews I should like to re-write completely; the majority, though, would be printed tomorrow as they stand now and are valued for the commentaries that they offer on the way in which the cinema and ourselves were changing.

I'm well aware that the balance of the book is tilted towards the American cinema. One of the reasons for this is that the majority of movies that Anglo-Saxon critics have to deal with come from there. Moreover, I believe the Hollywood cinema is particularly rich in the elements that interest me, the links between the cinema and society. A director working in the European tradition usually tells one much more about himself, and sometimes can create a personal vision of society that goes a long way to being a metaphor for it; but the Hollywood cinema responds more quickly, more rapaciously perhaps, to the movements it senses or can exploit in the society to which its films are to be sold; so that when a public nerve is touched, or, increasingly frequently today, can be artificially stimulated, the film's reception can provide a crude but powerful clue to the collective consciousness. A critic is part of the information being fed into that consciousness—and, as I have said, far less able nowadays to withstand the competitive cries of the other media which are there for hire. This doesn't mean that he should be any the less vociferous: but it does mean that he should perceive society as much as its films, which is why the running commentary of a book like this can be useful, and also why the 'double takes' express my growing sense of unease with both films and society in the 1970s. The British cinema of the last decade, the 1960s, offers some of the most fascinating material for critic and sociologist; but as I have dealt with it at greater length in my book *Hollywood, England*, I hope I shall be pardoned for omitting reviews of certain British films of the period whose inclusion here would amount to repetition, rather than reprinting.

In looking back over all the material I have brought together, I must express my gratitude to the people who let me write it in the first place, to the editors of the newspapers and magazines which offered adequate space and (except in one case which I have noted) complete liberty to express what I felt about the most exciting art and industry this century. 'Communicate' was the only obligation laid on me: the only rule I observed was 'Please yourself'. For such living-space as these precepts provide, much thanks.

Alexander Walker, London, 1976

Ladies First

When I re-read the following half-dozen reviews, I ask myself, 'Where have all the women gone?' Women on the screen, *dominating* the screen, is one of the things that separate the films I started off reviewing from the ones I now review. Wrecking marriages, redeeming cowards, murdering husbands, saluting heroes, holding homes together, bitching other women: there seemed so much for women to do in the movies *then*. Today it's the rare experience to find a film built around a woman: when they make the running today, women do it off-screen—of which, more later. But part of the pleasure—and still a good part of the profit—of the pictures I saw professionally in the mid-1950s came from the women in them.

Even so, I was aware I'd missed the Great Matriarchal Years; for a lot of the female stars who had ruled the roost at Warners, MGM or Columbia (at least, when the men-in-charge at the studios permitted them to do so) were passing through the middle-age of their emotions, and menopausal parts were regarded as the next stage to granny's rocker. Better less work than that kind of work. So of Lana Turner, Betty Grable, Rita Hayworth, Bette Davis, Joan Crawford, Barbara Stanwyck and many another, I saw increasingly less at the Press shows and what I did see revealed women uncertain of their years, their looks or their roles now that the women-dominated audiences of the 1930s and 1940s had begun settling more comfortably into the living-room easy chair with the TV set and the studios that once sustained morale and built careers—whatever other penalties had to be paid in return—were only too anxious to cut the expensive pay-load by turning their stars loose to try their luck as freelancers. Usually, the independent producers to whom they now had to look for work lacked time, money or interest in building up a continuing career for women who were on the wrong side of the date line. So unfair, that a man's maturing looks become an endowment policy for his old-age, whereas a woman's declining ones load the insurance business against her—but there it was.

I suppose Monroe was just about the last of the female superstars to come out of the industry machine: she, fortunately, was spared the enormity of the self-destruct process that is ageing, though, God knows, one wishes she could have found some gentler way out. Elizabeth Taylor, of course, keeps on going strong, though she belongs to that group which gains public notoriety through the life they lead off-screen: they feed

3

the public appetite for themselves by the way they live that life in terms of their own screen fiction. They are a phenomenon made by the media, not by the movies alone.

It was so much simpler for Hollywood to put its faith in wooing back its declining audience in the 1950s—by 1950 only half of every 'leisure dollar' was spent on filmgoing, against 75 per cent in the 1940s—by investing in technical innovation (Cinerama, 1952; 3-D, 1952; CinemaScope, 1953). Ultimately, even this novelty lost its magnetism; and new sources of attraction had to be sought. The very pluralism of the cinema audience—so unlike the monolithic 'family group' that went to the movies in the 1930s week in, week out—came to the rescue, as the opening split in the generations revealed the seam of gold in the 'youth pictures' and in teenage idols like James Dean. And so the women were pushed still farther back from the story's centre of interest. The new 'Method' style aided and abetted the displacement of interest from female to male; since that dazzling generation of Dean, Brando, Clift and Newman were graduates of a drama school that was nominally co-ed, but in practice male chauvinist. For all that Kim Stanley or Julie Harris brought honour on their Method mentors, their graduation exercises were necessarily less impressive. The 'torn blouse school of acting' was no match for the glamour of what some still called, sceptically, 'the torn T-shirt' variety. The increasing sexuality of what the screen showed, or, at first, suggested between the lines of the still enforceable Production Code and Legion of Decency boycott threats was something the older generation of women stars weren't equipped to handle— and not just because of their age.

Hollywood which had sold the Dream back to the American people in the 1930s, by way of exhortation and consolation to the victims of the Depression, was well on the way by the mid-1950s to selling the Disaster to people whose views of society now came principally from television and their own personal experience of a breakdown that wasn't economic but psychological and social. The so-called 'woman's picture' had been *the* Problem Picture in earlier decades: now the problems were all over the lot—kids on motor-bikes, split families, drugs and blackboard-jungle violence—and women had hardly the leading role in any of them. It was a pity. As Michael Wood said in his illuminating book *America in the Movies*, referring to the great days of the screen goddesses, 'the activity of women is virtually the only intelligent activity in the movies, because men (in the stories) never have time to think'.* Even where women might have hoped to hold their own, in the best-seller novels bought for the screen which often revolved around women, or were narrated by women (or young girls), the 'denaturing' process of the screen adaptation cheated them of their printed-page pre-eminence.

The 1950s was a decade when best-sellerdom often appeared to producers like Zanuck, Jerry Wald and Preminger the way to bring new, 'controversial' themes into movies: to some extent, but only to a partial, point-begging, retrospectively issue-dodging extent, they succeeded. We have to measure them against the way such themes were treated in the next decade; by *that* standard of comparison, they look limited and self-serving, though often, in a film like *I'll Cry Tomorrow*, for example, they have a residual energy that is highly watchable. Today, they would be probably duller, since so many of the issues, like the partition of India in *Bhowani Junction*, would be benumbed by portentous self-awareness. Say what one likes about Ava Gardner dominating the screen to the exclusion of national destiny, it is at least a more enjoyable movie than the pretentious *Nine Hours to Rama* in the early 1960s.

I find that re-reading the number of reviews I wrote about the 'English School' of Hollywood actresses—Jean Simmons, Deborah Kerr, Audrey Hepburn—generated in me a feeling of slightly surprised gratification. I can't think of one equivalent talent today—I suppose Julie Andrews is about the last of the class who gained Hollywood stardom without surrendering her essential Englishness. 'Class' in another, more vulgar sense of the word was their precious attribute. It's doubtful if there's a market for it today, even if there were a way of adequately displaying it. Psychological realism has done for the well-bred stylisation what these girls carried out of school in their satchels. Only Hitchcock today wants a lady. And significantly Claire Bloom, their only natural successor, has kept the lifeline to the stage firmly in her talented grasp.

I wish I had written more about these actresses when I reviewed their films in the 1950s; but then we didn't know how women's role in the movies was going to give way to other pressures on the box-office—some of which, paradoxically,

America in the Movies, by Michael Wood, p. 65.

were going to come from women in society, a feminist counter-attack that, unfortunately, hasn't yet replaced what was reviled with anything as unique or enjoyable.

STORM OVER AVA/*Bhowani Junction*

If *Bhowani Junction* were merely a picture of India at the crucial moment before partition, when the British are pulling out, it would have some serious claim on our attention. Unfortunately, far, far more of it is about the fate of a single Anglo-Indian lady (Ava Gardner) once the British have gone, and on this score it only rates as minor melodrama. The reason for the imbalance is clear enough, in all conscience: the fate of Asia is already history, but the fate of Ava is contemporary box-office. One may believe, with Henry Ford, that history is bunk; but if so, be assured that the labour pains of India are not half as much bunk as the romance of Victoria Jones, daughter of a Hindu lady and a Welsh engine driver.

Miss Gardner, who expresses what is going on within her through her hair styles, alternately dishevelled or lacquered, dallies in short order with an Eurasian like herself (Bill Travers), with a dark-skinned Sikh—an affair ended prematurely by a rush of warning voices to the head—and with an ageing British colonel (Stewart Granger). She has a costume for every multiracial occasion—except when an unforeseen train crash catches her unsuitably clad in wispy white—and a complexion that also matches the man of the moment, thereby ensuring compatibility with filmgoers of every race or colour. Between affairs she is attacked by a British cad whom she brains, for which act she is acclaimed a 'heroine of the new India', and she is also bounced off the back of a motor-bike, abducted by the Communists and bound and gagged by the villain. In the end she settles for the colonel, who has been beastly to her all through the film—thus testifying to canny film buffs their complete and ultimate suitability.

In fairness, such a part merely requires Ava Gardner to go through the film reacting to whatever fix she is in. She has only a few positive moments when she can suggest the genuine confusion of a girl who cannot choose between a sari and a skirt. Bill Travers, on the other hand, catches the very essence of Anglo-Indian character. With his shrill petulance, his sola topee and club blazer, his adopted vocabulary of 'ruddys' and 'jollys', his assumption of an equality with the British that is never quite acknowledged in return, he is a credible inhabitant of a racial no man's land; and, as such, has pathetic truth. But the fate of such Anglo-Indians—Miss Gardner apart—is submerged in the scenes of seething humanity that director George Cukor has created on location. His shots of jammed streets and clogged railway stations are the best things in the film. You experience the blind power of Asia to inflict wounds on itself, sense that time is running out and tempers are burning short. Close-ups reveal the odd, often ironic character of the struggle to make the British quit—Gandhi's passive resisters, for instance, scrupulously equipping themselves with platform tickets before lying down on the rails in mute protest. And here there is a superb cameo of an agitator by Abraham Sofaer, bold, cunning and mercurial, who lies athwart the sleepers hugging his black brolly—for all the world like a crusader stretched in effigy with his broadsword.

But masterly as is its sense of time and place, *Bhowani Junction*'s perspective of both is fatally and indeed insultingly interrupted by the shape of Ava Gardner crowding out of the picture some of the millions east of Suez.

Birmingham Gazette, 8 October 1956

EASY COME, EASY GO/*I'll Cry Tomorrow*

Many people, I am told, regarded Billy Wilder's *The Lost Weekend* as a hilarious parlour game when they first saw it, with Ray Milland playing Hunt the Bottle. But none, I think, will mistake *I'll Cry Tomorrow* for a comedy.

Someone in the film calls it 'the story of a girl who had one drink and found she couldn't stop'. The girl was Lillian Roth and the binge lasted 16 years. Lillian, the film suggests, was goaded into stardom by her mother, and escaped from it by marrying the first man who asked her. She stumbled into a second marriage while on a bender and kept on hitting the bottle relentlessly until rescued by AA and starred on TV.

The candour with which this penthouse-to-flophouse descent is chronicled might be a mite more compelling if it contained a particle of perceptive pity and compassionate grace. We are shown Lillian blundering gawkily on stage, Lillian knocked sprawling by her sadistic second husband, Lillian lurching down Skid Row, Lillian prostrate among the hobos, Lillian in rags, mop-headed and raddled. . . . But by emphasising physical degradation in nearly every frame, the film makes her less an object of acutely personal concern than a street casualty seen remotely from the top of a bus.

7

Even the few intimate scenes between mother (Jo Van Fleet) and daughter wear the look of a private moment bathed in the public incandescence of a flashbulb. The tone is strident. The violence is counterpointed by a crude emotional barrage. Susan Hayward is reduced to howling for the bottle as quickly and flamboyantly as were Frank Sinatra and James Mason for their dope. Be sure that when critics urge the cinema to look squarely at life, we do not mean it to entertain us with sensationalised case-histories of the heroin addict, the dipsomaniac and the cortisone fiend. These records of horrific symptoms and their deceptively swift cures have little link with life, or with an earlier class of film where the subject was certainly sensational but the treatment realistic and sober.

The wonder is that a film as emotionally vulgar as *I'll Cry Tomorrow* yet contains a performance by Susan Hayward to astonish those who, like myself, rarely saw more to her than perky features and a determined chin. Brass-lunged and vibrant, she spares herself nothing. She has such drive and resilience that it would be an understatement to say that she walks off with the film: rather, she knocks it back.

Birmingham Gazette, 29 October 1956

ADMINISTERING ANGEL/*This Could Be the Night*

It is Jean Simmons' name that will bring most people to see *This Could Be the Night*. She plays a school-teacher who takes a spare-time job as secretary in a New York night-club. It is a witty, racy, pungent and moral story the film spins around her, one that illustrates the civilising influence of a college education.

In no time at all Miss Simmons has the night-club staff looking better, feeling happier. Under her guidance the proprietor takes to dieting and quieter neck-ties, his junior partner puts his bachelor flat in order, the vocalist changes her tune, the strip-tease dancer wins a cookery contest, and the trolley-boy passes his algebra exam. Plainly a *Viewer's Digest* of a film: bright, positive and containing a generous number of 'unforgettable characters'. And just that teeny-weeny bit didactic. It is unlikely to figure among the six, or even the 12 best films of the year: but here and now it is a likeable piece. Particularly because of Jean Simmons.

She reminds us that Hollywood which has—rightly—long since ceased to look to our butter-faced actors for its leading men still acknowledges that this is the only land to look to when in search of what I can call the 'head girls'. That chin-up, shoulders back look, the discipline of the crocodile line, the aplomb to plough through the most astoundingly witless dialogue as if it were the terminal hockey report and must therefore be taken seriously, the purity of character without the primness of manner, the angelic features with the hint of iron in the jaw line: these are things that nowhere grow under California's sun. On the old Hollywood studios, actresses of this type have the same effect as the commingling of innocence and education had on Damon Runyon's gangsters. They gaze on the phenomenon with simple wonderment. Then pulling out their chequebooks, they ask shakily—as if these were qualities that had been left on bequest to the nation—'Can we buy?'

Studios lucky—and rich—enough to get the services of Miss Hiller, or Miss Kerr, or Miss (Audrey) Hepburn, or Miss Simmons, behave like provident finishing schools and reserve the right roles for their wards. In general, career-girl parts are out: no stenographers, fashion models, gossip columnists or chorus beauties—all the great avenues, films teach us, of advancement in American society. Occasionally a head girl, through sheer will-power, will break bounds and startle the school by her example—like Miss Kerr in *From Here to Eternity* allowing the sea and Burt Lancaster to possess her simultaneously. But such rebels are soon back in line. The approved, the really OK roles, are the girls with vocations: school-teachers, nuns, bookshop assistants, Salvation Army lasses (commonly known as dolls), housemasters' wives, Anglo-Indian nurses, foreign princesses—though these are on the way out—any of Shaw's head girls and any of Shakespeare's, too, if Greer Garson is not immediately available. These are the lamps that Miss Simmons and Co. keep tended. All over Europe they are going out: in Hollywood studios they burn brightly still.

For years Jean Simmons has been my favourite lamp-tender. In *This Could Be the Night* all she really does is give another reading of her part in *Guys and Dolls*, without the songs and dances. But she coaxes a new warmth into her small voice: she plays the part of a Good Influence with a firmness that never allows it to turn into a goody-goody influence. Her sense of comedy is vital ballast for the soulful overtones that creep in near the end of the film. She works her wonders, so to speak, earthbound at the secretary's desk. She is an administering angel.

The Birmingham Post, 4 June 1957

I am slightly embarrassed today as I read the last paragraph in the preceding review (though I have retained the concluding phrase that the sub-editors seized on with delight as the headline). But Jean Simmons has worn well; so well in fact that 14 years later my enthusiasm for her was still like dam water, threatening to spill over and drown the review. It was odd, though, to come on a 'woman's picture' that had surfaced, like the coelocanth, in the 1970s. Even the phrase 'woman's picture' has a prehistory flavour to it, denoting, I suppose, the amount of inordinate masochism that the heroine accepts until the therapeutic value of her suffering is revealed to her and the audience. Nowadays the 'women's pictures' have toned down their sexist pitch and become the sentimentalised 'youth pictures' such as Love Story . . . but that's another story, for another place in this anthology. What happened to The Happy Ending, I don't know—but I suspect the accountants wouldn't reach for their black ink to reveal it. Anyhow, I liked it—and her—and still unrepentantly do.

AGE DIFFERENTIAL/Love in the Afternoon

Audrey Hepburn plays delightfully in Love in the Afternoon—and indeed why shouldn't she? It would be far stranger if she did not. For she has in effect been playing the same part, under different names in different films, for the past five years. Which part is this? A few weeks ago, writing of the school of English actresses who appear mainly in American films, I referred to 'head girls'. Miss Hepburn, I'm inclined to think, is the tom-boy of the form. I see her, like Iris Murdoch's heroine in Flight from the Enchanter, running away from finishing school to enter the School of Life—swinging, of course, on the common-room chandelier before she goes.

Parents are absent from her world—or, if present, they are there to be disobeyed. She is the princess in Roman Holiday who gives her advisers the slip to go sightseeing incognita on a Vespa. She is the chauffeur's daughter in Sabrina Fair who ignores her father's class-conscious scruples and sets her cap at his millionaire employer. In War and Peace she possesses the gamine wilfulness of Natasha—as well as her softer qualities. In Funny Face she is the waif in a Greenwich Village bookshop whipped off to Paris by a fashion photographer whom she then leads a dance—for is he not Fred Astaire?—through the *caves* of the Left Bank. Truant and pert, she bubbles along, sticking her oval chin impulsively out to seek love, and then accepting it with wide-eyed innocence. No, 'innocence' is hardly the right word; for in her arsenal of seduction, her chief weapon is to pretend to maturity. She flatters men, she captivates them as uncles are sometimes captivated by their nieces, for they see through the adolescent affectations to the child beneath. What they do not see, however, are the sophisticated wiles that the child doesn't scruple to use against them. Here, to my chagrin, I have to confess that an American critic has already lit on the only phrase that exactly describes Miss Hepburn's technique. It is 'like watching Red Riding Hood gobble up the wolf'.

Film after film repeats the gobbling-up process. To Audrey's 'Junior Miss' attitude is opposed the experience of an older but vulnerable man of the world: Peck, Bogart, Holden, Fonda, Astaire—and now Gary Cooper. In the light comedy of love, they are all *old* hands: mark where the stress falls. The stories they figure in—barring *War and Peace*, of course—might have been made up by Françoise Sagan in a (rare) moment when she was feeling especially gay. Take *Love in the Afternoon*.

It is set in Paris. In the spring, naturally. Its style derives from Lubitsch. A single mood permeates it—slightly fantastic, lightly satirical. I think Billy Wilder is the only director left who can do Lubitsch so well. It is about an American millionaire, an ageing Casanova played by Gary Cooper, 56, who is waiting for Mme 'X' in his suite at the Ritz when a strange girl appears with the pressing news that a M. 'X' is outside with a gun. Grateful for the warning, Cooper turns his attentions on his rescuer, but fails to learn her name (Ariane) or who she is (a music student at the Conservatoire), or what her father does (he runs a detective agency). Champagne, soft lights and his personal four-piece gipsy orchestra are of no help. So what does Casanova do? He follows the essential logic of this kind of comedy and hires Father (Maurice Chevalier) to detect his daughter's identity.

This is the shell of the film: the kernel is Ariane's attempt—drawing on Father's files where her imagination fails her—to convince the elderly *roué* that she is just as worldly as he. The literally last-minute abduction of the girl by a Casanova now head-over-heels in love is a neat QED to the affair—no more. Everyone is in perfect unison. Gary Cooper, though far from the saddle and homestead, easily adapts his laconic casual manner to the sophisticated way of life; Maurice Chevalier playing on the home ground makes the most of it; and Audrey Hepburn bubbles over with the qualities I've noted—being careful, in moments of real pathos, to remind us that bubbles sometimes burst. She plays delightfully. But then, as I've said, why shouldn't she?

The Birmingham Post, 23 September 1957

HOUSEWIFE'S CHOICE/*The Happy Ending*

The Happy Ending hasn't one. But what it does have more than makes up for the loss. In short order, it has wit, truth and acting—all brought to bear on a dilemma that could have been simply heart-sob stuff, but isn't. Why does marriage kill romance? The question is at least as old as Elinor Glyn. But it's asked against the background of a sharply observed contemporary America and the heartlessness with which the social scene is caught more than keeps the human crisis from melting into sentimentality.

Jean Simmons plays a Denver housewife, 16 years wed to the same man (John Forsythe) who starts the day by telling her to start his eggs. The crisis that begins in the flesh of every middle-ageing woman has now spread to the spirit. A smoker's cough, a trayful of breakfast pills, the bottle of vodka stashed away in the snow-boot—is this all that's left to live for? On their wedding anniversary she takes a pep pill and a one-way ticket to Nassau. And flashbacks keep her company on the journey into love and marriage in the American style. It begins with suspicions of her husband's infidelities, her own fear that her looks are letting her down. A hush-hush visit to a beauty clinic for a face-lift is followed by the flat feeling when no one back home notices. Life is lived amidst friends, but the social basis is business connections. All the guests at each anniversary party—how well the hideous occasions are described!—are not really friends, only tax-deductible clients of her husband's. Domestic rows have an uncommonly life-like spit and growl. The peep into a beauty parlour tenanted by bored wives mortifying the flesh has a misogynist bite. 'Look,' says one wispy client displaying her new bosom. 'Silicone—do you think it's dishonest?'

Jean Simmons isn't called on to get thoroughly sloshed—even the scene where she's hauled in for drunken driving and can't toe the line without a steadying arm is pathetically funny, not repulsive. So, too, is the desperate spree she gives herself in a gown shop, using a charge account to compensate for the loss of her husband's softer affections.

Her acting is faultless. She gives the unsettling feeling of a woman not on a bender, but on a continuous light tipple. She makes emotional desperation into a many-faceted thing, some of them funny, all of them true. Maybe the fact that writer-director Richard Brooks is her husband contributes to the feeling—not so common in films—of an actress knowing precisely the character's place in the script and *her* place in the character. Brooks very skilfully interweaves her past with the present escapade in Nassau where Shirley Jones appears as an old college chum whose life as a professional 'other woman' experiences its own acidly funny crisis when she meets with a marriage proposal. And an ex-pop singer who used to be called Bobby Darin turns in his sharpest-ever performance under the name Robert Darin as a hotel gigolo who used to be quite a marksman with rich women and now has trouble reloading.

The truth about the process of ageing is what binds this film together like cement, even when Michael Legrand's obtrusively lush score is trying to prise it apart like layer cake. It shows how well the Hollywood formula for entertainment can be constantly revitalised if the will is there—and, of course, the talent.

Evening Standard, 30 April 1971

In spite of the next review, I never had the 'thing' about Ingrid Bergman that others had. I found her effects forced and unsubtle when I was a child film-fan in the 1930s, though, heaven knows! by the standards of Davis and Crawford then prevailing she was *pianissima*. By the time I was writing reviews for love, not yet for money, she was in eclipse—well, to put it bluntly, she was in 'disgrace', the victim of Hollywood hypocrisy which took it out on her for shattering that carefully and expensively nurtured screen image of someone in whom romance ran strong but pure. I was unimpressed by her 'penance' in *Anastasia*, for all its clever parallel with a woman seeking to regain her identity and reputation (or perhaps *because* of this); I winced at her obvious discomfort in *The Visit*, where her director, Bernard Wicki, did little to 'protect' her in some cruelly unflattering location work. But in a comedy like *Indiscreet*, she was in secure hands: they knew the attentions she needed and saw that she got them, in spades—or, rather, to keep up with the style of it all, *en suite*.

13

Nothing has been too good for *Indiscreet*. I don't know when I last saw a romantic comedy as well provided for. Stanley Donen, who made it in England last winter, has plainly determined that only the best that money can buy shall go into it—starting with Ingrid Bergman and Cary Grant. Appropriate enough: for it is the story of two people who have everything.

Their names are Anna and Philip. She is an actress with a suite next door to Buckingham Palace; he is a diplomat and commutes between his suite and a Nato post in Paris. Together they move in the best company, dine at the Garrick Club, then on to Covent Garden, go shopping at the Leicester Galleries and, lovesick, let the Rolls-Royce follow them while they dawdle along the Embankment, just like an ordinary couple. She is the last word in style and taste: Dior, Balmain and Lanvin-Castillo have closed forces to clothe her; Dufy, Rouault and John Piper furnish her apartment; three dozen Picasso sketches flank the chimney-piece. Both of them are terribly talented. She shines in a West End hit, though mercifully we don't have to see it; he sets shrewd City heads wagging approval with a speech on hard currency, which mercifully we don't have to hear. And both are hopelessly in love. When the French Cabinet have kept him up late supping, he is prompt to telephone her and explain. He woos her with a yacht, a bracelet and a Matisse. It all goes famously. Even the man at London Airport who sees him in and out is happy at the affair: he smiles a secret, knowing smile and stamps his passport tenderly.

Indiscreet has more than good looks, is more than—as someone has remarked—'an occasion for appreciation'. It is a film to which you would not hesitate to take your architect, your jeweller, your home decorator, your dressmaker and your domestic staff. It also has wit, spirit and two exuberant artists. Cary Grant who looks made from choicest pigskin with hair that's been dunked in silver dip, behaves with engaging deftness, and a radiant if somewhat Juno-esque Bergman lets him pilot her securely through a style of comedy that may not come quite naturally to her. The direction is assured and just that bit stylised to support an affair that is built on deception. For our Philip, though a bachelor, has pretended to be married, thus keeping himself safe and letting waiting women know where they stand. Does Anna care? She does not, until she finds out the truth; and then she cares. 'How dare he make love to me', barks Miss Bergman, 'and not be a married man?'

The trap set for the bounder is sprung with juicy relish; and the passages leading up to it are the gayest in the film, with Philip all unaware of his doom throwing himself light-heartedly into an eight-some reel with Anna which, this being the film it is, they perform in the Painted Hall, Greenwich, on Diplomatic Night, with a hundred pipers an' all, an' all.

The Birmingham Post, 5 January 1958

I am afraid my teeth were set on edge by the Ingrid Bergman 'woman's picture' of the 1970s, *A Walk in the Spring Rain*, whose cuteness and ecological opportunism were wildly at odds with the menopausal genre to which it belonged. Coming out at a time when Hollywood's anxious shibboleth of movies 'for the under-30s' had been succeeded by total panic *diktat* of movies 'for the under-20s', it looked its age even more and seemed to call for the charity of parody rather than the curt dismissal I dare say it deserves. However, the notice exudes a kind of compensatory enjoyment of the film's very badness, which is not uncommon with film critics.

THE COUNTRY DIARY OF INGRID BERGMAN/*A Walk in the Spring Rain*

3 SEPTEMBER: We are going to be so happy here in our cabin in the Great Smoky Mountains. The way my husband Roger put his pipe in his mouth tonight, I know he is going to write a *good* book. And what do you think! A neighbour called Will Cade had already put hot bricks in our bed to air it. 'Do you want *me*, too?' I asked Roger. 'A brick only goes so far, Libby,' he said. Back home Roger may be a Harvard professor, but he is still the man I married.

4 SEPTEMBER: My moss-green up-country suit today. It seemed the only thing. Will Cade came round before breakfast—everyone in these parts calls him 'Weeel'. Can't get out of my mind how much he looks like Anthony Quinn. He brought us an armful of sweet-gum wood and told us he calls it 'tradin' wood'—the wood you cut in the spring to trade for the widow's favours in winter. My, this Will is *quite a man*!

5 SEPTEMBER: The gum wood made the smoke go out of our chimney all twisty. Will soon put it straight.

6 SEPTEMBER: Roger was just a little bit annoyed when Will dragged him away from his book on constitutional law to take us frog-hunting. I can never bear to see any wild thing killed, so *I* pretended that what interested me was the jug of moonshiner's hooch Will had brought along. If the Bridge Club could have seen me trying to swing that jug over my shoulder! Looked in the mirror tonight. You know, I know I *am* a grandmother, but I still have that radiant quality.

10 OCTOBER: Snow, snow, snow. . . ! 'What do you do for green vegetables this time of year?' I asked Will. 'There's cress in the branch stream, Mrs Roger,' he said. He even carried me out to it. Told Roger I would love some animals about the house, but he is deep in his book.

11 OCTOBER: Will came round with two beautiful little baby goats! The 'billy' kind—not the 'nanny', which smells.

11 DECEMBER: I have just *got* to set this down. This Will Cade and his world of animals and plants and seasons makes me tremble strangely in my tweeds. 'I can love a woman so the roof jumps clean off the house with the happiness inside,' he told me the other day. I believe he could, too! Roger read me a bit out of his book tonight, but somehow I kept seeing pictures in the fire and couldn't concentrate on constitutional amendments.

23 FEBRUARY: I am afraid Roger is becoming just a little bit of a pedant.

24 FEBRUARY: I was in the barn. Will came in. It happened. We did not do anything as vulgar as roll in the hay, but we pressed each other's hands together the way Roger and I were taught to do when we took that course at the Essalin Institute last summer so we could *experience* our marriage more truthfully. My white hands in Will's baked-clay ones, my bosom against his rough denim shirt . . . I looked at myself in the drinking trough afterwards. I was radiant!

25 FEBRUARY: The most terrible day of my life. I hardly know how to set down what happened. First, I was planting seeds when our daughter Ellen arrived from Boston. I immediately thought: 'Her marriage has broken up!' But it was worse! She is going to college! 'It's not every day that Harvard accepts a *female* law student,' she said. This means she wants me to come home and act as baby-sitter while she works for her Master's. In other words, leave my Will. . . ! Well, I refused there and then. Are only the young free to choose, to get taken by rapture, to find joy. . . ? But this isn't the worst that has happened. I was walking down the country road in my simple pink frock with the tie belt that matches the dogwood when Will's son—the one he calls 'Boy'—laid hands on me. I resisted. God knows what might not have happened had his father not appeared and knocked him down. It appears that in falling Boy sustained a brain lesion.

28 FEBRUARY: Boy was buried today. Will turned the sod himself.

I MARCH: Roger and I are returning to Harvard. His book has not turned out well and he will be glad to get back on to full pay. Will wanted me to stay. Well, I am genuinely sad for him, but these country people recover quickly. 'It passes as quickly as marshmallow in a cup of cocoa,' he used to say. It is a fine philosophy. Meanwhile Ellen has begun her law classes and I can look forward to a life of collecting our little grandson Bucky at the school gates—and to all this talk of Women's Liberation, I say 'Shute!'

Evening Standard, 3 September 1970

The next three reviews are all of films derived from best-sellers: a process that usually levels the 'best' to the condition of the 'worst', and here proved to be the case. Why this should be so, and whether it matters a damn in most cases, are topics too grave to be analysed lightly here. But as it happens, the only one about which I have any regrets is the fate of Nancy Mitford's *The Changeling*, here re-titled for the screen—and how ominously!—as *Count Your Blessings*. Not just because it is a far finer piece of writing than Sagan's *Bonjour Tristesse* (though less important as an illumination to its time and mood), but because no one today would *dare* make a movie so steeped in class snobbery, feudal privilege and all the other things that might remind filmgoers how 'disadvantaged', to use the euphemism of the Welfare State, they are compared with the folk once known and looked up to as 'their betters'. *Nostalgie de la boue* has still its commercial viability: I am afraid its anti-type, *la vie du château*, has not, unless the people who live in the *château* are portrayed as lackeys of capitalism, or, failing that, break into song. I got a certain pleasure out of seeing privilege put on the screen with total disregard for the implications: but only enough pleasure to make me regret there wasn't more.

With Sagan, I knew that the literary artifice of her three best-known novels was going to be converted into production values the moment I heard that three of the glossiest entrepreneurs in the business, Preminger, Negulesco and Litvak respectively, had got hold of them for filming. An ironic fate for one of the most 'French' of post-war writers: today, one likes to think, such works wouldn't float totally beyond the writer's capacity to influence their screen versions, though I'm not so sure.

I've included *Bonjour Tristesse* because it's the first Sagan to be filmed and what went wrong was symptomatic of what went very grievously wrong with two of the others: *A Certain Smile* and *Aimez-Vous Brahms* (re-titled as *Goodbye Again*). To this day I can still see the second film's credits, in Twentieth Century-Fox violet italic script, 'introducing' us to Miss Christine Carere against a Seine-et-Oise hamlet all poplars, cobbles and dormant anglers (not for nothing did Mr Darryl F. Zanuck spend time in France). A pert, healthy, chip of a girl, and not heard of much after her 'introduction', Miss Carere had the task of incarnating the dropsical Dominique who deserted her boy-friend for his middle-aged uncle. Rossano Brazzi (he of the splendid nostrils), Bradford Dillman (he of the campus long shanks), and Joan Fontaine (she of the pencil slim skirts and sharp smile of martyrdom) contributed their jarring accents to the international miscasting and the overdressed, deodorised adaptation.

At least Mr Litvak's production of *Goodbye Again* was more fun—and by the third time around, one had ceased to care for the book's anguished but rewarded authoress—since it so plainly relished exposing and exploiting what had been Miss Sagan's formulae: what happens when the man who is afraid of Growing Old (Ives Montand) and the woman who is afraid of Being Alone (Ingrid Bergman, a likely candidate) meet the teenager who is trying to Find Himself (Anthony Perkins). It was the sort of picture in which no one could open their hearts without first opening a dinner menu—well, at least *that* was French—and a line of *de luxe* dialogue was slipped in on every possible occasion, so that when Mr Perkins dashes from London to Paris in order to woo Miss Bergman at his mother's dinner party, he cries out to the cabby, 'Heathrow Airport, but first call at the Dorchester'.

The 1960s ended Hollywood's love affair with Sagan. An unconsummated one. But the sound of this trio of directors panting after Sagan's listless ho-humming is the characteristic one for me of a certain part of the era and of the belief that emotional heartburn, at a certain level of income, becomes not merely bearable—but box-office. By substituting sex and violence, the next decade simplified that belief still further—and verified it more frequently.

ON THE MEND/*Bonjour Tristesse*

Part of the trouble with *Bonjour Tristesse* is that it glows with good health—a quality hardly to the fore in Françoise Sagan's story of the too-close attachment between a father and his daughter. Otto Preminger has produced and directed the screen version; and I see it occasioning a few malicious smiles in the authoress's old Left Bank haunts. For this is Sagan not so much translated as traduced—opened out, smartened up, the sickliness overlaid with Riviera sun-tan.

The Sagan scene was sultry and languishing: Preminger's on the contrary has a 'race you to the water' vitality. Her characters exuded a graveyard fragrance; his are simply bursting with beans. One early moment sets the new mood and simultaneously betrays the old one: it shows Cecile and her father on tip-toe, drinking in the morning ozone. Can anyone credit that a breath of air ever penetrated the enclosed passions of the two in the book?

Briefly, this is the story of a philandering father and his daughter in her teens, who tolerates his infatuations so long as nothing comes of them. When one takes a serious turn, the girl plays a cruel trick that sends the woman to her death. It looks like a car accident: it might have been suicide. At heart, though, father and daughter know better. On they go with their round of pleasure-seeking: only now they have made their acquaintance with a new sensation—pain. *Bonjour tristesse!* Granted, it is hard to film so atmospheric a tale. At the start the director seems to be making a brave shot at it, by using black and white to express the current melancholy of the pair, then going into colour for flashbacks to the carefree life on the Riviera. Sometimes a coloured image drifts hazily over a grey one: then indeed the book's soft, wreathing torpor is caught. But Preminger cannot hold it in the longer stretches. A director versed in the tradition of decadence to which *Bonjour Tristesse* belongs—Claude Autant-Lara for choice— might have extracted the right mood of sensuous perversity. Preminger, falling far short of this requirement, lays bare what should be left implicit with the subtlety of a broom scouring away the cobwebs.

The story has an incestuous core, has it not? Right: so he sets father and daughter dropping Christian names and pecking each other's cheek *ad infinitum*. Cecile's is a bad case of infantilism, isn't it? Right: so he resorts to the Teddy bear at the bedside and shows her committing her thoughts to a nursery-schoolroom slate. If some psychological states defy this kind of crude manifestation, he pops them into her mouth—so that Jean Seberg has to recite, in her passion-less little flat American voice, such inanities as 'Part of me was happy, part of me was angry, all of me was excited' while the camera shows her neither happy, angry nor excited but making her way into the Cannes municipal casino with great circumspection. Nor are the rest of the cast of much help. David Niven, as the philandering papa, suggests only a genial English *roué*. Mylene Demongeot is one of his mistresses (sunburned and cast-off), Deborah Kerr (chic and doomed) another. Seen tantalisingly across a restaurant for a few moments only at the start is Juliette Greco, singing the title song in her smoky voice and wondering, perhaps, what she is doing in this *galère*.

All Otto Preminger's appetite for novelty to which some shock value can be attached probably impelled him to direct *Bonjour Tristesse*:

all his instinct should have warned him that these particular *fleurs du mal* were not for the likes of him to pick.

The Birmingham Post, 12 May 1958

REJECTION SLIP/*The Best of Everything*

Rona Jaffe's best-seller *The Best of Everything* was just the sort of omnium gatherum of murky private morals and dubious business ethics which a film producer might have been expected to welcome in with gently smiling jaws. Mr Jerry Wald has done so: and speaking for myself, his digestion is welcome to it. It is a cautionary tale sensationally told, in which it is presumed that every illustration of immorality is redeemable if accompanied by after-effects of varying strengths of unpleasantness.

Set in a New York firm of paperback publishers, all rubber plants and coloured veneers, where the drinking fountain is used mainly to cure hangovers, it concerns three girls in the typing pool (Hope Lange, Suzy Parker, Diane Baker) who go astray with various philanderers (Stephen Boyd, Louis Jourdan, Robert Evans) and end up sadder, wiser or just dead. The direction is in Jean Negulesco's glossiest style, without a fingerprint of character on it. It is sad to spot amidst it all the Hollywood veteran Brian Aherne, playing what Synopsis, with unconscious levity, calls 'a wolf in grey flannels'. Older filmgoers, however, may relish Joan Crawford's relatively brief role as Amanda Farrow, manuscript editress, glowering over her minions like the serpent of the Nile, and treating new authors with the same disdain. 'Sailor and virgin on island—Trash,' she pencils on one MS. Such a film invites similar brevity.

The Birmingham Post, 8 August 1959.

HONS AND SNOBS/*Count Your Blessings*

Count Your Blessings, adapted from a novel by Nancy Mitford, is a piece of whimsy about a French marquis (Rossano Brazzi) on a spot of leave in London who finds his best friend has left his position undefended, and promptly marries his *fiancée*, Deborah Kerr in ATS uniform lightly powdered by the blitz. True to his aristocratic function, which is to lead, he heads back to the wars. Grace, with feudal precedent, too, takes up her tapestry needle. Nine years and a few wars—Algeria, Indochina—later, he returns; she is just finishing stitching, and a son, Sigismund, has grown up and insists on still sleeping with Mother. 'Run along to the guest-room, dear,' says Grace to her husband, adding helpfully, 'At the end of the hall.'

After a move to the de Valhubert Paris house, occupying a commanding site next door to the Petit Palais, relations improve but rupture again after Grace takes a dim view of an old French custom of the Marquis's: paying the rent and dress bills for a friend. The family splits up, divorce begins, and Sigismund, finding himself spoiled first by Father in Paris and then by Mother in London, thwarts all efforts at reunion.

Count Your Blessings is mildly amusing and always elegant. Great thought has been put into the furnishings; and the visible result enchants. Deborah Kerr manipulates some marvellously foolish dialogue with the cool dexterity of someone officiating over afternoon tea; Rossano Brazzi is porous with charm and leaks it all over the place; Maurice Chevalier is there as the Duc de St Cloud fussing over vintage cars and other incunabulae while patching up marriages; and Master Martin Stephens as Sigismund presents what I hope is a well-simulated little horror of a pi-eyed darling. But best of all in the film—and what one feels will endear it to Miss Mitford—is its acceptance of high and gracious living as part of a natural order, complete with stooped retainers, a stout nanny to buttress aristocratic prejudices in the growing young, the English language being employed as the least ostentatious index to status, and indeed no sign of much effort being related to money-making. Love, in short, in a 'U' climate.

The Birmingham Post, 6 June 1959

Players Please

In general, the cinema isn't a place for actors. Personality is what it catches, cultivates, magnifies, multiplies—and the most constant element in star-making used to be the way that the aspirant's personality was rotated quickly and methodically, in role after role, this facet and then that, until one lucky combination caught the public's attention, amusement or affection. And on that, loyalty was built by sheer repetition, the habit of moviegoing being confirmed by the certainty that the moviegoers not only knew what they liked, but, even more, liked what they knew.

For actors, it is not a happy state; and the history of Hollywood is riddled with the frustrations of performers who were not allowed to stretch themselves, or even to *change* themselves radically, in roles where their acting reach might exceed their grasp on the public's allegiance. There are plenty of cases where the greatest actors have never become screen stars: for every Garbo who disproves this, there is an Olivier who confirms it. In general, I am happy—well, I am resigned—to settle for the metaphysics of a screen personality and, if I'm lucky, see the annealing process at work on its owner and analyse the appeal that he or she may make, from time to time, to the perceptions of the crowd. Stars used to be archetypes: today they're trace elements, usually aids to diagnosing what ails society.

But all of this means that the *acting* in films tends to get summarised in a sentence or two of the review, usually at a tangent to the main theme or opinion. It worries me, this neglect, to which I plead as guilty as anyone, except that in two books, *The Celluloid Sacrifice* and *Stardom*, I've tried to make amends by describing personality and performance in ways that I hope would suggest the mechanics and metaphysics of both if the films that contained them were to be lost—which in some notorious cases has actually happened.

But journalism's constraints encourage the art of impression, not analysis. What I hope the reviews that follow will indicate is the sheer pleasure of that rare thing, a screen performance. If there's any common element, it's surprise—the unpredictable. The sensation of not knowing how, from scene to scene, from look to look, a player will perform. That's rare in movies: in most cases I'm sure we could all forecast fairly accurately, the second that credits have faded, where the predestinate lines of the playing will take us.

Brando, for me, will always be the pre-eminent male

performer just because, good or bad, he will always astonish me. I could have nominated half-a-dozen other roles where he generates the sense of risk-taking inseparable from the great explorers of stage-craft and self-knowledge, but I have included his performance in *Reflections in a Golden Eye* for the chance it gives to add a few notes on John Huston. Another reason is, when I think of the film I *hear* Brando as well as see him. He begins with the voice, I'm told, when elaborating a character—just as Orson Welles is supposed to begin with the nose—and it's an education to go back over Brando's films and just listen to his vocal variety. There's hardly another male film actor, except Olivier, who uses his voice to insert his interpretation of the role into the film. Even Brando at his most capricious, like the foppish high-falutin' diction he bizarrely adopted for Mr Christian in *Mutiny on the Bounty*, reminds us of how meagre the use is that most actors make of their voices, though they work in the medium of 'the Talkies'. Sometimes Brando's vocal 'models' assert themselves, proving how fine his mynah-bird's gift for mimicry must be. If one closes one's eyes to *Reflections in a Golden Eye*, it is Tennessee Williams speaking; in *Queimada!* it is Sir Alec Guinness. Such undertones don't matter. Despite everything self-indulgent and self-destructive about the man, I shall always be grateful to Brando for renewing in me the delight at the supremacy of the player.

As I glance through this batch of reviews, one other dread thought occurs to me. Except for *The Prime of Miss Jean Brodie*, not one of the films made what one could call 'money', and most of them hardly broke even. It must make one wonder what the cinema audience goes for. I am glad I don't have to think of this too often. I please myself—why else be a critic?

OBJET DE VERTU/*Billy Budd*

The hardest kind of character to play is one who is absolutely without a single bad quality. Terence Stamp, who played the devilish schoolboy in *Term of Trial*, has had this horrendous task set him in what was actually his first film—*Billy Budd*. And it is not just his blinding good looks that get him through it and make his acting of the angelically tempered young sailor in Nelson's navy one of this or any year's most masterly debuts.

Billy Budd is a sea story one can rightly call unearthly. At one level, it is a totally absorbing account of mutiny and court-martial aboard a man o' war: the story of a boy hanged for murder—hanged in the name of justice, but actually done to death as a necessity of the legal codebook of ship's discipline. But below the story's Plimsoll Line, it is about the consuming need that Evil always feels to destroy God whenever the two meet.

Billy is goodness personified. When first we see him in the resonantly prophetic opening of the film which Peter Ustinov directs, produces, co-scripts and acts in, he is hanging like an Eiger climber in a merchant ship's rigging. A perch for only those with sure feet and free souls. He is the sailor nearest the angels, and so handsome he could be mistaken for one. But on his lips is an ominous shanty about a hanging; and soon he is being plucked down out of his element and pressed into service aboard a warship captained by Ustinov. Now watch Stamp subtly making Billy's sweetness attractive. He effectively puts on the frankest accent in England—a West Country burr. His eyes blink like a soulful calf's—but beware, his arm packs a bullock's kick. Great gentleness goes with great strength. His simplicity adroitly laps against simple-mindedness. When the enlistment officer (Paul Rogers) asks him what he is, this Bristol foundling answers, 'A bastard . . .' He is guileless—and the crew love him for it.

But Billy has one defect: a speech impediment that, when agitated, renders him speechless. And it is this that destroys him. He is accused of inciting the restless crew to mutiny by the satanic petty-officer Claggart (Robert Ryan), who hates his goodness the way that a less metaphorical figure of evil would hate his guts. Struck dumb by shock, Billy answers his accuser with a fatal blow. By all the justice in heaven, he is innocent. But by all the laws of King George's navy, he is guilty and must hang. The summary court-martial draws one near to tears and does in fact draw tears from Ustinov, whose hitherto slightly over-calculated performance—the effect of keeping an eye on so many of his own talents?—now throbs into heartfelt life. What makes the tragedy of Billy Budd so unbearable is the knowledge hammering away inside each officer's brain that it need not happen at all. They love Billy as dearly as the crew: by one word, one scratch of the quill, they could free him.

Ustinov rounds out this impressive illustration of the law's inhumanity with a hanging scene that shocks one utterly, from the noose dancing its grisly come-hither, to the noise of Billy's buckled shoe clattering pathetically down on the deck boards. The film has many novel touches—like the spoken credit titles, with each actor announcing the character he plays as Robert Krasker's helicopter-borne camera looks down on the sailing ship and the voices multiply spectrally in her shrouds. Among an excellent crew played by Ronald Lewis, John Neville, David McCallum, and Lee Montague, I shall only single out Hollywood's veteran Melvyn Douglas as the vessel's most ancient mariner. But first and last, it is Terence Stamp's film. He has achieved the near impossible, and done it all on the white notes of acting talent, by making a symbol that was virtually unactable into a character that is human and memorable.

Evening Standard, 20 September 1962

GRANDMOTHER COURAGE/*The Whisperers*

Her age, 79, is all Edith Evans has in common with a character that she and her writer-director Bryan Forbes have created together; but their partnership is so unified that to ask where direction leaves off and acting begins is as futile as asking which part of the air we breathe is oxygen and which nitrogen.

Mrs Ross, the old lady who is almost killed in *The Whisperers* by the good intentions of the world, has a 'dot and carry one' hobble, ears like radar dishes that pick up imagined whispers in her cluttered flat, and a nose like a fixed bayonet for challenging strangers. She is poor, but not pitiable. She fills her day with enough self-busying eccentricities to make the Queen of England footsore. With unsentimentalised sympathy, with music by John Barry that plucks pathos out of the sooty air, with Gerry Turpin's photography that falls like North Country light on the end of a life, benign but clear-toned, the film admits us like invisible visitors to make Mrs Ross's acquaintance. We watch her paying a routine call on the tolerant police, to report her 'voices', drawing her National Assistance dole, cannily putting in for a new pair of shoes ('nicely styled, but not too racy'), assisting at a Salvation Army sing-song that is like a scene by Hogarth—but Hogarth tempered by mercy. Dame Edith invites our chuckles, and cunningly fends off premature sentiment, by giving the old woman a wintry haughtiness and the airs and graces that go with gentle birth and expectations of wealth—all fantasies hanging on from her days 'in service'.

Ironically, it is when one fantasy comes true—her petty crook of a son (Ronald Fraser) stashes a parcel of stolen notes in Mummy's flat and she finds it—that her life is undermined by a cruel subsidence. An avaricious acquaintance (Avis Bunnage) hijacks her for the loot, and very nearly kills her as well. In hospital they strip off her insulating illusions in the name of therapy. They trace her fly-boy husband (Eric Portman in an impeccably cagey performance, husky with kow-towing insincerity towards authority, glinting with every fast-dodge opportunity) and re-unite the two mismated people so that one can 'support' the other. Finally they spring-clean her flat and when she opens the door it is like a rehabilitation centre, not a home. The world's wickedness, says the film, is not nearly as fatal as the world's charity.

The Whisperers confirms Bryan Forbes as among the country's most mature, sensitive filmmakers. His only 'showy' effect will disquiet some, but comes off perfectly for me: a chandelier remembered from some grand old house she served in floats into Mrs Ross's drugged mind like a star galaxy and finds a sinister echo in the glittering folds of an oxygen tent. Forbes's one discursive passage, when Portman gets mixed up with crooked bookies, is so entertaining that I pardon the time it takes us away from Edith Evans. His cast fit flush into the story with such generous self-effacement that it seems almost a shame to single out for mention Nanette Newman as a shrewish wife, Gerald Sim as the soul of charity and Kenneth Griffith as a nervy health visitor. But ultimately it is Edith Evans' film and in a hundred strokes—none more marvellously intuitive than the crying-laughing fit of disbelief when she finds the stolen money—she proves that in the last lap of her career she has reached her peak.

Evening Standard, 24 August 1967

OUT OF UNIFORM/*Reflections in a Golden Eye*

Brando and Rod Steiger are almost the only American actors I value for their unpredictability. I go to their films never knowing what to expect: how they will play the part, or what new inches it will add to their stature. Neither seems to care a damn whether the part will add to or take away from his box-office popularity. They sink themselves, sometimes unrecognisably, into the roles—thus throwing away the star's strongest (sometimes only) asset, which is the repetition of a recognisable likeness, an expected personality. They bring a dazzling technical detail to their playing, yet seem to reach the truth of the part by underground means—by intuition. I'd dearly love to be able to compare their two new films in the same column—for in *Reflections in a Golden Eye* and *The Sergeant* both play homosexuals, repressed by the cruelly conformist pressures of Regular Army life. But Steiger's performance I'll have to wait for: Brando's I can salute this week.

His is the only performance in a hothouse of a film that wouldn't be shrivelled up by the cold blast of realism. The hothouse is Carson McCuller's novel, which is set, geographically, in the doldrums of a post-war Army camp in Georgia, but also in a literary latitude of perverse artificiality where only the most exotic types of human abnormality are deemed worth cultivation.

Julie Harris is an officer's wife whose bad experience with a baby has made her amputate her nipples—'With gardening shears,' someone insists, as if kitchen scissors would somehow have legitimised the business. She's mothered by a fey Filippino houseboy (Zorro David) who chatters tweely in French and wears shirts cut out of his mistress's spare dress lengths. Her husband (Brian Keith) is all weary tenderness, but takes his own comfort with a brother officer's wife—Elizabeth Taylor. Dieting seems to have given Miss Taylor's cheeks back their seductive hollows. Her hair styles (by the ever-faithful Alexandre) look a bit chic for a backwoods Army base, especially the confection with the pearl caught up in the front wave, but she plays the part with the right dash and determination of an oversexed woman who's not getting what she demands from her husband—Marlon Brando.

Brando has deliberately put on weight for the part. The effect is of a man whose secret kink is locked deep inside a heavyweight hulk that at times is immobilised by the self-knowledge it bears. His face is tight as a balloon skin—tensile with inner trauma. He fidgets over details in a way that signifies the dammed-up sex drive of a man who lives in loneliness with himself amidst the fraternisation of Army life.

The film as a whole is coarser—and John Huston's direction lazier—than Brando's own subtle performance. Surely it must be only for the hicks in the audience that he's seen poring tenderly over a postcard of a male nude Greek statue. But some scenes go through to his private agony like armour-piercing shells. The moment his wife strips nude to taunt him and turns him apoplectic with impotence; the moment he rides her favourite horse with vengeful mastery until it throws him, and leaves him crying with vexation. Especially the moment he lays eyes on an Army private (Robert Foster) who's in the habit of riding naked, and Brando's self-discipline crumbles before his need for the other man's affection. From then on, the film is a study of emotional breakdown, climaxed by jealous murder.

In catching the pain of such a condition, but avoiding the laughs it could expose him to, Brando takes more risks than ever before. He even shows us himself making a piteous scoop into his wife's cold-cream jar, like a shy girl unsure of her looks. But his boldest moment is the speech he makes justifying the moral right to be a square peg. He makes it almost to himself, in an extraordinary tone of voice—dreamy but high-pitched, mingling pride and envy. The sense of his words is sometimes muffled by the thickness of his accent—but the plea is pitched beyond our misunderstanding. Here is a great actor, provided with every gift except one—finding a film really worthy of him.

Evening Standard, 18 April 1968

John Huston presents a problem that possibly only his own memoirs—should he get round to writing them—will solve satisfactorily. How come that a man of such talents should be no longer in the forefront of the creative fray?

The uncharitable thought occurs to me that for some American directors, the 1950s should have never ended. Huston is one of them. His Hemingway-like characteristics—his preferred themes of the 'loner', of group loyalty and individual treachery—appear *passé* in the cynical 1960s, the anarchic 1970s. His painterly eye for colour and composition (*Moulin Rouge*, *Moby Dick*, even *Reflections in a Golden Eye* which the producing company unforgivably robbed of its impressionist tints before its general release) no longer distances him from his peers in these days of superlatively imaginative colour photography. Trying to re-establish himself, he has made all the 'right' subjects: spoof thriller (*List of Adrian Messenger*), picaresque period-place (*Sinful Davey*), 'youth' movie (*A Walk with Love and Death*), spy melodrama (*The Kremlin Letter*). All competent, all undistinguished. Even his 'maverick' reputation for being at odds with the 'front office' is largely an obsolete factor in the respect, if not renown, now accorded him, since the 'front office' has given way to the 'independent producer'. And his *macho* temperament—somewhat to his credit, this—has proved no match for the bloodier excesses of Aldrich, Peckinpah or Leone.

Someone says '*Fat City*?' Certainly that 1972 movie was his best for a decade: the first, perhaps significantly, he has made in America since *The Misfits*, in 1961. My main reproach, then

31

and now, is that it felt as if it might have been made even ten years before *that*. Its theme about two boxers was a throwback to the down-beat movies about 'making it' of the late 1940s and early 1950s. Its nice touch was its modesty: Huston didn't force anything. He looked mellowly on the run-down life-style of a town where the Depression smell still hangs in the air and poor whites hoe a row in the fruit fields beside chattery blacks. Young Huston used to be a pro boxer himself thereabouts, and old Huston's eyes sparkle sharply over the details of gym and ring. It's a homecoming of a kind—but to what? To an America where kids still try to 'make it' and Fat City is the worshipped capital of success. I don't see any relevance to a single sign, sound or social issue of 1970s America. It is as if Huston had come home in a sealed train and seen nothing en route of how the land has changed.

Just before he moved out of his impressive home in the West of Ireland, I visited him with a television team and gained a disturbing impression of the splendid isolation he created around himself. He treated us all with impeccable yet distancing courtesy: the Great White Father trading beads of courtly geniality with us respectful Indians. He 'performed' for the cameras as if to the manor born—and what a manor it was, forming the backdrop. A former abbey, with a granite 'Big House' grafted elegantly on to it, Huston had filled it with *objets d'art* that all recalled the movies he had shot around the world. Beyond the moat, the fountain, and the huge stone lions were rooms that held his collection of Impressionists, original posters by Lautrec, a medieval wooden Christ astride a donkey, Indian jade deities, African sculptures, heads from New Guinea, six-foot high candles and silk screens from Japan, Spanish Colonial chairs, a bed which belonged to Napoleon, a myriad pieces of Inca and Aztec handiwork, and everywhere so much gleam of gold that it looked as if it wasn't the Galway Blazers that the host followed, but the Royal Hunt of the Sun. Such movie mementoes as 'Oscars' and scripts were tucked away, invisible, in a dusty remove room downstairs. The effect upstairs was of a well-ordered treasure house into which the living Pharaoh would ultimately retire himself. Huston had arranged his own pyramid: an impression that was oddly, almost risibly confirmed when Gladys Hill, his long-time friend and skilled collaborator, was recording her 'piece' for the TV camera and remarked in an aside that Huston's love of antiquity led him to stay at the Teatro Marcello whenever in Rome. For other folk, a hotel: for him, a national monument.

The feeling I took away with me was one of awe and dis-enchantment—of a man who has used his films to construct his life-style. His passions have attached themselves to *things*—rare, beautiful and precious things, but things that are impedi-menta to the creative will-power. The temptation of playing roles—to which he has unwisely yielded in well-rewarded but sub-standard films directed by other people—had found its apotheosis in playing The Role. The saddest thing in the world is seeing an erstwhile iconoclast set himself up in his own temple.

WEEKEND PASS/*The Sergeant*

The eyes are like stones in a dumpling face. The belly overhangs the soldier's belt. The head tilts on one side, monitoring the world with a squinting stare. The exterior looks battle-hardened—and it is. The man is a total product of the army whose master-sergeant's stripes he wears.

Rod Steiger giving a character-study as painfully deep and pitiable as the one in *The Sergeant* makes us appreciate what unsparing rigours he goes through in each performance. I think this is one of his best. It is certainly the definitive portrait of the repressed homosexual whose condition is aggravated by the all-male society of army life and the loneliness that gradually breaks down his self-discipline. Directed by a new name, John Flynn, and set in the muted colours of provincial France in winter-time, it shows how Steiger smartens up a slack supply unit and is inexorably drawn into a too-close relationship with a coltish young private (John Phillip Law). What starts as fatherly concern for the boy turns into an oppressive buddy-buddiness that makes the sergeant string along with the boy and his girlfriend (Ludmilla Mikael) and is then triggered into tragedy when the older man's need for love compels him to make a pass at the younger one.

It is really a one-man film. Steiger's performance sometimes seems to burst out of the screen, the way he bursts out of his uniform. But his insights into the character—like his disgust for women, which makes the sergeant trap the private into taking the girl to a demi-brothel—give it detail and subtlety. It is not to be missed.

Evening Standard, 20 February 1969

The most refreshing thing about *The Prime of Miss Jean Brodie* is that the people in it are acting. Well you ask, why not? Isn't this what actors are paid to do? Yes, but so seldom on the screen these days are they given the chance to do it. In the 'new-style' movies, filled with jump cuts, flick-of-the-eye flashbacks, slow-motion and theme-song overlay, the stars' performances often look as if they had come out of a vegetable shredder and then been further obscured under the top-dressing of commercially applied 'style'. Lost, too, is that wonderfully refreshing sense of seeing characters created and kept alive in front of your eyes.

This year's Royal Performance Film may be considered orthodox—all right, then, *old-fashioned!*—in its avoidance of everything but the skill of the cast to tell a story and keep us absorbed by the drama, irony and humour. But what pleasure this is to watch—what sheer entertainment value it offers!

Take Maggie Smith. Her playing of Miss Brodie, the Edinburgh teacher with the power of good and evil, is a bewitching spectacle. Not just on the surface, either. She has absorbed Miss Brodie's personality through her very skin pores. From the moment you see her cycling to school, you know from her imperious traffic signal that here is a woman with a predestinate sense of where she is going. A woman as intolerant of others as she is sure of her own inspired behaviour—as likely to be the cause of a nasty accident as she is the custodian of impressionable children. Miss Brodie is a dangerous romantic. In the age of the dictators—Hitler, Mussolini, Franco—she is a bit that way herself. She reveres strong men of action, without asking where their action is leading the people. Her history lessons have a habit of turning into romantic reveries about Hugh, her lover killed in Flanders—and in all probability a dull chap. She sleeps with the bashful bachelor music teacher (Gordon Jackson) and infatuates the impetuous married art teacher (Robert Stephens), but won't commit herself to either, because that would spoil her romantic vision. She keeps herself for her girls, the Brodie Set led by Sandy (Pamela Franklin). And she talks of being in her 'prime' as if it were not a condition of age, but a kind of divinity. Ultimately, she requires a romantic sacrifice from her gym-tunicked disciples—and like many a Messiah, she meets her Judas.

Maggie Smith physically projects this enigmatic woman without dispersing her strange spell. Her long, slim body stalks along with the certainty that her halo is in place. Her hands forever move as if to the strains of some music only she can hear. Her voice is mesmerising: a Scottish sing-song, insinuating, smug and insolent, yet resonant with sex appeal. The Pre-Raphaelite tones of her dresses—cherry, emerald, peacock blue—strike the right note of perverseness in grey Edinburgh. Even her complexion has the cold-cream vanity that sets her apart in the soap-and-water conformity of the staff-room. I measure her against Vanessa Redgrave's stage Brodie—and find Maggie Smith superior.

But running her close for applause in director Ronald Neame's film is Celia Johnson as the shy, old-maidish headmistress. For all of us who know how Miss Johnson excels in showing the warm side of English womanhood, this purse-lipped, starchy pedagogue with the vindictive glance is a revelation. Pamela Franklin skilfully grows from giggling schoolgirl filled with sniggering apprehension of sex—to hear 'saax-ual interrr-courrrse' uttered in a Scots accent is practically aphrodisiac—into a precociously perceptive adolescent. I can't deny that by opting for straight story-telling techniques, the film fatally sacrifices the novel's curious echoes and fatalism—the sense of shifting back and forth in time and anticipating Miss Brodie's comeuppance even while she is celebrating her prime. But what one loses in prophetic ironies, one more than gains in impeccable performances. Prime, Miss Smith, just prime.

Evening Standard, 27 February 1969

BLIND SPOT/*Laughter in the Dark*

Though it comes from a novel by Nabokov, Tony Richardson's new film sounds like a painting by Hogarth. *Laughter in the Dark* has the Englishness and heartlessness of that 18th-century delineator of man's follies and where they lead him. It could be subtitled, 'The Ruin of a Man of Taste'. Sir Edward Moor (Nicol Williamson) would be an ornament to Bond Street. He shines resplendently in the art dealer's Establishment. His little finger lifts the bidding by tens of thousands at Christie's and Sotheby's. On the telly, he is the nation's guide to good taste and art treasures. Wealth, influence, possessions, the town house and the country home: it is all beautifully English even down to the wife (Sian Phillips) whose stock answer to the night-time query of 'Shall I come in with you, dear?' is 'It's late, darling.'

With sure, fluent strokes Tony Richardson, his scriptwriter Edward Bond, art director Julia Trevelyan Oman and set dresser Ian Whittaker sketch in this secure, enviable life—then destroy it utterly. For Sir Edward's only error of taste is the girl he has chosen for a mistress. She is a cinema usherette. He is obsessed by her, and as the laughter in the dark explodes around him at some comedy on the screen, the scene is set for the tragedy of a man who falls victim to his irrational impulses—and then is victimised by a very cruel, rational conspiracy. For the girl (Anna Karina) is a taker and, in secret partnership with a shady young art dealer (Jean-Claude Drouot), she sets out to take Sir Edward for all the money in the bank. Blinded by love, he lets home, family, reputation break into pieces while he obeys this predatory pair's plans without realising that they are laughing at him behind his back. Then a car accident—and now love really is blind. As Williamson realises he has lost his sight—one of the most horrifying moments I have witnessed—his mistress cries affectionately, 'And now I'm happy because you really need me.'

The rest of the plot is set in the blinding sunlight of the Riviera— Dick Bush's photography perfectly suits the psychological climate as well as the meterological one—and centres on the bizarre *ménage-à-trois* in which the blind man has to substitute an ear for an eye to know that his mistress is feeding her lover at the same table, sleeping with him in the next room, making love with him just a foot away.

Judged by reason and commonsense, and by how we think we can control our own passions, it is an improbable story. But I would never be bold enough to scoff at the unlikelihood of an art connoisseur falling for a cinema usherette. It is in the nature of infatuation to send the victim off at a tangent to normal life. And Nicol Williamson's performance makes it plausible as he moves flawlessly through the stages of the embarrassing first encounter, the alarm of having to cope with the sudden return of his wife and family from holiday while his mistress lies stripped in the bedroom, the pain of having her inflict her own ghastly taste on his home, and then the Hogarthian descent into rashness, folly and ultimate madness. The horrendous shriek he emits on discovering the truth about how he has been gulled is ripped from the very innards of his gut—and is harrowing indeed.

Evening Standard, 28 August 1969

TRIBAL WARS/*The Reckoning*

Nicol Williamson is our only screen heavyweight. He turns the scales of drama to a mark that would daunt any actor less well equipped than he is to make every pound and ounce count in characterisation. He stays on his feet till the last round. And the contests he goes in for are physically gruelling, morally self-destructive. He excels at playing contemporary man in the grip of obsession. Guilt obsessed his solicitor's conscience in *Inadmissible Evidence*, infatuation his blind lover in *Laughter in the Dark*. Now in *The Reckoning* it's the power drive that takes over the soul and destroys him inwardly while appearing to reward him outwardly. It's the story of the struggle between who a man is and what a man wants—between his origins and his ambitions.

Williamson plays a Liverpool boy from the back streets who's got on fast in a big London business and raised himself on the bodies he's done in till he's one floor below the boss—as he coolly reminds the boss. He cuts himself into the film from the opening seconds—the finger-snapping executive, swallowing aspirins on the run, doing the dirty work in boardroom vendettas. His business aggression is manifested even in the morning rush-hour, in some disturbing, nervy, driving sequences. But the impatient foot on the accelerator also shows the suicidal reality of the success story. He's in the act of knifing yet another rival when news arrives that his father is dying. And the old man's death summons him back to his roots in Liverpool amid the neat decencies of a working-class household and the haunting fantasies of a father who lived his life as an Irish romantic and used to taunt the English with rebel ballads. The prodigal's conscience is touched.

Something deeper responds when he learns the old man's death was no accident and Irish tribal law expects him to take revenge on the pimply yob who killed him. Williamson lets filial piety push him into an act of violence that differs only in bloody directness from the mayhem going on in the economics of big business. The parallel is persuasively suggested by John McGrath's well-honed screenplay—and by Jack Gold's direction that plucks depth and feeling from a man's return to his birthplace. The Merseyside scene has a physical contact with life personified by Rachel Roberts as a randy housewife with poker-work eyebrows and by the beery ambience of Bingo, pubs and wrestling that Ronald Shedlo's detailed but unfussy production has re-created entirely in the film studio. The story's 'Power Game' side is socked across too stridently—but entertainingly all the same in the playing of Paul Rogers as a chicken-hearted executive and Douglas Wilmer as a tiger-clawed one.

But it's Williamson whose massive physicality of performance embodies the theme of moral sell-out most effectively. He opens scenes inwardly like the swing-doors of a bar-room. His own rebellion breaks loose at a cocktail party when he summons up the least corrupted part of him—the Irish song his father sang—and rubs the words into the well-groomed faces before laying his company director out on the pile carpet with an uppercut. The film itself does not sell out with any last-minute repentance. Its ending is breathtakingly cynical. It would be unpardonably immoral, too, if Williamson hadn't cracked the character open for our inspection and let us see, inside the shell, the soft meat of piteous self-loathing. He's made himself what he is— the reckoning is still to come.

Evening Standard, 15 January 1970

Kenneth Tynan, a braver soul than I, has actually seen Nicol Williamson up close, in the flesh, and lived to bring back the story of the actor's solo performance before President Nixon at the White House in 1970.* I have only once confronted Williamson, when Sam Spiegel, who was standing conversing by my side, abruptly edged away from it as the actor approached us both, jocularly swinging a champagne bottle. I recount this to show I am as impressed with Williamson off screen as on it: and of few actors can a critic say that truthfully.

Tynan quotes Jonathan Miller, 'I enjoy sacred monsters, but preferably in zoos', and that description of the uncomfortableness that Williamson sows around him, hoofs pawing and nostrils flared to catch the scent of blood on the wind, is what gives me a sense of excitement and even peril. Williamson on the screen doesn't need the stamina that sustains him on his vast stage marathons and I suppose that's why in some of his movies there is a fractional feeling of impatience with his fellow actors, as if he'd saved his energy for the heavyweight championship and found he'd climbed through the ropes of a welterweight contest. In the Hollywood cinema he would have been a natural *genre* ruler: one of those transcendental character actors, like Marvin, Scott, or Bronson, who have become stars by the secular rather than the divine power they radiate— except that Williamson's intelligence as well as his intransigence might have been a bar to his advancement. Where the British cinema is concerned, at least at present, there is the greater bar that one can't advance across a void. But even when

The Sound of Two Hands Clapping, by Kenneth Tynan, pp. 13–57.

we *were* turning out British movies, we never accommodated ourselves to Nicol Williamson—and why the hell, he no doubt asked himself, should *he* do so to us? The loss has been ours, as I later pointed out in a piece in *Vogue*.

STANLEY KOWALSKI, WHERE ARE YOU?

A researcher from one of the international news magazines telephoned me the other day with a labour-saving query. (Her labour, not mine.) Did I, she asked, know of any English film actors who had particularly deep voices? Before I balanced myself for the plunge into deep thought to come up with the answer, I quipped, 'Most English film actors I know sound as if their voices haven't yet broken.' And then I realised this *was* the answer.

The besetting sin of our national cinema, and, in large part, our stage, too, is the way its young leading men are encouraged to stay suspended in handsome adolescence until well into the advanced years of middle-age—veritable Peter Pans of the profession. We have the most resourceful reservoir of acting talent in the Western world, as the American producers who keep coming here to siphon it off keep telling me. But one species that our films and plays, our acting schools and television studios, do not encourage to grow—or at least *grow up*— is the aggressively male star. The kind who can show the wear and tear of the world on his face, never mind his T-shirt, who can carry a charge of muscular manhood around with him that lends an interest to even his most perfunctory performance. We don't breed *machismo* kids like this: we just breed kids. Perhaps it is because ours isn't a society that puts a premium on proving yourself a man and doing so preferably by virile suffering, by both accepting pain and doling it out, the way that Marlon and Clint and Steve and Jon and Jack and Burt can all do, in the saddle, behind the wheel, beneath the trench-coat, down the mean street, up the Eiger. So different from the persona of our own stars like Terence and Roger and Michael and Malcolm and David and James (Fox, that was), all of them sensitive actors, all of them fine performers in the right role. But their physicality—the only word for it, regrettably—is a mite on the lightweight side, and charm today, I'm afraid, no longer tips the scales when what is needed is the state of mind of the hard man, a certain contemporary 'cool', an un-feelingness that distinguishes the 'man in charge'.

Whatever other revolution they have worked in the theatre, the last generation of English playwrights have not provided roles for the kind of actors who have been annealed in the masochistic self-scrutiny that Lee Strasberg's pupils submitted to as they worked their way through the roustabout studs, bruised siblings and butch gigolos of Inge and Williams. Pinter, Orton, Anthony Shaffer and Stoppard are writers whose sense of theatre feeds on party games, cerebral masquerades, rather than robust romanticism; and their interpreters on the stage are encouraged to cover up the first intimation of violence with at least seven veils of ambiguity, which a Stanley Kowalski would have shredded as brutishly as he did Blanche's pretensions. English actors let their power go to their heads; Americans, to put it vulgarly, to their balls.

Life has taken a hand, too. I always smile when I think of Ian Fleming's ultra-civilised little comment, in writing to a friend, when he heard that at long last they had found an actor to play James Bond. 'Saltzman thinks he has found an absolute corker,' Fleming wrote, as his biographer John Pearson recorded it, 'a 30-year-old Shakespearean actor, ex-Naval boxing champion, etc., etc., and even, he says, intelligent.' Now indeed Sean Connery is intelligent; he has been a Shakespearean actor; but the side that showed 007 up to such world-wide advantage was the one represented by the 'ex-Navy boxing champion', not to mention the 'etc., etc.' It is not just a matter of keeping in trim, which I am sure the gym classes can do at RADA, but of being interestingly marked by the world in a variety of outside experiences before you turn actor. Where the British star has modelled himself on Peter Pan, the American one has been a Jack London. Garage mechanic, lifeguard, hash slinger, ski teacher, lumberjack, bar tender, dock labourer, carnival barker, bookie's runner, even reform-school recidivist: such are some of the free-wheeling vocations that the top American male stars filled temporarily before matriculating to acting lessons.

There has never been a tradition in Britain for letting life groom you for stardom in that rough-and-ready manner. Yet the instinctual self-awareness it elicits, quite apart from the interesting physique it reinforces, helps give the American his classless appeal, his aggressive assertion that life as many people view it today is a brutish business where bone and muscle count for more than good looks and breeding. All right, a film industry that thrives on school bullies has its dangers. But it is much more fascinating than a cinema of head prefects.

Vogue, 15 October 1975

The camera swings with the slow pendulum rhythm of lonely people's eyes over the crowded lounge of a Grand Hotel on the Venice Lido in 1911 and comes to rest on a beautiful face. A girl's? At first you think so. The features are so fine, the hair so full, the delicacy so overstated. And then its owner rises to go in for dinner and you see it is an astonishingly beautiful 14-year-old boy. By this brilliantly bold bit of casting, Luchino Visconti not only preserves the perfect tone of Thomas Mann's novella, *Death in Venice*, but also secures the total success of his film.

To call it a story of homosexual attachment between a middle-aged composer convalescing from a breakdown, though actually surrendering to a burnt-out career, and this god-like boy is to lay too heavy and contemporary a hand on its hidden chords. Mann meant them to vibrate with delicacy, not lust. Visconti sees that they do. The almost feminine looks of his boy actor Bjorn Andresen spiritualise the flesh without effeminising the character. The gravest risk in the film becomes one of its greatest strengths. The other, of course, is Dirk Bogarde, though why I say 'of course', I don't know. I've long admired Bogarde. But never have I had more cause for delight in an actor's skill and nerve than watching him in the role that will surely be the capstone of his career.

Gustav von Aschenbach (Bogarde) is a man who has held back on his nature to the frustration of his art. He is a musician in the film, the only departure from Mann's story, and the change is justified by the use to which Visconti puts the ebbing and rising music of Gustav Mahler to combine in harmony with the other Gustav's dying fall. Beauty belongs to the senses, runs the film's argument, which Visconti states in brief 'flash' cuts back to the composer's breakdown. But can the senses lead an artist to the discovery of the spiritual? The fatal debate that has caused the musician to relapse into formal mediocrity is settled by the encounter in Venice. It is an encounter in looks and longing only. The aching gap is emphasised, not the carnal connection. Bogarde trails the boy on beach, terrace and through Venetian causeway with his eyes only—not one word is spoken between them— encouraged only by a rare, tiny smile from the boy that might even be mockery.

Bogarde makes every moment transmit its telepathic signal. His playing is minute and masterly. He suggests a world of physical trepidation when the glimpse of a playmate planting a kiss on the boy's cheek forces the physical side of passion into his sight. Oppressed by hopelessness, he tries to leave Venice in a progress down the Grand Canal like a dirge. Then fate decides otherwise and he returns to the hotel with almost a swagger, all shamefulness dispersed Visconti makes the city an ally in the gathering tragedy. For plague is on the way up the coast of Italy and the ugly splotches of disinfectant and the bonfires of decontamination in the alleys counterpoint the composer's moral and physical dissolution.

He brings his film to a swelling climax that snatches pity, irony and revulsion from the fate of a man with all self-command gone, who lets a barber touch his lost youth back into his cheeks and hair with cosmetics and dye and finds, too late, that it is not life he has restored, but the mortician's counterfeit appearance of it. 'The time left us is like hour-glass sand,' says the composer. 'To our eyes it appears that it runs out only at the end.' To *our* eyes, watching *Death in Venice*, it appears like a miracle the way that Visconti and Bogarde follow that trickle of life from first to last shot until the vessel that held it collapses, emptied and alone.

Evening Standard, 4 March 1971

It was, in commercial terms, almost the gravestone of Bogarde's career. Simply no one came to see the film in anything like the numbers Warner Brothers needed to recoup their investment; and Bogarde had to wait for *The Night Porter*, a piece of *porno-kitsch* linking the Nazis with exotic perversions, to repair his box-office credit. I can sympathise with the bitterness I detected in him whenever we met in the intervening years: he would contemptuously refer to the pressures that Visconti had resisted to turn Mann's homophile *novella* into a Lolitaphile pursuit by switching the boy's sex to that of a little girl. Would that have saved the film commercially? Who can tell—and who cares? The point is that it exists beyond the considerations of profit and loss, which is how most art has to be got on to the screen even while attempting to satisfy avarice.

Among those who *did* go, some found it too slow; others insisted they detected an element of 'come-hitherness' in the boy's attitude that vulgarised the relationship; and even greater purists resented Visconti's obvious identification of Von Aschenbach with Gustav Mahler, in spite of there being evidence that Mann had had this in mind, too. The fact is that even the literate public, never mind the cinema masses, just didn't come, thereby missing a wonderful piece of acting, ungrudgingly at the service of a true *maître*, and confirming my own private hunch that even the beauty of such a film doesn't exist in the eye of the Anglo-Saxon beholder, for generally he turns a blind eye to any visual elegance on the screen less obvious than a Martini commercial or a Lelouch romance.

GRAND SLAM/*A Doll's House*

Ibsen's definition of a wife and mother as 'a woman who has shared her bed with a stranger for eight years and borne three children by him' profoundly shocked nineteenth-century society. The shock still comes through to us like the bang of the door—subtly amplified in Patrick Garland's film of *A Doll's House* as it sinks into the consciousness of the husband whom Nora walks out on at the end. But the actress who plays Nora has to *open* a door before she can close it—the door into herself. And this Claire Bloom does as if she'd been in training for it all her life.

It's a most intelligent, satisfying film we have here. Not the most cinematic kind of film. But good in a clear honest, involving way just because the director has relied on the play to grip and on a cast that no theatre could muster for very long at current prices. And the special quality of Women's Lib timeliness, extracted from the play and not shoved into it, makes us gasp at its contemporary relevance. But it's Claire Bloom who makes it all work. Given the details that cameras can register, I'd say she's even better on the screen than on the stage. She shows us Nora as a childish, spoilt, dependent wife by a dozen little tics of expression and gesture. Toying with a muff, babyishly prising hubby's fingers apart as if to extract the money from between them, pleading guilty to buying bonbons, knowing full well his male ego is flattered by her dependence and boosted by his forgiveness—this makes his wife doubly his. She consents to her kept status like the pet squirrel she mimics. Life is nuts and pats and sugar lumps.

But with the arrival of her husband's bank clerk, who'll blackmail her for a past sin of forgery, Miss Bloom also shows us the clever woman under the fripperies. Clever and ruthless and heartless. An intriguer who secures the man's job at the bank for her old schoolfriend Kristine—and so traps herself into having her sin revealed to her husband. At which point she has simultaneously destroyed herself and liberated herself. 'No man will sacrifice honour even for love. Millions of women do.' The words bite into us through the decades since they were written. The confrontation between husband and wife, as she contemptuously sees his panic in case her less-than-perfect past should destroy his affluent present, is a memorable one. Miss Bloom makes no slip: she is not an advocate for a cause, she is simply a woman speaking her mind—a mind she always had, but only now dares to voice. It would have been more than enough to give the film distinction, were Patrick Garland's other virtues not so obvious.

The adaptation hasn't admittedly done much to avoid Ibsen's creaking coincidences, implausible resolutions like the sub-plot of love between the blackmailer and the heroine's best friend, and the dreaded bits of exposition as characters tell each other what they already know all too well. But Garland's direction of the cast—plus Christopher Hampton's ruthless pruning of Ibsen's verbosity—keeps us at full stretch. The players are flawless. Anthony Hopkins as Nora's husband is never so priggish as to resist our pity and consequently triumphs in his adversity; Denholm Elliott as the blackmailer is perfectly motivated by unfairness, not malice; Anna Massey's Kristine rides the improbabilities of the most thankless role by sheer good nature; Ralph Richardson's doctor, the play's symbol of corruption and contamination, diagnoses his own death with professional relish; and even Dame Edith Evans catches and holds the eye in the nanny's role, a part so small you might miss it if you blinked.

Evening Standard, 19 April 1973

Minor but Masterly

Every critic has films he feels almost ashamedly affectionate towards. They're mostly, I find, the unrequited love affairs, the ones the public hasn't gone to see, so that inevitably there creeps in an element of personal protectiveness. They're usually minor works, too, though often from the hand of a master or, sometimes, a skilled beginner. I suppose the classic case is Hitchcock's black comedy, *The Trouble with Harry*, off-beat and now rarely seen and, quite certainly, never repeated by a filmmaker whose personal fancies are now carefully pre-tested against public expectations.

All the movies that follow demand small frames—except *The Night They Raided Minksy's*, that's obviously destined for the great gold rococo 'pride of place' portrait behind the saloon bar. But even it has the intimate care of many professionals lavished upon its individual colours and looks. In any case, one doesn't need to strain to take them in: one doesn't need to rise to the occasion, that obligation which damns so much pleasure in the viewing and reviewing of films. Truffaut and René Clair have a purity, a sense of style that could only come from people very much in love with movies and what can be done in movies: artistically speaking, one might be the son of the other, and indeed the genesis of Truffaut's *Day for Night* resides in a Clair-like love of people and the absurdities they create around themselves: in *La Peau Douce*, it is tragedies they create, for which they are none the less loved and pitied; and though the *ballet* in this film is very much *mécanique*, its movements have the stylised perfection of Clair's early casts. I'm especially fond of *The Hireling*, which I saw one cold morning in its rough-cut form when I was selecting films for the Cannes festival and immediately it ended rang up the producer, who had begged me to exercise mercy, to tell him it must go. It did and won Sarah Miles the acting prize. Hardly anyone went to see it when it opened in Britain, and Alan Bridges, its director, is still waiting for another film really worth his talents. With fondness for some films there is mingled sadness: if only mass audiences were interested in small matters of the heart and senses.

Imagine a film where instead of the pit-pat of a lover's heartbeat as he telephones his girl, one hears the buzzing of an engaged line; where one of those 'cannot live without you' moments in a man's life is conveyed by a pencil totting up the words on a telegram form; where the ardour of a man who has fallen for a girl half his age becomes a kind of visible inner wattage as he elatedly goes round his hotel suite switching on all the lights; where the clicking of a camera's delayed-action shutter fixes the moment of truth for a suspicious wife who finds the damning snapshot that the camera took; where even the tricky mechanics of loosening a suspender strap do duty for the usual scene of threshing limbs.

If you imagine such a film to be either pretentiously tricky or coldly mechanical, you are wrong. François Truffaut's *La Peau Douce* is a love story as different in style from *Jules et Jim* as a temperature graph is from a spiral of bubbles—but just as audaciously original. Love, says Truffaut this time, is a human emotion you feel in your skin: but everywhere love-life is getting more and more mechanical. Look, for example, at how many movements a man must make when he wants to telephone his mistress. As they drive home, his skin may be on fire with desire, but he still has to make all the changes on his car's gears correctly.

Sometimes Truffaut photographs the mechanics of filling a petrol tank in such minute detail that it looks like an Esso commercial. But generally it is with more concern for subtlety that he breaks down a *crime passionel* story into the fleeting shots of mechanism or human movements that habit has made mechanical, like the way a girl changes from flat heels into stilettos. And the fixed ways of the machines counterpoint the erratic destinies of the characters. Even the characters are not what one expects.

The lover is no bedroom athlete, but a French man of letters who looks both ways before he crosses the road and who spends some of the funniest scenes wondering and worrying whether 'people will talk'. The girl is no good time minx, but an air hostess who flies by regular timetables and admits that although she likes making love, she can do without it for a time if need be. And the wife is no cold bitch, but a full-blooded woman who would bring many another man hurrying home from the office. When she finds out the truth, she kills her husband with his favourite shotgun in the corner of his favourite café. Reported in a French newspaper—where it has been a hundred times— such a story would perhaps hardly rate more than a 'Ça, alors!' But filmed by Truffaut and acted by Jean Desasilly, Françoise Dorleac and Nelly Benedetti, as if they didn't know a camera was within miles of them, it is marvellously human, tender and tragic. One of the most skilful marriages of style and story that I have recently seen.

Evening Standard, 5 November 1964

MENU FOR BATTLE/*Les Fêtes Galantes*

René Clair is a filmmaker who would sooner raise a soufflé than roast an ox. A juggler who works with his finger tips. An illusionist who lives for the moment of surprise. A joker who uses a wink and would disdain anything as vulgar as a punch-line. Such airy, elegant, aristocratic arts are out of fashion in today's muscular hit-or-miss, leave 'em laughing screen comedies. All the more reason then to savour a rarity like *Les Fêtes Galantes*, which Clair made recently in Roumania. Minor Clair it may be; but it is unmistakably pitched in the master's key.

It is a satire on the 'gallantry' of war in the 18th century, when the niceties of birth or breeding dictated the conduct of the battle and the treatment of the troops, when cannon balls bounced about like iron pumpkins, when honour was the preserve of the nobly-born and martial engagements were broken off by mutual agreement when the bugle sounded the retirement for luncheon. The action springs from the daft inaction of two rival armies bogged down in the siege and going through the motions of war-like defiance and defence. Clair keeps the cloudless panorama—as in a second-rate historical painting, it's always fair weather for fighting—filled with dozens of delicately engineered sight gags. A sweaty corporal gallops up with the army standard he has saved and the flag is passed from officer to officer till the dandified *aide-de-camp* who actually hands it to the commander collects the grateful decoration. The besieging general's dinner menu is bawled out over no man's land as gastronomic propaganda to weaken the resolve of the castle's starving defenders.

Clair is master, too, of the accelerating gag, like the fortress's last chicken getting loose on the parade ground and turning the goose-stepping evolutions of the troops into a shambles as they march in hungry pursuit. He can also revive the obvious gag so that it seems totally fresh, like the general's own men ducking whenever he fires a musket. He can produce the unexpected with a smothered chuckle, like the order 'Sound the alarm', which is then sounded with mellifluous inappropriateness on eight French horns. Under his direction, people appear to lose their weight as they move—a soldier tip-toes down a pile of cannon balls as if they were soap-bubbles, a man who falls into a trench gets thrown up by the men he falls on over and over again like a ball on water-spouts.

Clair is the best ballet-master at work in films, and it's this that helps *Les Fêtes Galantes* keep its aerated good-spirits, even when inspiration deserts him and he has to settle for the conventional. To a degree rare in anyone's films, you feel his cast were totally in sympathy with him, especially Jean-Pierre Cassel as a wily corporal, and Philippe Avory who has the country innocence of the lucky third-son in a fairy-tale. It is a film that commands something rarer than respect: it commands affection.

Evening Standard, 15 December 1966

PROTUBERANCES/*The Night They Raided Minsky's*

'Where there's smoke, there's salmon,' says the worried Jewish owner when the vice squad come nosing round his theatre. In New York, in the 1920s, you could have truly said, 'Where there's burlesque, there's Minsky's.'

Minsky's was the temple of variety in the days when comics wore red noses, girls jiggled like table jellies, funnymen fell on their prats, daring French books were sold between the turns and the clients were warned not to take them out of their plain wrappers till they were ten blocks away. A tawdry, vulgar, zestful era in Jewish-American showbiz history. This film is the story of how they raided Minsky's one night and caught the daughter (Britt Ekland) of a strict Amish patriarch in the act of artlessly inventing a new art form—the strip-tease.

The basic anecdote isn't to be taken seriously: but the beauty of this superbly entertaining film is that everything else *has* been. Don't think it'll be too vulgar for you, or too parochial for us. Its wit is out of the best Jewish pickle-jar. Its appeal is as international as the hamburger. Producer Norman Lear has done an expert hands-across-the-sea job in picking British names who shine like Broadway bulbs on the US scene. Imagine finding Norman Wisdom here! *Imagine finding Norman Wisdom funny!*

The locale is exactly the same as *Funny Girl*, though far juicier and sharper. If they wanted a new title, they could call it Naughty Girl.

The cast is not only in character, but something rarer—it is in period. Jason Robards is almost as good as Olivier was in *The Entertainer* as the slick song-and-dance man whose lecherous patter tempts him to sweet-talk his way up to a new girl and then helps him to smooth-talk his way (with a cardiac wince) back to safety when her six-foot husband appears. Norman Wisdom as the clown who's always being used to wipe the stage is funny because he's been sat on firmly in other ways, too. Denholm Elliott as the vice squad man pops with public decency and looks for offence everywhere. Harry Andrews marches out of the Old Testament to save his daughter from exposing 'thy protuberances'; and the late Bert Lahr, who died during the filming, pads in white spats through a vaudeville that gave him birth and died long before him.

But all of them—and I mustn't forget Joseph Wiseman's Minsky Sr, Forrest Tucker's gangster, or Rudy Vallee's voice as narrator—are only excuses for re-creating the era and its entertainers. And this is an impeccable joy.

The Fanny Brice country on the Lower East Side is stunningly brought to life—every face a snapshot of yesterday. Colour floods the screen off and on, and only then can one tell where yesterday's newsreel footage and today's feature film begin and end. Every stage act bristles with authenticity, for one of the surviving Minskys advised on the candy-floss chorines, the bump-and-grind floosies, the patriotic tableaux, even down to details like the pianist with a racing paper instead of a music sheet on his keyboard. A triumph for director William Friedkin, photographer Andrew Laszlo and designers William and Jean Eckar. Even the accidental invention of the strip-tease is made to appear a likely happening, though we're spared the sad news that the art of vaudeville began to die once the strippers became a part of it. With Britt Ekland, red-haired and ravishingly innocent, Minsky's imported the seeds of its own destruction. But what seeds, what destruction!

Evening Standard, 17 April 1969

DRIVER'S LICENCE/*The Hireling*

The Hireling proves conclusively that a film in which a man and a woman have no carnal contact with each other is more erotic than one in which total permissiveness is the state of the union.

Beautifully balanced at the precise point where post-First World

War society was about to give way to the hectic licence of the Bright Young Things of the 1920s, the test of *The Hireling* is that we feel if its story had been set just a month or two later than it is in 1920, Sarah Miles' titled lady and Robert Shaw's uniformed chauffeur would have wound up in bed together, instead of keeping the places God appointed them to—the back and front seats, respectively, of a Rolls-Royce. The class barrier is the electric fence between them, separating the man's yearning from his fulfilment and communicating its erotic tingle to every feature of the film and its relationships. It just requires Shaw to roll up his shirt sleeve at one point—for a perfectly innocent purpose— and the tattooed snake on the forearm of the ex-RSM has almost the shock effect of some more intimate exposure.

Based on L. P. Hartley's story, *The Hireling*'s irony is the pathetic failure of two people ever to 'meet'. For this time there's no 'go-between'. The chauffeur is a lonely man, missing the regimental home and companionship of the trenches now that he is a proprietor of a small hire-car business. Out of sympathy for the aristocratic lady he collects from a nursing-home, where she's had a breakdown precipitated by guilt at her husband's death, he invents a wife and family for himself. His enviable if fictitious domesticity revives the lady's wilting spirits—and his own sexual desire. But just when he is ready to make his play, he finds that all he has done is turn Milady on for the well-born young chancer (Peter Egan) to pluck for himself.

Alan Bridges' direction is impeccably, painfully true. Cold Cotswold countryside, freezing mist in the air, passing shadows of impoverished tenant farmers drawing politely back: the world outside the Rolls-Royce is as set in its ways, its feudal ways, as that inside the great country houses, town mansions, provincial fêtes and candle-lit dinner-parties. Yet the thaw, one feels, might set in tomorrow. Sarah Miles' performance, wan, withdrawn, then brightening into touching life before finally frosting over with class heartlessness, must be reckoned her finest work on the screen. Robert Shaw has much the less showy role, but he does as much with considerably less. The virility of the man, held in check by the class-conditioned society, almost bursts out of the screen in anguish, so that when he does give way to his feelings, it is like a sudden storm—overwhelming. And as for Peter Egan as the ex-officer romantically reciting lines from Rupert Brooke's war while Shaw's old sweat gets barely an acknowledgment that it was *his* war, too—Egan is an actor to watch as he fills in a hollow man and supplies substance to a light-weight parasite.

Evening Standard, 19 July 1973

Six of the Worst

Coward's line in *Private Lives*—'How potent cheap music is'—has its echo in every film critic's memory. 'How potent bad movies are.' Why the bad ones afford instant recall whereas—I find, anyhow—the good, the very good ones shimmer hazily like an oasis in desert heat (and sometimes disappear if one rides up for a second and closer inspection), is difficult to explain.

Less difficult, but a shade more shameful, is why the bad ones are so often highly enjoyable, though perhaps not in the way their makers intended. I think it's because they allow us to relax our standards and fall in line with theirs, provided the latter conform to our escapist enjoyment, our shrugging off of the required aesthetic responses. There is a great deal of fun to be got from running wild (and naked) in the streets. The appeal of bad movies is the freedom that the streaker feels—an irresponsibly frivolous type of exhibitionism, but an escape from High Culture into some rudimentary craziness. There is a kind of 'punk art' around nowadays that, just because it comes along less frequently, is enjoyed more refreshingly.

In the old days, every week seemed to deliver some piece of Hollywood fatuousness, based on the movie industry's own preconceptions and on the audience's own ignorance, so that in the meshing of the two there was a release of trashy fun that didn't have to be placed inside the aesthetic or significant tradition. Nowadays, when even movies as atrocious as *Mandingo* or *Goodbye, Norma Jean* or *Mahogany* make some basic, spurious bid for importance, there's a lot less tolerance to be extended to them. They should know better: and the point is, they *do* know better, for even producers aren't totally lacking in sophistication nowadays, but they play us for suckers, for *schmuck* who can be manipulated by the media into thinking they're respectable, even in some hideous way 'important' people, be it only in the deplorable way they can exploit flesh and blood and legend. They and plenty of others like them may be all right for what I heard described as a 'good Friday night picture', but even then you feel the people who talk this way have not got the remotest knowledge of how entertaining the old, unwised-up movies could be, the ones that didn't take themselves seriously, but used the opportunity to have fun, knowing that this was all that was expected of them by those who would eventually pay to see them.

I am sorry to say that I began writing film criticism when the movies were just starting to show life as it is and putting behind them, like the evidence of a misspent past at best, or a criminal record at worst, the plentiful examples of life as Hollywood used to stylise it. There are now whole areas of contemporary movies ungoverned by the Hollywood rules that once determined how we should react to life. Take the 'woman's picture', for example. It's almost disappeared now, as I have already remarked, and, along with it, have gone the conventions of the genre. For example, no woman in a present-day picture ever carries a handbag. A small thing, yet it is connected with such large changes as the disappearance of the studio wardrobe department—or, in some cases, the studio itself. Likewise hats. Hairdressers are fortunately a hardier commercial lobby than handbag makers or hatters; and make-up is still kiss-proof, rain-proof, sleep-proof and, in this era of towering infernos and earthquakes, disaster-proof. Just as well, really, since there is now seldom anywhere to freshen it up; for as social realism has familiarised us with the long invisible 'men's room', so the powder room, which was once the scene of the bitchiest set-tos, is almost unvisited. (The double sex standard perhaps.) Women's footwear has become more practical since Marlene Dietrich set out to march with the Legion across the desert in high heels in *Morocco*. Slumberwear for both sexes has almost passed out of recognition, as no one nowadays appears to resort to a bed for sleeping purposes, or, if they do, it is invariably in the nude. I should not like to predict the return of the day when a man will keep his pyjamas in the airing cupboard, at least in order to offer the runaway heiress something in the way of night attire.

A mark of such movies' glorious inanity used to be the fulsome attention paid to the star's wardrobe. When films were simple, when they were still *fun* and hadn't become social phenomena, then every crisis was within a woman's experience —and purse. She was sure to have something in the wardrobe to match it. There are a couple of examples of this in the next few pages. I can only offer apologies and plead the self-limiting ordinance of 'six' of the worst films I have seen in my time, if someone's favourite has been left out. Even now I have regrets about omitting *The Game Is Over*, in which Jane Fonda (of all people!) flirted with her stepson in stripped chinchilla, deceived her husband in black sequins, abandoned herself to adultery in a white-silk wrap, Eskimo-hooded and marabou-trimmed and provocative if a mite restricting, switched to jealous yellow when betrayed, wrapped her murderous thoughts in a doeskin hunting jacket and didn't let her dress sense desert her even when she committed suicide in the lily pond. She went under in sealskin. It's a film I always want to draw up a little gilt chair to, and watch again. But to have included it here might have been *de trop*.

I regret including a couple of examples from directors who certainly didn't set out to make bad films, but, lacking a sense of proportion to guide them through their effects, found it turned out that way. Badness in great ones, as was so nearly remarked in *Hamlet*, must not unwatched go.

BLANK CHIC/*A Place for Lovers*

You know all's not well with Faye Dunaway when she turns up at this uninhabited palace outside Venice and flops down on the best four-poster after simply dropping her valises on the front doorstep, where they remain for the next 48 hours. Dying, that's what she is—so why unpack? What seems like half-an-hour of screen-time later, just when you're wondering if the makers have forgotten the credit titles, she revives slightly to send for Marcello Mastroianni to come and keep her company. After that, the only thing left to wonder at is, have the people also forgotten the movie?

A Place for Lovers is one of those costly, empty films that look as if they've been made with someone's blank chic. It's filled with Beautiful People. People like Miss Dunaway, who may be on her way to death's door from some nameless cinema disease that doesn't interfere with her looks, but *en route* has scooped the wardrobe empty of Theodora Van Runkle's jet-set creations. Each crisis she passes through, on goes a new gown. Mastroianni can only look at her in that quizzical Italian way which may denote love, amazement or just envy. The luxury of how the rich die! And, oh, the lethargy of it, too! Five scriptwriters have laboured—collectively or consecutively, it's not stated—to do as little as possible in the way of providing a story, and after 88 minutes have merely managed to move things from the marchese's Venetian palace to a millionaire's Alpine chalet. There Miss Dunaway, who's taken to posing to show how her spirits are sinking, decides at least to die generously and gives away all her pretty things to the local pig-keeper's daughter and then, when she changes her mind about dying, is caught above the snow-line in an above-the-knee-line number while every other sensible person is in woollies.

Just to show his sophistication, director Vittorio De Sica—yes, *the* Vittorio De Sica—throws in a house party where a guest shows lantern slides of the erotic sculpture of Hindu culture; and there's a bit of free dealing-out of bed partners for the night, a process that is less stimulating to watch than a hand of Bridge. Acting honours—the competition is not hot—must go to Caroline Mortimer as the heroine's best friend who comes all the way from Paris to tell her, 'The doctor wants you back *at once!*' (It took five writers to write that?) The two stars try to out-act each other in seeing which of them can get nearest to falling asleep standing up without actually letting their eyes close. Mastroianni loses by a blink.

Evening Standard, 12 June 1969

CORNFLOWER/*Sunflower*

Welcome back, amnesia. And give a big hand also to the husband everyone thinks is dead—everyone but his wife, that is. How *Sunflower* takes me back! You'd think nothing had happened in the world since 1945 when this was the cinema's most fashionable malady and also its most cliché-ridden plot. Actually we all know what the big event is that has happened since then. Carlo Ponti has opened up Russia so that his wife, Sophia Loren, can make a film there.

With 42 Italian technicians Signor Ponti covered the USSR last year, which just happened to be the 200th anniversary of Napoleon's birth. It must have been quite a comeback, if we're to believe the hand-out. Where once the Emperor shivered in lonely retreat, Sophia walked with modest step and absolutely no make-up as a hapless seamstress in search of her missing husband. 'The Russian public recognised her instantly,' we're told. Even the custom-dyed grey strands in her hair, to show her genuine *concern*, didn't fox them. Nor did the plain woolly cardigan the character wears, to show her basic *simplicity*, hide who she really was. These Marxists can still tell a film star when one of them sets foot in town. So, I think, will filmgoers.

Sophia mingles with the crowds under Lenin's dome, outside Stalin's tomb, as she seeks Marcello Mastroianni, the husband who went missing on the Russian front, and now and then accuses stray Muscovites of looking like an Italian, 'because of your hair, your walk, the colour of your eyes.' All she keeps getting in reply is 'Nyet'. Heartbreaking? Not exactly. Sophia does her one-note best to look woebegone, but the camera keeps making it all look like a Big Occasion, as if she was really on her way not to find a husband, but to seek an audience with the Pope. Perhaps it is hard to shake the dust of Italy off your clogs. 'They remind me of Neapolitans,' Miss Loren told the hand-out writer about the Russians. 'They wear their friendliness where you can see it—on their faces.' I wonder what their faces will show if the film is ever premiered in Moscow.

Sunflower's first half-hour is a flashback to the characters' youthful courtship. Plainly it's a strain on Loren and Mastroianni and their cameraman. They talk Basic Peasant ('These are my mother's eggs'), share love-bites with the mosquitoes, have an orgy of omelette-making and generally behave like film stars doing what they imagine the simple folk do. The second half-hour is another flashback to Marcello's winter hell on the Russian front. Helpfully for him, most of it takes place in old newsreels whose worn looks are covered by the Red Flag flapping symbolically over them. He comes out of it with amnesia, frostbite and a slight limp and marries and their child says 'buon giorno' as Miss Loren happens by one day during her search. Encounter, separation, renunciation: the rest of the plot can be summed up—and is—in all-purpose looks of zombie-like intensity.

Sunflower has a story that an illiterate chambermaid might consider a bit beneath her customary standards. It moves along with the pace of scene-shifters at La Scala. Every so often someone announces, 'The war's over', or 'Stalin's dead', or, plainly at a loss what exactly to report, 'Oh, so many years have passed.' Dubbed American floats in the air in the general vicinity of the Italian characters while their lips babble on fiercely in the rush to catch up with it. For all the help Russia is to the story, everyone might have stayed at home and made the movie more comfortably in the Tuscan hills or on the back lot at Cinecitta. The director is Vittorio De Sica. Odd how he once made a picture or two that caught the spirit of their time precisely and made us think he was an important name.

Evening Standard, 13 August 1970

A GIRL FOR ALL WEATHERS/*Ryan's Daughter*

Down in the forest something stirs. Spiders' webs palpitate. The sun peeps through the branches like a voyeur. A dandelion discharges its seeds and a couple of horses graze flank by flank, the way their owners are apparently doing, too, in the undergrowth. Rosy Ryan, the publican's daughter, is at last losing her virginity and all Nature is in heat.

The heaving and ho-ing that goes on in the green woods of Kirrary is absolutely typical of the way that the elements behave in the new film directed by David Lean, a filmmaker who has always manifested a mistrust of the flesh and who, in *Ryan's Daughter*, prefers to express physical passion in terms of high waves, rough Irish landscapes and every orgasmic wind that he and his screenwriter, Robert Bolt, can whistle up to their assistance in telling what the posters describe, a fatal shade too preciously, as 'a story of love'. It would be cruel to say that at the budget it reportedly cost to make, *Ryan's Daughter* represents 14 million dollars worth of bad weather magnificently photographed by Freddie Young. But even acknowledging Lean's proven ability to please vast audiences with the cinematic equivalent of publishers' best-sellers, it is still right to query the cost, the cast and the care—the excruciating, suffocating care—he has lavished on a tale whose basic triteness places it in the class of palliatives designed in earlier and more innocent decades to lighten the hard lot of kitchen maids. Only craftsmanship of a high order, performances of a high-definition kind that need to be capitalised, and the ever-changing scenery of the West of Ireland (with a detour into South Africa for matching locations that come complete with the kind of spectacular storm denied the film unit in Eire) can excuse a story that needs a novel built round it to flesh out the characters and fill them with more than wind and weather.

Rosy, played by Sarah Miles with twitching mouth greedy for sexual experience in the priest-ridden village, jumps into marriage to the ageing teacher played by Robert Mitchum—Mitchum is cast against his usual role and his is the only performance of any depth, a careful, thoughtful portrait of a man whose wedding night is limited to a few, despairing hugs and then a face-to-the-wall future. After trying to arouse passion in her spouse by serving him his tea while he's stripped to the waist after a little gardening—a rather awkward scene of domestic sensuality that aroused laughter at the Press show—Rosy takes up with the aristocratic English major drafted to the west of Ireland to tackle the gun-runners—the time is 1916.

To suggest the illicit liaison of these two, Lean uses symbols of the clumsiest kind. Assignations are arranged by Sarah Miles standing in a patch of priapic lilies; the major (Christopher Jones) is forever being seen in romantic silhouette on the skyline like a visitor from another planet. The couple's horses whinny ecstatically at each other from their respective paddocks. And instead of transmuting their lust for each other into true love, the very reticence with which Lean films the couple's clinching encounter simply draws attention to his artful placing of the obscuring foliage—a perfect case of not being able to see the nudes for the trees. Love founders in a terrific storm—the film's most spectacular scene—where gun-runners are battered by waves that pour like scalding steam off the rocks and launch themselves like torpedoes out at the cinema audience.

Rosy gets the blame for betraying the 'patriots' to her Army lover— whereas it's her turncoat father (Leo McKern) who is the informer— and the film reaches its climax in muted tragedy, rather marred by the tendency of the vengeful villagers to act as if they were on hire from Rent-a-Peasant. Amidst all this—and the 'all' includes Maurice Jarre's insistent score which makes for nearly as much music in the film as weather—Trevor Howard and John Mills stand out: the one as a village priest with a craggy face like a rock formation, the other as the dumb and deformed village idiot with a face like a handful of squashed putty. Christopher Jones is effective enough, though the part calls on him to look comatose much of the time; and it's highly unlikely that such an obvious shell-shock casualty, whose traumas in the trenches Lean presents in jarring, subliminal flash cuts, weirdly at variance with the style of the rest of the film, would get command of even a kitchen patrol, never mind an outpost in turbulent Ireland.

Breadth of landscape and the inimical nature of the elements gave Lean's previous epics, *Kwai*, *Lawrence* and *Zhivago*, a binding force. But the story here stubbornly resists being pressed into the epic mould and remains one that needed intimate telling. By exteriorising emotions in effects more worthy of meteorology, Lean has simply added inflation without achieving insight. Instead of looking like the money it took to make, the film (at 195 minutes) feels like the time it took to shoot. At least it does to this film critic, though I freely concede there is probably an audience—the kind that rarely goes to the pictures today—which will settle down comfortably to be told a story, shown recognisable, easily explained characters, and not have to fear that a full frontal exposure will be sprung on them. If so, I hope they enjoy *Ryan's Daughter*—but remember, no laughing.

Evening Standard, 10 December 1970

FREAKING OUT/*Beyond the Valley of the Dolls*

The scene: a Californian beach house. The showbiz host has just plucked the lacy ruffles off his Superwoman costume and revealed himself to have been a female all along.

A gigolo in a Tarzan loincloth lies on the expensive rug, minus his head. The houseman, wearing a Nazi uniform, sprawls in the waves on the beach stuck through with a sword. In the master bedroom a top fashion model had been kissing a pistol when it went off . . . And behind the bar cowers her lesbian dress-designer, nude except for a drift of fishnet. The orgy continues . . . the night is still young.

And what are film critics doing as they watch the entertainment that bears 20th Century-Fox's trademark and has been made by the 'King of the Nudies'—16mm sexploitation pictures, to you and me—by the name of Russ Meyer whose talents the studio co-opted to pull it to the top of the heap again? Are we putting on our most censorious faces, preparing to pen notices reeking of 'disgust', 'affront' or 'obscenity', and generally arising as one man against a film whose commercial hypocrisy begins with its very title which a prefatory note on the screen claims has no connection with the Jacqueline Susann bestseller *Valley of the Dolls*?

I hope we are not doing any of these things, otherwise we shall emerge as greater hypocrites than anyone connected with the movie. I have seen it one and a half times and on both occasions my colleagues and I came out clutching our sides like bad lumbago cases, only emitting whoops of laughter, not cries of indignation, in short overcome by a film whose total, idiotic, monstrous badness raises it to the pitch of near-irresistible entertainment.

Beyond the Valley of the Dolls is the kind of movie that a maladroit Mack Sennett might have made if he had worked in a sex shop, not a fun factory. To see it perpetrated in—or on?—a major Hollywood studio adds richness to the gravy. (To know it is going on release in the same bill as *Myra Breckinridge* makes one fear for the indigestion of cinema audiences.)

An all-girl rock band who've squeaked, bubbled and popped their way to the top gets involved with a cast of Hollywood freaks who are drawn and acted with the subtlety of strip-style characters in pulp-paper comics. The story is simply an endless series of party-going. And at the end of it all, a voice like Moses comes up on the sound track to underline the high morality of it all by summing up what was wrong with virtually every one of those in whose antics the film has wallowed like an elephant in slow-setting jelly.

'Lance Rock, half-actor, half-gigolo,' it booms, 'generous of his body, he never truly gave of himself. Super-agent "Z-Man" Barzell forgot that life has many levels and chose to live on one. Ashley St Ives, movie sex-queen, believed men were made for her enjoyment. Casey and Rozanne, the lesbians whose love was not evil though evil came of it. And Otto, the Nazi butler, is his death an end to Martin Bormann. . . ?'

'You must each decide what your life will be,' the Voice continued, chiding us critics as we remembered the high points in the film—the seduction in the Rolls-Royce with the radiator symbol intercut with the threshings and gropings on luxury upholstery; the 'shock' cut from an abortion scene to pancake batter dropped on a sizzling skillet; the pop ballads with titles like 'Look On Up at the Bottom'; the race to the rescue at the end, when a paraplegic hero in a wheelchair cries, 'My toes . . . I can *feel* my legs!'

'If love is in *you*,' the Voice intoned, as we critics groped our way out into the street, wheezing like people caught in a tear-gas raid, 'then guiltless will be all *your* life as you walk beyond this valley.'

As we all walked down the Haymarket, love was in us all right—and you couldn't hear the traffic for the laughter.

Evening Standard, 11 February 1971

Roger Ebert, the film critic who wrote the scenario of *Beyond the Valley of the Dolls*, has assured me that the parody was intentional. Maybe so. But Fox hired Russ Meyer with the perfectly serious aim, and mouth-watering hope, that he would repeat the highly profitable experience of his string of skin-flicks. And if the ingredients were better, the logic ran, so much bigger must be the box-office. Seeing how it was turning out probably convinced everyone to make a virtue of necessity. It remains my—and many people's—best-ever 'worst film'. I should record that the makers saw a profit at the end of the valley.

SIEGFRIED FOLLIES/*Mahler*

Ken Russell will try anything in order to keep the class attentive. But *Mahler* may leave the schoolboy, for whom it was presumably made, quite giddy with shock.

Such a boy, for instance, will learn that Gustav Mahler's life was continually interrupted by people posing as friends, acquaintances, even strangers, but all of them actually the rankest kind of dramatic 'feeds', who, on every possible occasion, would say things like 'Why were you forced to leave the Vienna Opera—anti-Semitism?' Or 'All your music is a hymn to Nature.' Or 'What you completed perfectly in your Fourth Symphony, Dr Mahler (nudge, nudge), a child's view of Heaven.' Or 'I understand you're searching for tranquillity, Mahler.'

Such a schoolboy will also discover that as the great composer sweated over the music paper in his lake-side hut, Mrs Mahler (Georgina Hale) ran about the countryside, soothing Nature into a *sotto voce* state more accommodating to composition, unhitching the cow bells, muffling the church clappers, confiscating the shepherd's pipe and buying a round of lager for the folk-singers so as to stop them in mid-stomp.

Furthermore, he will learn that the Mahler family resembled nothing so much as a rabid pack of East End London Jews who gabble out their money-grasping ambitions for the boy pianist in between gobbling up mouthfuls of hot food.

To his continuing surprise, our schoolboy will find that the youthful Mahler learned about 'the birds and the bees' on an *Out With Romany*-kind of study tour ('When does the moon rise?' 'What brings the north wind?'), after which he begins to espy the roly-poly type of bird and beast in a profusion that may make him suspect that Mr Russell, like Mr Disney, has salted the woods with them in advance.

If he enquires further into the composer's source of inspiration, the schoolboy will be told that the brass bands in Mahler's work were associated with seeing his parents having it off—the phrase is in keeping with the vulgarity of the film—in the outside shed. He will also deduce the stumbling block that Mahler's Jewishness was to his career from a tastefully staged scene in a lunatic asylum where the deranged composer Hugo Wolfe (David Collings), posing as the Emperor Franz Josef, orders Mahler to let down his trousers. 'As I thought,' he says, looking under the shirt, 'a Jew.'

I assume that a schoolboy, be he even a mite backward, will be able to distinguish between such plausible supposition and the ensuing sequence of rampant fantasy as Mahler tries to purge his Semitic characteristics by submitting to the Aryan 'disciplines' of a Cosima Wagner, got up for the occasion as Miss Boots-and-Whip and turning Wagner's *Ring* into a song-and-dance show such as might be put on by a classy sex-parlour—The Siegfried Follies of 1895.

After our sixth-former has witnessed Mahler slay the smoky dragon and eat the flesh (which has turned into a pig's head served up with a glass of milk, to further knock the Kosher image), I hope he will still be in a state to appreciate the subtlety with which Mr Russell inter-poses a theme song, which goes something like, 'No longer a Jew Boy Now you're a Goy.' And supposing our schoolboy has seen Visconti's *Death in Venice*, he will smirk with recognition at the sight of a little boy in a sailor suit provocatively lounging round the character got up to look like Dirk Bogarde in his Aschenbach gear, whom Mahler observes from the train window. Lampoons may not have much to do with Mahler, but they have everything to do with a film based, like so much of Russell's work, on the belief that anything's worth doing for effect.

By this time the observant schoolboy will have noticed that the story is happening in flashback aboard a train that seems unduly crowded by Mahler's friends, enemies, admirers and even his wife's lover (Richard Morant) who invites her to join him for good at the journey's end. Quick thinking on the composer's part averts this. 'Don't you remember the second subject of the Fourth movement? That's you, my love.' A marriage is thus saved by instant musicology, and the lovers exit, centre platform, murmuring a line worthy of the worst Hollywood weepie: 'As long as our music lasts, our love will last.'

The pity is that with his unequalled visual flair, Ken Russell combines an apparently unbreakable addiction to the most jarring and naïve symbolism. Setting out to reveal his chosen genius, he ends up raping him. Seeking to interpret, he merely vulgarises. Mahler is ably impersonated by Robert Powell, who is put through virtually every kind of experience including literal hoops of fire. But what chance has he to register a consistent character when the composer's life is pictured in a constant state of hyper-tension? What springs of genius can he suggest when the performance of any of Mahler's works is broken down into Ken Russell's own subjective and frequently objectionable interpretation of them?

Mahler is a film for the kind of people who want to 'see' symphonies, the way that *The Forsyte Saga* was a telly serial for the kind of people who want to 'watch' a book.

Evening Standard, 2 April 1974

CLOSET QUEEN/*Night Watch*

Elizabeth Taylor's gowns are by Valentino, her jewellery is Van Cleef and Arpels, even her kitchen is by Westinghouse. And she is *still* going out of her mind.

It is a good rule that if you've a bad picture, what you should do is dress it expensively. How hypnotic crime is among the rich. Just to see the awful experience Miss Taylor undergoes in *Night Watch* is a mortal comfort to the rest of us scraping by with under £40,000 a year in relative sanity. A police inspector in the film says 'Probably the menopause . . . the rich get nervous,' when he's seeking a motive for Miss Taylor seeing corpses with their throats cut in the old dark house opposite her own smart new one whenever it's a stormy night in London Town (which in *Night Watch* it often is). Myself, I'd have said that what accounts for Miss Taylor's nerves is the standard of living she's got to keep up: it would drive the Queen of England nuts.

In keeping with Walker's First Rule of Insanity—*'Those who lose their wits never lose their dress sense'*—Miss Taylor is forever ringing the changes on her Valentino wardrobe. A champagne-hued suit for potting out plants in the garden where their mysterious neighbour Mr Appleby (Robert Lang) is digging flower-beds (or is it graves?) in the middle of the night. A dove-grey housecoat with blue lapel interest for the edgy run-up to her first glimpse of the corpses by the lightning-flash. A flowered silk nightie for the actual crisis-point. And then a sombre descent into burgundy with silver waist-clasp for going off to the Swiss lunatic asylum.

I forgot to mention that Miss Taylor plays an insomniac—hence the *Night Watch* title. This is presumably why she never takes off her make-up at bedtime—I mean, if you're going to wake up at all hours of the night and watch corpses, you might as well look your best. It's tough on Billie Whitelaw, playing a suspicious house-guest who hasn't been supplied with the *haute-couture* distractions that the main role merits. She has to get by on sheer enigma rather than style—Is she in love with Miss Taylor's husband? He is played by Laurence Harvey. He's a top investment broker. You know he's at the top because he can't get away on holiday so long as the *Financial Times* Index keeps soaring, though on other occasions he says to his wife, 'Panic on Wall Street—every time the Viet Cong start an offensive, I'm late home for dinner.'

Tony Britton plays a posh psychiatrist. 'In the meantime, try to act naturally,' is the advice he hands out to Miss Taylor. Dangerous advice in a film like this, and impracticable too, when you suspect your husband and his mistress are out to do you in. But *are* they?

Billy Williams' photography abets the awful watchableness of such a movie. The final spooky sequence in the old dark house creates a nice atmosphere of suspense over who'll finish up dead in the wing-chair. In fact the only thicker atmosphere in the film is the one of constant snobbery maintained towards the Police (Bill Dean) who are only good for tea and Alka-Seltzer at the station, or letting themselves be patron-ised by Mr Harvey saying 'Do be seated', or telling the Spanish maid-servant, 'Show the gentlemen the way to the garden'. The moment I particularly relish for its totally mad unlikelihood is Mr Harvey calling up the police station and saying, like someone ordering Stilton at Fortnum's, 'Hello, Inspector, I'd like to report a murder.' Have *you* ever got through to a police inspector in one go, just like that? No? Nor have I. The rich, alas, they have all the privileges—even when it comes to reporting their own murders.

Evening Standard, 6 September 1973

Saints and Sinners

Besides the relative absence of women in star roles, one of the other changes in cinema fashion that a critic learns to accept in the 1970s is the total absence of God or his earthly disciples from contemporary production rosters. It's true that we recently had a *Moses* and Franco Zeffirelli has made a *Life of Christ*. Both were intended for 'the box', though, and it's interesting that the Zeffirelli project began life some years ago in the then current mode of 'conspiracy' films—like *Day of the Jackal* and *Executive Action*—as a secular thriller called *The Assassination of Jesus Christ*. It was nudged back into orthodoxy and ecumenicism by its new TV sponsors.

Nearly all the old and hallowed rites of such productions have been cast into limbo by the widespread advance of scepticism among the once worshipful masses. I particularly miss the disappearance of the Scandinavian type (Jeffrey Hunter, Max von Sydow) who usually appeared as Christ and, once shooting began, retired from public view and, we gullible ones were led to believe, neither smoked nor drank nor engaged in such worldly, hubristic activities as giving interviews. Somehow the self-denial involved in not talking to the Press seemed the ultimate earnest of Hollywood reverence. Nowadays it all seems as historical as the Beatles.

Part of the explanation—but only part—is the regrettable eagerness of those who still promote the Christian religion to meet the world—never mind the flesh and the Devil for the moment—on *its* terms, rather than on theirs. If you are purveying religion today, you have to sell it as something—*anything*—other than religion. As psychedelic experience, for instance: which has had a long run, a good trip, though to judge by the mocking disbelievers who greeted the last of Carlos Castanedas's accounts of his apprenticeship to Don Juan, the Yaqui sorcerer, its promoters may have pushed their peyote a bit too far. Religion recast as 'showbiz' is still around, though it's doubtful if the track record of the Bethlehem Superstar can be repeated. The next Big New Thing may well be religion conceived as 'international incident', with films like *Escape from Entebbe* assuming the contemporary role of the Flight from Egypt. I doubt if the drama to be wrung from the new-style ideologies of terrorism and politics will show us anything as exemplary (in a way) as the old rituals of Hollywood's periodic attempts to help Mammon sell God without actually incurring a loss.

If we are to go by what we see on the screen in *Sodom and Gomorrah*, then clearly Biblical reports of the twin cities' wickedness have been greatly inflated. Nothing my roving eye could detect in this rigorously heterosexual epic deserves to be called to the attention of the Wolfenden Committee.

On the contrary, it is disconcerting to find that people who were reputedly so corrupt and depraved should have had such a dreary time of it—in Sodom, anyhow. (Gomorrah, being the less publicity-worthy municipality, is soon forgotten.) The usual dancing girls waft around the court in mid-afternoon in the usual Oriental undies. The wicked Queen of Sodom (Anouk Aimée) occasionally tilts her eyes lecherously above her drinking cup at her current female favourite, but the worst she gets up to is casting a pearl into the asses' milk on the girls' bath-night. The wicked Prince of Sodom (Stanley Baker) curls his fly whisk round nymphets' chins, but the only improper suggestion he makes is to the captain of the bodyguard, and this the censor has properly deleted, as the jump cut in the action will still tell you. The worst torture anyone suffers is suffered decoratively by Miss Scilla Gabel whose pneumatic charms are irreparably punctured by a man in a spiked undervest. Heigh-ho! afternoons must have dragged in Sodom. . . .

Across the river of Jordan, there is hardly much more action in the tents of the Hebrews led by Lot in the improbable person of Stewart Granger complete with a complexion like a peach-fed ham, a prophet's robe, a Moses wig, grey elder-statesmen side-curls, and advanced ideas on slavery. The story, written by one Hugo Butler, follows the Bible with touching literalness if not total literacy. It contains at least one mad, memorable moment. No sooner has Lot taken in one of the Queen's ex-slaves (Pier Angeli) and replaced her sheer-line finery with a sack-cloth shift that the ungrateful girl clearly thinks even a Hebrew wouldn't be seen dead in, than in runs his own daughter (Rossana Podesta) in a Sodomite gown given to her by the Prince which laces—but only just—down the side. '*How dare you appear in clothes like that,*' thunders Lot. '*What would your mother say!*'

To shorten a long, 153-minute story, the Hebrews rout the Helamites and then, since their encampment has been burned down, move in with the Sodomites on an 'equal but separate' footing (wise rule in the circumstances). But though their table manners show immediate improvement, their morals sag badly, and they are sobered up just in time by a pair of visionary angels who unfortunately phrase their greeting so that it reaches filmgoers' ears as, 'We have a message for you lot.' Jehovah finally strikes the Sin Cities which brings the special effects men into their own with a jamboree of wrack and ruin, fire and earthquake. A pity they then try to cap it by showing Lot's wife turning into a pillar of salt, and only bathetically prove how curiously Divine wrath anticipated Henry Moore.

I commiserate with Robert Aldrich—directing a religious epic is like getting run down on your own slipway by an ocean-going liner that then promptly sinks—and impatiently await his next film, *What Ever Happened to Baby Jane?* in which the twin cities will no doubt be shown a trick or two in wickedness by Bette Davis and Joan Crawford cast as twin sisters.

Evening Standard, 29 November 1962

SAINT BAMBI/*Brother Sun, Sister Moon*

Other ages, other drop-outs. Franco Zeffirelli's new film sees St Francis of Assissi as a thirteenth-century Flower Child. A viable concept, I suppose. But did it have to be so glib and facile, so sweetened into picturesque superficiality, so reverentially unquestioning in its deference to the hippy life-style?

'War is beautiful,' declares young Francis (Graham Faulkner) the night before his call-up for the Perugia battle-front. However, staggering back badly rattled months later, he is put into the convent's intensive-care unit where nuns speed his recuperation with a Donovan special ('*Flowers in the meadow, rabbits in the orchard*,' it runs). Out comes a changed teenager who casts looks of compassion at the working classes—they stare back and wipe their noses with the backs of the hands to show their commonness. Rejecting his war-profiteer father, he casts off middle-class respectability along with all his clothes in a chastely angled scene in the main street and goes off without a stitch on to lead the hippy life of commune-building along with other distempered children of the middle-classes and a girl-friend called Clare (Judi Bowker).

They have a rotten time in the rainy season till Francis reminds them that there's still a place for sex in the brotherhood. After that, things go so well at the wee kirk in the valley, where Donovan's lyrics introduce a mild swing to the litany, that they steal the local bishop's congregations. Reprisals follow; whereupon, breaking off bathing the halt and lame in the brook to the sound of Donovan's babbling lyrics,

Francis goes to Rome and gives them St Matthew, verses 19–33, which is badly received by the over-dressed house till Pope Innocent III (Alec Guinness) shrewdly gives his endorsement to this new brand of soul-food by kissing Francis's tastefully made-up toe.

Bro-oth-her Sun, Si-his-ter Moon, as Donovan's song re-phra-hases the title, has been called a marvellous spectacle for the eye. Well, so it is with its tangerine sunsets, pointilliste poppy-fields, water-colour limpid woods and virginal snow-plains. But what can't be endured is its being beautiful all the time, every one of its 122 minutes looking like an art-gallery masterpiece. The overall effect is one of suffocating chicness, so that even the Papal scenes, which are *meant* to look suffocating, come off looking as if *Vogue* had put out a Vatican issue. There was always a suspicion of blandness in Zeffirelli's films that left me uneasy. Now it's the *only* thing in this one and it's as opportunist in its evasive way as the glib contrast between false piety and true poverty which is represented by cutting quickly from bloated bishops to suppurating beggars. It can only please those who prefer their religion to spread more easily than butter.

Evening Standard, 12 April 1973

PROPAGANDIST/*The Gospel According to St Matthew*

I have often wanted to see on the screen a life of Christ in which the characters didn't look as if they had read the Bible in advance and knew how they should behave. With *The Gospel According to St Matthew*, I have found it.

Pasolini's remarkable Italian version opens with a close-up of an unshaven, suspicious Joseph glaring at an almost furtive looking Mary. The camera moves back and confronts us with what he sees— the unwelcome fact of her pregnancy. The notion of a virgin giving birth is thus stated with all the sexual suspiciousness it must have aroused at the time—and only then does the Angel of the Lord appear, with the utmost naturalness, to set the record right. If I use worldly terms like 'set the record right', it's because Pasolini encourages me to do so. He meets the Gospels head on. His film treats facts as facts— and the miracles as merely superior facts. Its faith is not specifically religious. It is the faith of a reporter's notebook: it sets down events as they happen and keeps hindsight to the minimum. Yet it grips the historical and psychological imagination like no other religious film I've seen.

For all its apparent simplicity, it is visually rich and contains strange, disturbing hints and undertones about Christ and his mission. Nothing meek or mild about Pasolini's Jesus. I suppose the features could just about pass for those sanctified by millions of altar portraits; but in action on the screen, it is the face of a near-despot, not a redeemer. Its eyebrows meet about the nose, its mouth looks printed on the pale skin, it's so sharp cut—and when it opens, it barks out curt commands. 'Come!' he orders, and his Disciples down tools and come—the lack of one single instant's hesitation conveying explosively the feeling of a land that's keyed-up, waiting, expectant. . . . Similarly, the Sermon on the Mount is split up into short, stabbing bursts of speech delivered in all kinds of light and weather—the tactics of a propagandist sowing his creed, rather than the usual long-winded exhortation of the top table's guest of honour at a public banquet.

Astonishing and welcome are many other breaks with Biblical orthodoxy and screen spectaculars. Herod's death is no State occasion, but a lonely series of elastic spasms suffered in front of impersonal courtiers. Salome's dance is almost demure, which makes her request for the Baptist's head all the more perverted. At Christ's trial, the camera keeps dodging about behind the spectators, trying to see over the shoulders—the documentary impact is stunning. Best of all, Pasolini holds back where Hollywood directors have busted their budgets. He *scales down* the Crucifixion—and we realise for the first time on the screen, perhaps, how an event that has become universal in time was once strictly local in place.

Pasolini has pulled in faces from the Italian peasantry recruited for the film that are amazing survivals from the age of Breughel, Lucas Cranach and Hieronymus Bosch and thus suggest earlier, wilder ages in history. Everyone in the film is a non-professional: its Christ is a young Spanish student.

Inevitably it will arouse controversy and disagreement, but one thing is certain: it is a tremendously personal film. No one has consulted the Pope, the Chief Rabbi, the Archbishop of Canterbury or even the Emperor of Japan before making it. One man has simply put his own vision of Christ on to the screen unimpaired by holy dogma or production diktats—and that in itself is a small miracle.

Evening Standard, 1 June 1967

All the same, for all my admiration for Pasolini, I have a residual regret for the passing of those holy pantomimes, now called irreverently 'Christpics', that used to roll along every five years or so with their load of piety and (hopeful) profit borne on the shoulders of an all-star cast, few of whom were more than a flash in the Panavision as they impersonated the Bible's best 'guest appearance' parts.

Remember the roll-call of *The Greatest Story Ever Told*, George Steven's mammoth PR exercise for God in 1965? Donald Pleasence tempting Christ with a rather off-hand 'How'd you like to be ruler of all this?'; Charlton Heston as John the Baptist bellowing 'Repent!' as he dunks the Roman soldiers sent to arrest him; Ed Wynn as a folksy native of the Holy Land who would look more at home in Disneyland; Van Heflin registering awe; Shelley Winters as the Woman of No Name (and barely two lines, either); John Wayne as a cavalry captain on Calvary ('Tru-ly, he is the Son of Gawd!'); Telly Savalas as Pilate; and Angela Lansbury scarcely doing more than flash him a 'Wash-your-hands-of-the-whole-thing' look. Remember the truly protean preparations to film such a hallowed rite as this, back in the days when the Legion of Decency was on hand, and in force, to make sure the box-office showed proper respect for the cassock? More than three years' researching . . . a pilgrimage by the leading technicians to Israel . . . scrutiny of 'every inch of the soil' on which Christ trod . . . 30 different editions of the Bible examined . . . comparison of the six major translations of every word Jesus spoke . . . consultations with religious leaders of every faith, including Islamic, Hindu and Buddhist . . . and finally all declared ready to roll in the Holy Lands of Nevada, Death Valley and California, at the no-doubt re-dedicated acres of the Desilu Studios.

As if all that wasn't sufficient to guarantee spiritual uplift, we were also promised 'Vital, Exciting, Intensely-Moving Theatre'. I always thought that promissory note held a slight note of self-doubt, a nervous catch in the 'Hosannas', amply justified when a film that was boasted to run 'for ever' had a hard time toughing it out in London's West End.

Nowadays, if they get made at all, religious epics are usually destined for the television audience. Why, I wonder, is the greatest story ever told no longer told any more in the cinema? It can't be because there isn't the finance. More likely, there isn't the faith—the faith that it would show a box-office profit of the same order as the film genre that has largely replaced the 'Christpic'. I mean, the lay 'disaster epic'. I suppose this was only to be expected—at least we can say so, now, with the smugness of hindsight. Every period of history which deserts God, or believes itself deserted by him, tends to re-distribute its fears and superstitions among such worldly phenomena as the insurance policies characterise in their fine print as 'acts of God'.

The proliferation of 'disaster' epics began, I suppose, with shipwreck in *The Poseidon Adventure*, in 1974—at least it showed the money there was to be made out of spectacular calamity—and continued, as I have described elsewhere in this book, with other elemental events such as air crashes (*Airport '75*,) conflagrations (*Towering Inferno*) and earthquakes (*Earthquake*) so that one soon began to hope that a non-proliferation treaty would be signed. All of these were contemporary melodramas devoid of overt religious uplift—though nuns and priests were on the passenger or casualty lists in some of them. But the disastrous event that was central to them all surely showed divine perspicacity in the way it singled out the virtuous from the wicked in spite of the distractions offered by the special effects. The audiences that paid to see disaster strike mustn't be allowed to depart unpurged, without seeing how it did God's work quite as thoroughly as Christ or Moses, confirming the courageous, exalting the righteous, punishing the faithless, exposing the malefactors, reuniting the separated, dignifying the humble, casting down the mighty and rebuking the adulterous, or, at least, giving them cause to repent when the flames are devouring their bedroom of high-rise sin on the 137th storey and 'the firemen can't fight anything satisfactorily above the seventh'.

An off-shoot of this is, of course, the 'Devilpic', and *it* can probably date its rise to box-office phenomenon from the very film, *Rosemary's Baby*, in which was featured a copy of *Time* magazine with the cover story slogan, 'Is God Dead?' Well, we may no longer intone 'Amen' as fervently as DeMille used to command us to do: but after seeing *Towering Inferno*, we can still affirmatively state that, yes, Caroline, God is alive and well and living above the seventh storey.

The spread of the occult has, of course, accompanied the proliferation of disasters, off screen and on. Certainly production
coin is quickly pushed across the desk nowadays to back any
film that deals spectacularly enough—which generally means
messily or bloodily enough—with the inexplicable—which
invariably means inimical—forces at loose in the world. It is an
off-shoot of the drug culture which in turn begat the rock-pop
'generation' which in turn begat the psychedelic experience
which in turn collapsed in on itself in the early 1970s.

I also think it's connected with the conspicuous rise to box-
office power of the black audience who, in some American cities,
are all that keep the cinemas going: they have generally kept
more faith with the moviegoing habit than the whites on the
run from the city centres and even suburban retreats to their
last redoubts in exurbia. Blacks have made up a large percentage of the audience for occult movies, and not just ones like
The Possession of Joel Delaney which have some sympathetic
coloration. Images of disorder and anarchy upsetting the
rational and usually predominantly white and privileged groups
in such films may have elicited a response from the generally
disadvantaged black audiences, though there are obvious
elements in race history that promote a more fervent, cele-
bratory attitude to religion among black than whites.

But the international success of films about occult influence
also indicates the genre's strong, non-racial appeal in a world
where 'un-reason' is the ruler and 'forecasting' by whatever
name it is known—'opinion polling', 'futurology', etc.—shows
the growth industry in augury and omens. I find it fascinating
to follow the way that the occult changes form and definition
as it pervades the old genre movies like the horror cycle and
fills them with a social appositeness we may not quite detect
till some time later, as was the case with me when I reviewed
Rosemary's Baby, the true begetter if not the onlie one, of
most of what followed.

SINS OF THE FATHER/*Rosemary's Baby*

The anguished heroine, who's just realised she's carrying the infant
Antichrist in her womb, is frantically dialling a friend for help. Outside
the locked door, the diabolist coven who have induced the satanic
pregnancy, are beating to get in.

Outside. . . ? Why suddenly two unfocused figures, like a threat glimpsed out of the corner of one's eye, tiptoe quickly up behind her. Have they dissolved the walls to get at Rosemary (Mia Farrow)? One is reminded of director Roman Polanski's earlier film, *Repulsion*, where an insane girl's fantasies of rape suddenly materialised in the shape of dark figures who gripped her an instant, then vanished. The explanation here turns out to be simple and natural. But the moment is typical of this brilliant film, it suggests so disturbingly the presence of evil magic in ordinary events, behind harmless objects, inside the most neighbourly acts of kindness and the most commonplace experience in the world—having a baby.

That dowdily fashionable apartment house in New York: it looks at the start such a cosy little warren. By the end it's become a possessive coven, a Gothic prison, a cradle for the Antichrist. . . . A girl can get trapped in its corridors. Its sub-divided rooms are resonating boxes for faintly heard chanting. Its musty colours have been subtly altered to emphasise the reds, yellows, ochres we only half saw at first—as if some door had been opened on to hell's glowing fires.

Polanski's script, plus William Fraker's insinuating photography, tip us hints—no, half-hints—about what might be going on. That chocolate mousse the insistent neighbours give Rosemary for supper—is there more in it than meets the taste-buds? The scratches on her body when she wakes up beside her husband (John Cassavetes)—was it just the night's love-play? The herbal drinks the doctor recommends for her pregnancy—are they sustaining or subverting the foetus welding itself so painfully into her? The actor's sudden blindness that gives her own actor husband his big break—was it just a coincidence or has *he* signed a contract with the Devil as well as Broadway? (The film, by the way, takes the sourest side-glance yet at the insincerity and opportunism of actors.)

The section of *Rosemary's Baby* that's been most publicly controversial—her nightmare of being raped by Satan, which the censor has unjustifiably cut—is actually its least successful. Though skilfully filmed in waves of nausea, its glimpse of magic rites and scaly hands contains the mummery of magic, not the menace. The simplest things in the film—the shot of a stranger's back waiting outside a phone booth for Rosemary to finish—are more unsettling than the carefully laid set pieces. One of the cleverest calculations is the exploitation of the 'generation gap'. The two young people are the victims of such old Hollywood hands as Ralph Bellamy, Sydney Blackmer and Ruth Gordon whose success in the roles may inspire teenagers with the suspicion that everyone over 30 is a diabolist. But the sharpest bit of casting is Mia Farrow. Her curious physical deficiencies are turned into advantages by Polanski who makes the thin, ravaged, angular, listless, anorexia-like appearance that the character presents, especially when Mia Farrow is shorn almost down to her scalp by Vidal Sassoon, into a pathetic counterpoint to the supernatural powers operating on her. I congratulate him on the pregnant performance he has induced in his star.

Evening Standard, 23 January 1969

I think there is a good case for going back to look at a film again when changing social patterns encourage us to see things in it that were missed the first time round. I had this opportunity with *Rosemary's Baby*.

ROSEMARY'S BABYFOOD

Even before the passing of the Sex Discrimination Act, one sensed that male chauvinism was changing its spots. Not changing its nature, you understand, but simply presenting a less conspicuous target to the sharpshooters of sex equality. The subtlety with which the creature still stalks the entertainment jungle can be seen if you look at what's been happening to the horror movie in recent years—ever since Rosemary had her Baby, in fact. Nineteen Sixty-eight, that would be, when Mia Farrow took one appalled look into the crepe-hung bassinette surrounded by god-parents from the neighbourhood coven, and discovered what the Devil had fathered on her.

That strain is still going strong. This spring alone sees two new horror movies, both of them based on the notion of woman as the progenitor of earthly evil through the agency of AID, or artificial insemination by a demon. *The Omen* is the title of one of them, in which Gregory Peck adopts a foundling of subsequently satanic disposition. The other film announces in tones that are staid enough for the back page of *The Times*: *To the Devil, a Daughter*. Moreover, it is only last year that cinema programmes were sounding like bulletins issuing from some maternity ward where brimstone was the likeliest analgesia. *The Devil Within Her* came along one month; *I Don't Want to be Born* followed a few weeks later; finally there was the grim communiqué, *It's Alive!* All of them dealt with demonic gynaecology—

the three-parent family, in fact, in which the husband was, consciously or not, the Devil's surrogate. At a time when social welfare was concentrating on the one-parent family and sex equality, it was an odd example of male chauvinism diving for cover (or coven), though it is one we might have expected in a male-dominated industry like the movies.

Such was the interest in the occult in the late 1960s that I think we were sidetracked. We quite overlooked the fact that *Rosemary's Baby* was filmed at the same time as Women's Lib was winning the front-page headlines and its first prominent converts in the United States. No one, I think, attacked the film at that time for being a male chauvinist fantasy laced with the occult, in which pregnancy is the last resort of a man who defines a woman simply by reference to her biological function. And in this case, you will remember, it was the final payment on a bond signed by Rosemary's husband, who was that arch-male chauvinist, *an actor*, and traded his wife to the Devil for a fat role on Broadway. The wife who stays at home and bears a baby while her husband goes out and does the exciting, prestigious things in the world, like acting: you couldn't have a neater statement of male chauvinism coupled with the additionally comforting view of woman as a blameworthy mate who introduces evil into the happy household. Reviewers might be a bit more pointed in identifying the chauvinism that was Rosemary's babyfood in the days just before Germaine Greer, Betty Friedan, Gloria Steinem, *et alii*, were signposting the road to sex equality. It is no accident that a film called *The Stepford Wives*, made by Bryan Forbes in America last year, has had a rather more muted welcome, even though it is based on another of Ira Levin's novels and deals in the same sort of twentieth-century witchcraft known as male chauvinism. Not just one sexist, but a whole community of them this time, the husbands in a commuter-country township, conspire to make their wives over completely into docile sex-objects, and do in fact turn them into female zombies. But somehow, because we have all been clued in now to what is going on by the Women's Libbers, the submissive mores of exurbia have lost their potency. The appeal has dated. You could of course say that the popularity of male chauvinism is directly related to its evil kick, that it just won't work in a domestic setting today unless it is given the added dimension of horror, which is where the Devil comes in. For he is the ultimate chauvinist. But even he had better watch out. In an era of sexual equality, even a man who pulls satanic rank on a sex-object can get into serious trouble. One of these days Rosemary could actually cry 'Rape!' Worse still, the message could spread to Salem, and before sunset the women will be forming branches of Witches' Lib and going in for abortion counselling.

Vogue, 15 April 1976

WHERE DOES IT HURT?/*The Devils*

'Have you thought of the pain to come?' asks one of the inquisitors. 'It cannot be different from the pain I have seen,' answers his victim. 'True,' comes the reply, 'except in its location.'

That lively exchange says quite a lot about *The Devils*. In fact, it says everything about it. The pain changes location on the bodies of Oliver Reed and Vanessa Redgrave every five minutes or so as one or other is put to the torture in order to drive the devils out of them. But one way or the other, one place or the other, it's all the same pain. Even if you are the star graduate of the Torquemada School of Film Direction, so undifferentiating an assault on the senses of your audience, never mind the bodies of your stars, is likely to provoke not horror, but indifference. Not reflection, but numbness. Not scandal at your own outrageousness, but concern for your artistic sanity.

Ken Russell's film depicts events in the demonology trials of seventeenth-century France which are lewd, obscene and blasphemous. It does so for the most part with plausible historical accuracy. But nothing the screen shows us is so monstrously indecent as the simple-mindedness of a writer-director who believes that the best way of approaching the problems of conscience and the ills of the soul is through the repeated physical agonies of the flesh. The film is a garish glossary of sado-masochism wildly at variance with the booklet put out by Warner Bros. which is filled with scholarly glosses on religious heresies and State politics in a pretentious and vain attempt to give filmgoers the essential 'perspective' on events which the movie itself ought to have achieved had it crossed the threshold of intelligence as often as it leaps over the threshold of pain. In the circumstance, the historical guidebook looks less like a crib than an alibi.

Inspired, it would seem, more directly by Dachau and De Sade than by either Aldous Huxley's book or John Whiting's play on which Russell has based his script, *The Devils* deals with the attempt by Cardinal Richelieu (Christopher Logue) and his lay and ecclesiastical minions (Dudley Sutton, Michael Gothard, Murray Melvin) to rid themselves of an obstinate priest (Oliver Reed) by alleging that the admittedly sensual man has used unholy means to infest the Mother of the Ursulines (Vanessa Redgrave) with erotic fantasies.

Almost every serious question raised by the historical situation is thrown away by Russell in order to flaunt a taste for visual sensation that makes scene after scene look like the masturbatory fantasies of a Roman Catholic boyhood. The exercise of statecraft by Louis XIII (Graham Armitage) is reduced to camp charades in drag, or an inexplicable glimpse of His Majesty gunning down Protestant heretics in feathered costumes with an anachronistic murmur of 'Bye-Bye blackbird'. (A trailer, maybe, for Russell's next film, the 1920s musical *The Boy Friend*?)

A good film could be made about erotic possession in the enclosed order of nuns. Indeed a good film *has* been made about it—in 1960, by Jerzy Kawalerowicz, whose *Mother Joan of the Angels* dealt with the very same events as *The Devils*. But where his film was austerely analytical, Russell's is grotesquely anatomical. In fantasy, the Mother Superior licks the stigmata of her lover, seen as a crucified Jesus, with erotic relish. Impromptu medicals are carried out on the altar table. Nude nuns massage church candles with lubricious glee. Hot-water enemas are applied at various points. Vomit is picked through for a crumb of undigested demon. A pectoral cross used as a makeshift dildo has proved too strong for the censor's stomach and at one point 'other means' are used by an inquisitor whose nature can only be guessed at from a bystander's expression. For this reticence, much thanks.

The hunchbacked nun played by Miss Redgrave has an initial physical power, like a bent ikon. But psychologically, her role is as expressive as tortured iron. Rather than perform it, she does the only sensible thing—she abandons herself to it. Likewise Oliver Reed, allowed a few noble speeches on tolerance and quiet reflections on the nature of celibacy versus marriage, is then subjected to a process of disintegration in which his head is shaven, his tongue stretched, his testicles pierced, his lower limbs split by wooden wedges and his body finally flambéed over a quick flame—but not so quick that you can't see every blister and boil on his blackening face portrayed in Technicolor close-up. One man comes out of *The Devils* very well: Mr Charles Parker, chief make-up man.

Evening Standard, 22 July 1971

This review involved me in the only assault—to date, anyhow—made on me by the director of a film I have criticised unfavourably. The BBC TV people who had been alerted, late in the day one might think, to the enormous brouhaha *The Devils* was provoking, rushed invitations to Russell and myself to appear on live TV on the very day my review appeared. We were kept in separate 'bull pens', tethered by lapel microphones to the cables on the studio floor, till the moderator, Ludovic Kennedy, got the signal to extricate himself from a fairly prickly interview with Denis Healey, then Minister of Defence, and turn his clip-board towards us. Battle was in the air, I judged, from Russell's tight hold on that day's copy of the *Evening Standard*. Kennedy had seen the film in the afternoon and, it was soon obvious, hadn't liked it, either. Tempers rose: the level of debate did not. Russell exploded, 'I don't make films for critics: I make them for the public.' 'The public don't seem too grateful, especially in America,' I retorted. 'Then go to America and write for the fucking Americans,' *Rat! Tat! Tat!*

The damage inflicted by a rolled-up newspaper on one's frontal lobes, even by an outraged filmmaker, is negligible: but having the explosive charge of a four-letter epithet behind it, it appeared as if a veritable cannon had been detonated—and all *live*, too! I remember seeing a monitor out of the corner of my eye on which the image of us both 'jumped' as if the camera operator had just been goosed: then Kennedy was saying, with surely a gulp of distaste for a topic that lacked the clean, sociable cut-and-thrust of nuclear strategy, 'Thank you, Mr Russell, Mr Walker . . . now back to the news headlines.' And it was all over: or rather, it was being continued in another sphere by viewers' indignant telephone calls, anxious BBC executives' private-line enquiries, intrigued Press calls, the whole outraged battery of reflexes that is swivelled on to target whenever national morality has been put in jeopardy. I fear the truth was that the burden of complaints fell on the language used and not the injury suffered.

The sequel was rather shabbier and less blood pounding: a letter from Russell that appeared in *Radio Times* alleging collusion between Ludovic Kennedy and myself in order to do him down. Since neither Kennedy nor I had ever before met professionally, or, as far as we recalled, socially, until he walked over from Denis Healey to begin interviewing us, it was a charge that was factually and demonstrably untrue, as the *Radio Times* subsequently acknowledged.

I am still surprised at the numbers of people who saw, or claim to have seen, an encounter that has become part of folk history at Television Centre. I suppose the sheer rarity of a live and unplanned bit of 'aggro' gives it a vividness that doesn't fade with the image or the years. Regrettably, if the incident was recorded, the tape no longer exists: though an earlier, still demonstrative but physically unassertive confrontation between Russell and myself occasionally gets shown, introduced last time by Robert Robinson with feral relish as 'The very Montagu and Capulet of critical feuds . . .' Russell and I have not met since, except in the newspaper columns, where he (vainly) requested that I be removed as critic during the week of *The Boy Friend*'s Press show. We have seen each other at a wary distance. I bear neither scar nor malice. Indeed I respect the man all the more for living up to his own image.

CRASH COURSE/*The Exorcist*

Exactly what are we watching when we go to *The Exorcist*? Easy to answer, you'd think. Easy and shocking. The invasion of a child's body by Satan and his 57 varieties of punishing (and highly photogenic) phenomena which manifest themselves in urination; pumping vomit into the priest's face; scars, wounds and blisters on the body; SOS messages for help appearing on the tummy; a furry tongue; a head that swivels 360 degrees on the spinal column; an ability to reduce the sick room to the temperature of a deep freeze; mutilation with a crucifix; a loss of weight until levitation becomes possible; and a gain in weight until the 12-year-old girl packs the punch of a heavyweight boxer. . . . There, I've got that out of my system for a start!

The Devil and all his special effects are the things people are flocking to see. Worth the money, they are, most of them. The head-turning trick is a bit muffed, I admit, since the camera turns *its* head away in mid-swivel; and the green bile comes out looking suspiciously like pea soup. But the sloshing on of the Holy water is impressive, every drop provoking an open wound on the troubled flesh. The Church in action all right—and, appropriately, on an 'Action Girl' doll (Linda Blair).

For, frankly, *The Exorcist* is nothing but a superior shocker. A very well-made horror movie with pretensions to something better (or certainly deeper) that never does more than stick its nose out, then hastily withdraw. For all its opportunity for delving into the spiritual state of being 'possessed', it does nothing but exhibit the physical state. Though posing as a serious film, it has hardly six lines of serious dialogue about the inner life of the afflicted—though it has a plethora of what you could call 'body language' about the innards of the afflicted.

Denied any real understanding of the events, much less sympathy with the people they descend on, we must settle for the freak show. And we emerge shocked, though not shriven. As all of it happens in modern Washington, DC, near Georgetown University's Jesuit campus (handy), to the child of a famous film star (Ellen Burstyn) who's making a movie on location there, it's a nice change from the non-sectarian Old Dark House horrors. But make no mistake: it's the same brand of the willies.

The acting is simply a function of the happenings: it's efficient-to-excellent, but nothing more. Jack McGowran is the director of the film-within-the-film who has his head screwed fatally round the wrong way while baby-sitting with Satan's child (a scene inexplicably not illustrated). Lee J. Cobb is a suspicious police detective, who's a film fan as it turns out, hunting more for autographs than criminals. Jason Miller is a young Jesuit, Max von Sydow an old one; and both of them read the 20-minute service of exorcism from the Roman ritual ('The large one,' says von Sydow, sending to the seminary for the prompt book) as if they were rooting for the home team at a football game. Considering the pair of them end up very dead indeed—Miller after one of the most awesome tumbles down a flight of stone steps that I have ever witnessed—the game's result isn't entirely reassuring to Our Side: it reads like Satan Two, God Nil.

But what I shall now be bold enough to do is interpret the film *my* way. Which is that, essentially, it is a screenwriter's allegory about filmmaking—a process that is represented as being sheer hell.

Under the surface of the events, William Peter Blatty the writer-producer (and it must have required some muscle to produce the film you've also adapted from your own novel and also demote the director, William Friedkin, to the place beneath the title) is showing us all the ills that can befall the creative writer, and his precious child of a film script, while trying to keep them both pure and protect them from the diabolical forces to be found around any Hollywood studio where the powers that be want to 'possess' the writer's idea and distort and transmogrify it. 'Film is an industry,' Blatty has been quoted as saying, 'in which writers are either broken, or wind up murdering people in the streets.' Which is exactly what the possessed child does in *The Exorcist*, beginning, significantly enough, with the film-director character.

Moreover, all the film folk in *The Exorcist* are viewed with venomous distaste. The movie-actress mother is an over-moneyed bitch who bawls out international telephone operators if they can't get her estranged husband on the line pronto. The director is a drunken bully who disparages film writers. The detective-come-film fan is just the kind of news hound you find sniffing round the perimeter of a closed set, hoping to pick up a bit of dirt on the stars. Even the film that's being shot within *The Exorcist* is entitled *Crash Course*, a neat synonym for the service of exorcism itself.

Indeed the only nice, trustworthy folk in the film are the two priests, Fathers Miller and von Sydow, the younger one a practising psychiatrist as well, the elder a famous archeologist. It's they who restore the child and deliver her from all the ills that flesh—or film writers—are heir to. When I reveal that Mr William Peter Blatty's own childhood ambitions were to be either a psychiatrist or an archae-ologist, and at one time he earned his living as a public relations man at Loyola University, I can quite believe someone will murmur, 'Elementary, my dear Watson. . . .' Or perhaps, in this case, 'Elemental. . . .'

Anyway, that's my theory and I'm sticking to it, come hell or Holy water.

Evening Standard, 14 March 1974

Trendy or Timely

It used to take time to reveal a 'trend'. Now it only takes a single box-office hit. I think that's what I find most depressing in current cinema—the speed of the follow-up. The ruthless diagnosis of some public symptom as soon as accident has revealed it—and invariably it is an *accidental* hitting of the nerve that produces the knee-kick reflex; for in the cinema the best-laid pre-plans of moviemakers are usually the ones that take them nowhere. But once the phenomenon has struck the box-office—then stand clear! There'll be a rush of follow-ups, rip-offs, second helpings of the same, strange mutations, anything that can cling to the original's coat-tails.

Pauline Kael has said the public no longer discovers movies, 'the public no longer makes a picture a hit.' I'd only disagree to the extent of saying that the public doesn't discover the *second* film once the trend has been located, or the third, or the fourth, or the forty-fourth. By *that* time, as Kael says, (the public) 'don't listen to their instincts, they don't listen to the critics, they listen to the advertising. Or, to put it more precisely, they do listen to their instincts, but their instincts are now controlled by advertising.'* That's certainly what happens with such media-created 'event films' that get (or hope to get) the benefit of the booster rockets fired by the first, really original movie to take-off. The rest often travel a long and profitable way in its jet stream. Thank goodness, though, that some films, some trends do catch us unprepared and give us that increasingly rare sense of discovery. I should really write 'me' instead of 'us', for, as may be seen in some of the following pieces, my excitement wasn't always shared by the public. Well, too bad for the public.

HAVE GUN, MAY KILL/*Dr No*

Moistening my typewriter ribbon with a spot of vodka Martini, let me introduce the screen's newest character. He has gun-metal hair, a figure that makes him a tall target for assassins, the patina of a playboy, the constitution of a commando and an Irish accent soft as peat smoke. Except for that accent—which gets over those awkward English vowels that American filmgoers find so irritating—and except that he hasn't got the famous comma of black hair falling in his eyes, this is

* 'On the Future of Movies', by Pauline Kael. *The New Yorker*, 5 August 1974.

Ian Fleming's James Bond down to the 60-guinea tailor's label. And in the person of Sean Connery, it is my prediction he will be around on the screen for a long time to come.

Dr No was made in Britain and Jamaica, in colour that does its Caribbean setting as proud as any travel poster. And there is never a moment—well, very few—when one feels the pace is palling, the invention running low, or the ways death is being dealt out are getting a bit repetitive. As a check-list for Bond fans, I report that Agent 007—the double zero means he is licensed to kill—gets chipped by gunfire, singed by a flame-thrower, tickled in bed by a tarantula, dogged by bloodhounds, grilled by electric fencing, drugged by coffee, swamped by sea water, steam-dried by a hot pipe and nearly atomised by a nuclear pile. He survives.

By putting their tongues often enough in their cheeks, the producers manage to turn Ian Fleming's sometimes unsavoury plot ingredients into what one could call sadism for the family. The beautiful women they have put in the film ebb, trickle and gush through it as if the makers had left running the tap marked 'Dames'. First in line is Sylvia (Eunice Gayson), a brunette whom Bond has just raked in with his gambling chips, when his soulless boss 'M' (Bernard Lee) speeds off on a mission. Pausing only long enough to make his usual tender farewell to the lady, who has somehow got into his Chelsea flat and is passing the time practising chip shots wearing only a shirt of Bond's—no doubt the brand-name that looks even better on a man—he enplanes for Jamaica where a sinister power (Joseph Wiseman) is diverting American rockets off-course from his off-shore islet. In Kingston he is lured into the foothills by a beautiful Chinese (Zena Marshall); but Bond's boudoirmanship is equal to this and in his own good time he has the lady transferred from private clinch to Government clink. When he lands on Dr No's private beach, the third and most bosomy lady, a honey-blonde child of nature called Honey, walks out of the waves at his feet. She is played by an actress new to me whose name is Andress, but whose line is undress.

Together they fall into Dr No's luxury lair-cum-lab, which resembles a combination of London Airport, Cary Grant's bathroom and a salesroom at Christie's. The climax with Honey staked out for the crabs, Bond wiggling through an obstacle race of interlocking torture chambers, and Dr No ready to blow up our American ally, leaves no switch unthrown. Directed by Terence Young, this thriller is content if it makes your mind boggle—which it does, with the powerful assistance of Ken Adam's sets—and then leaves you smiling tolerantly at your own naïveté. But it manages some felicitous subtleties. Such as when Bond, on his way through Dr No's living-room, spots a painting that looks familiar. Is it? It is! The National Gallery's stolen Goya of the Duke of Wellington. So that's where it went!

Evening Standard, 27 September 1962

Yes, I know, I know . . . We are so much more sophisticated nowadays about the stupefying virility and chauvinist sadism of 007; and I was in a minority when I thought the first portrayer of Bond, Connery Mark 1, (before he lost the rough-cast look and became the smooth-planed James of the later series), represented him as Fleming desired. 'People who have read my books will be disappointed,' Fleming wrote to me a few weeks later, when the review had probably been 'brought to his attention' (he was assiduous in his withdrawal from anything as vulgar as movie huckstering, which probably included reviews). But he conceded: 'Those who haven't, will find it exceptionally good entertainment.'

He was right—and wrong. People who had (and hadn't) read Bond said 'Yes' to *Dr No* in such phenomenal numbers that the most lucrative myth of the 1960s was given a momentum that took it well into the next decade. In *Hollywood, England* I have suggested the reasons in more detail, but they are already present in the review: the 'play-time' mood of death-dealing nonchalance, the dimension of fantasy, the hint of cruelty beneath the sexual charm, and the ideal of the swinging life that was at the same time presentably pro-Establishment and properly subservient to authority. As one of the earliest symptoms of internationally viable permissiveness in the 1960s, Bond's appearance was perfectly timed. I'd only add two things. One is that I erred when I identified Connery's voice as 'Irish': it is Scottish, in fact. The other is that if today's fantasies have kept pace with inflation, so have the prices of Savile Row suits and the '60-guinea tailor's label' would give the fastidious Fleming a tasteful shudder, if he were alive today.

DO MAKE WAVES/*Il Mare*

There is still time for filmgoers who don't mind being in at the end of a trend to make their own 'New Wave' movie. The kind in which whatever it is that happens to the characters, nothing whatsoever must seem to happen on the screen. After seeing a beauty of the species, *Il Mare*, I offer the following instructions.

Begin at the beginning with THE TITLE. Do not go overboard. Stick to simple words like *L'Avventura* (*The Affair*), or *La Notte* (*The Night*), or *L'Eclisse* (*The Eclipse*), or *Il Mare* (*The Sea*). A title like *Last Year in Marienbad* indicates a lack of discipline.

THE ACTORS: Engage Italians if possible—preferably Italians of the new, non-voluble generation. They must be good at saying nothing for long stretches of the film. If you cannot afford Marcello Mastroianni, Monica Vitti and Alain Delon (who now passes for Italian), hire people as much like them as possible. *Il Mare* has Umberto Orsini, Françoise Prevost (who can pass for Italian) and Fino Mele.

THE CHARACTERS: You *may* get by with two, but you *must* have no more than three—preferably two males, one female. The whole purpose of the film is to tell the audience as little as possible about the characters, so pay attention to:

THEIR NAMES: You *may* give each character one first name (no more), but it is better to call them simply 'A', 'B' and 'X', as in *Last Year in Marienbad*. In *Il Mare* a compromise has been reached: they are called simply The Man, The Woman and The Boy. Quite enough to be going on with, for if you reveal more about them you risk having:

A PLOT: Leave this strictly to the filmgoers. They don't want to know what *you* think is going on between The Man, The Woman and The Boy in *Il Mare*. Let *them* ask themselves, Is The Man deserting The Boy in favour of The Woman? Is The Boy coming between The Man and The Woman? Is The Woman trying to attract The Man and The Boy? Audiences will enjoy themselves figuring out what such relationships are at any given moment. It is as stimulating as geometry. But of course even a plot like this must have:

A SETTING: Very, very important. As empty and devoid of life as possible. If you don't favour city suburbs between the rush hours—as in *La Notte* and *L'Eclisse*—the very next best thing is an island. *Il Mare* is set on Capri—*but in wintertime*. Grey skies. Weak sun. Not a tourist in sight. You never get the idea that Gracie Fields is anywhere in the vicinity. This would be fatal to:

THE ACTION: The essential part of this is known as THE WALK. People take minutes to walk to their table from the restaurant door. They trail each other down Capri's alleyways, up street steps, along hotel corridors—the tempo may be varied by the odd violent action, such as spitting in the sea, but nothing should be too definite. Take great care over such an element as LOVE. Keep your head. You may show close-ups of ear-lobes and knee-caps. But skip the night of frustrated passion: enough to show The Man retrieving his socks at dawn. Impress on your cast that this will confer on them tremendous advantages when it comes to:

THE ACTING: Since nothing is explained for sure in the film, critics approaching it will have nothing to check the acting against. Dialogue should be spoken flatly like a recorded language-course—e.g. 'What time does the express connect with the Naples boat?' To some, the acting may look like sleep-walking, but there will always be the critic who will call it 'brilliantly understated'. Your leading lady's face may look as if it has been set in plaster-of-Paris, but some critic is sure to describe her as 'Garbo-esque'.

The golden rule is: *Make the audience work.* 'Less is more' should be your guiding aesthetic; and the less people have to go on, the more they can assume the function of the filmmaker. After all, Do-It-Yourself has invaded practically every other human activity: it is about time it took over the cinema.

Evening Standard, 5 March 1964

GOOD TRIP/*Easy Rider*

Easy Rider, which marks Peter Fonda's debut as film producer, is the tale of two drop-outs (Fonda and his director and co-star Dennis Hopper) looking for freedom on a motor-cycle odyssey from California to Louisiana that takes them through the mythical country of the American Western. The parallel with the old frontier is there, though this sophisticated, observant film doesn't force it. But the hippy communes where young boys have the straggly-moustached look of ageing pioneers, are throw-backs to the covered-waggon days if they are anything. And the mindless violence and indifference to taking life which ultimately thwart the two freedom-seekers is the same that once erupted on the wild frontier—yesterday's bandit is today's bigot, that's all that's changed.

No attempt is made to hide the fact that what finances the journey is the sale of cocaine. (A drug, says Fonda, chosen because it's rare, so far, in hippy circles: but, of course, fetching a higher price on the market.) But lawlessness is the fate, not the object, of the pair as their steeply raked bikes whisk them through scenery of prismatic beauty, backed by the rock numbers of Steppenwolf, Jimi Hendrix, The Electric Prunes and the Holy Modal Experience amongst others. They get unjustly jailed, meet an articulate alcoholic, winningly played by Jack Nicholson, and drop in at a bordello where the LSD episode is the film's flashiest and least successful part. The amazing thing is that *Easy Rider* finds time to exhibit a kind of poetic concern, like Walt Whitman after a bad trip, over what the hell happened to a country which preaches individual freedom, yet destroys the free individual. Even if you can't go along with the slightly fatuous self-importance of the hippies, or Fonda's tendency to bless all he approves of like a teenage Pope, the film remains one of the most perceptive in years to have come out of the direct experience of its makers.

Evening Standard, 4 September 1969

And it remains so . . . It was made for a few hundred thousand dollars and its subsequent box-office take ran over the 30 million dollar mark. There was no hope for it—it just had to be a *trend*. And so Hollywood began to churn out the small-budget 'youth picture'. Fortified by the vast return for small investment, James T. Aubrey, then production chief at MGM, decreed that no film in future should cost more than two million dollars and that all pictures, if possible, should dispense with the stars of one's grandparents' age-group in favour of the bright-eyed, bushy-tailed (and cheap) 'youth' stars. This proposition was made all the sweeter because it came at a time when the major studios, with few exceptions, had run themselves into near-bankruptcy. Any straw was worth grasping, particularly if it cost little.

There followed a succession of movies that made the show of getting deep into the concerns of youth, either on the move or on the rampage, since speed was an essential ingredient in each case, and almost every week seemed to bring a 'road picture' or a 'campus picture'—*Two-Lane Blacktop*; *Bike Boy*; *The Strawberry Statement*; *RPM*; *Drive, He Said*; *The Revolutionary*, in most of which the drug experience represented the culmination of liberalism and violence was invariably an 'other directed' event suffered by the free spirits or the 'Give Peace a Chance' militants. The hollow opportunism of Hollywood has seldom been more nauseatingly exposed in these few years, until it was brought home to the sponsors that such messages as were designed to win friends and influence the box-office were doing neither. Youth will be served all right: but not by cynical entrepreneurs. Fortunately (or unfortunately, depending where your money was) *Airport* came along in 1970, Ross Hunter took over again, James T. Aubrey departed, budgets began soaring, profits outclimbed them, and the stars who were one's grandparents' generation came in from the cold. . . . *Easy Rider*, however, retains its credentials intact, an extraordinary manifestation of the youth culture's thwarted utopianism. I am glad I recognised this at the time, being neither youthful nor utopian: I only wish I had said more about Jack Nicholson. But I have made it up to him since.

Girl meets boy in little, tired Main Street. Shyly, he shows her a gun. Teasingly, she dares him to use it. Like a lover embarking on courtship, he there and then holds up a store and takes a wild shot at the first of 18 people the pair of them will finally kill. 'What's your name, anyway?' she asks in an afterthought as they roar out of town in a stolen car. 'I'm Clyde,' he says. 'I'm Bonnie—pleased to meet you.'

This is the opening, chilling in its depiction of casual violence, riveting in its brilliant, shorthand illustration of two psychopathic characters, to what is, in my considered view, the most significant film to come out of America since *On the Waterfront* over ten years ago. Like that film, *Bonnie and Clyde* has been made by people who are one hundred per cent certain of what they're aiming at. Violence is their theme. It brings an episode of American folk-lore alive and bleeding— and bleeding buckets!—on to the screen, but with a seriousness of intention that can't be convicted of excessive indulgence in sadism and mayhem. Add to this, direction of the kind that cracks characters wide open for inspection, acting of impact from a largely unfamiliar cast, authentic distillation of the Depression Era atmosphere. Above all, constant concern for the social and economic chaos of the time and the public enemies who, like some of those in our time, used it as an alibi for their own criminal impulses.

Warren Beatty, making his bow as producer, may not be history's idea of Clyde Barrow, but he realistically incarnates an all too likely teenage hoodlum living life for kicks. Slack-jointed in the atmosphere of a wild spree, hideously tense in moments of sudden death, he exudes a butch charm that hides a pathetic sexual inadequacy which one astonishingly candid scene makes apparent and thereby adds motive to his reliance on his gun to impress his girl friend. Bonnie Parker is played by Faye Dunaway with a vulpine rapaciousness for experience that more than matches her mate's.

Drinking in their notoriety like oxygen, pulling up at mail boxes to steal a newspaper and read the communiqués on their progress of robbery and murder, they cut a trail through the backwoods of the American South-West, an area of timeless townships evoked by Burnett Guffey's pellucid grey, green and brown photographic hues like those in a Wyeth painting and orchestrated by a ricky-ticky country-and-western type of theme tune that brings a touch of baroque homeliness to the bloodiest escapade. Travelling companions and partners in crime include a hillbilly boy (Michael J. Pollard) with the face of a fallen angel some careless person has stepped on; Clyde's married brother (Gene Hackman), a snap-happy moron who totes a camera as well as a gun; and his wife (Estelle Parsons), a preacher's daughter who stuffs her fingers in her ears during the gunfights. Coming along for the ride, these people find they're hanging on to the tail of a comet.

Bloody scenes of police ambushes and bank robberies alternate almost incredibly with wild slapstick explosions, or scenes of perilously balanced comedy, as when a courting couple in their automobile are hijacked for a lark by the gang. But director Arthur Penn never fails in his ability to choke the laughter off in one's throat. Many moments are vividly etched into my memory: the aftermath of an ambush with the back-seat of the car turned into a blood-pit of wounded, lamenting humanity; the rough-and-ready surgery performed by the light of headlamps; the dawn call to pick up water at a hobos' camp when the refugees from the Depression recognise in Bonnie and Clyde their own avenging allies against the society that ruined them. Most of all I shall remember the audacious sequence, shot in pastoral quietness and lit in dusty, golden tones like a *pointilliste* canvas, when Bonnie takes time off from her odyssey of slaughter to go picnicking with her mother.

Make no mistake: *Bonnie and Clyde* is a film from which we shall date reputations and innovations in the American cinema. Owing nothing to the *techniques* of the European 'new wave' films, it has nevertheless been inspired by their example to shake off old, received traditions, to develop a new, confident, exciting approach to movie-making in America. It cries out to be seen.

Evening Standard, 7 September 1967

And it *was* seen. I think it was its attack on the audience's expectations of this kind of film that gave it that sense of audacity then new in Hollywood cinema. We thought it was comic in patches—then it turned horribly real. We thought it was romantic in patches—then it turned unbelievably bloody. We thought it was nostalgic in patches—then it shuddered with the contemporary characteristics of the psychotic. We were fooled, shaken, elated, shocked, purged: the whole gamut of filmmaking that didn't take anything straight any longer. *M*A*S*H* was to offer even wilder variations on this a few years later; and in both films blood is the common element that adds grisly reality to the absurd goings-on. 'Good taste' was one of the first casualties of the New American Cinema—thank God!

Not so long afterwards Sam Peckinpah's *The Wild Bunch* took the dance-of-death ending of Bonnie and Clyde—to which, I find with alarm, I never referred in the review—and used it as the whole concept of a film, allowing the eye to see in slow-motion what formerly the mind couldn't grasp. (I've more to say about this in the section entitled 'Blood 'n' Guts'.) Peckin-pah's technique spread like a virus through world filmmaking: everyone caught it, some people not once but several times in a fever of bloodletting for bloodletting's sake, till eventually it snuffed itself out (an appropriate end) in general weariness, plus the nervousness of television at showing such mayhem on the home screen.

The other dimension of *Bonnie and Clyde* that I find intensely interesting is the making of public heroes out of a pair of public enemies. *Sugarland Express* and *Dillinger* were later films in the 1970s that expanded the view of the criminal as a man who behaved like a film star—and sometimes *not just* the criminal, since Ben Johnson's G-man in John Milius's *Dillinger* enjoys watching his myth being made through the newspaper head-lines quite as much as Warren Oates' gangster does through his daring bank robberies. Money and publicity are fuel to the myth of supermen, whichever side of the law they operate on, just as they are to superstars on-screen and off. Gangsterdom, it's easy to see, has always had its hometown fascination for Hollywood, where so many of the local boys used its tactics on promoting big business into bigger box-office. How apt that the 'New Hollywood' of the 1960s should be born out of the same fixation. Audiences, I think, feel this 'self-identification' in their bones: they know when they're looking at stars who have grown out of some aspect of the material, maybe not the aspect that's bleeding all over the screen, but an aspect of the char-acters or the theme of the movie that clicks sweetly with the ethos of stardom and produces that laminated sense of total engagement with the material. And that's when movies take off. . . .

Peter Hall's new film, *Three into Two Won't Go*, may prove to be every
bit as much a landmark movie as *Room at the Top*. It has the same
feeling of taking characters who are a sample of British life at one
particular time and cracking them open for our inspection. That time
is now.

Class differences and how they could be exploited for gain by a
ruthless young man on the make: this was the subject matter of *Room
at the Top* in 1958. But age has replaced class as the great divide in the
permissive Britain of the 1960s. The new film is about the generation
gap and how it traps a married man who casually makes use of a
teenage girl for his own sexual pleasure, only to find that today's
teenager is more than a match for him in every way. It is a witty,
sardonic, biting, truthful film. Edna O'Brien's screenplay picks the
situation down to the painful quick. The film touches a nerve in
contemporary life because it knows all about its three characters—
husband, wife, girl interloper—and where they fit into society. It is
also, quite simply, the best-acted British film in ages. You know how
every second of time, every move made by the stars, is going to pay off
in character revelation from the very opening scene of Rod Steiger, a
company salesman, picking up Judy Geeson's white-jeaned hitch-
hiker.

Right away the girl imposes her totally uninhibited authority on
him. She just stands and waits—and lets him reverse the car back to
her. 'Do you always comb your hair forward?'—with this early,
prickly query she pierces his self-esteem and reminds him of the
receding hair-line and thickening waist-line of the over-forties.
Everything emphasises the man's growing bafflement, the girl's
growing control of him. Her supple young body is displayed, both
clothed and in the nude, as a rebuke by her generation to his. The
candour of her morals takes his own hypocrisy by surprise. When she
paints her lips like Carmen Miranda and points her lower lashes into
cat-like spikes, she's parodying the little whore which is all the man
wants her to be—someone who can be safely paid off. Instead, she
pays him back in kind. She turns up at the house on the new estate
where Claire Bloom, as his wife, is trying to make a home in the hope
that it will remake her failing marriage. And established there, somewhere between *au-pair* girl and weekend guest, Miss Geeson becomes
her generation's revenge on their elders.

To tell more would be grossly unfair to a film that, for a welcome
change, tells a story in which the characters at the end are not the

same people that they were at the beginning. It also tells its story in the round. With great skill, it explores the married couple's set-up: the quick, intemperate Steiger longing for a family; the sad wife with some hang-up that dates from her displacement out of a once-affluent social class. The adults are as solidly there on the screen as the teenager —and that's rare today—and just as solid is the awful, eternally in-transit feel of the new housing estate and the acres of loneliness between the few yards of back gardens.

The acting is the magnificent sum total of everyone working to effect on everyone else—and the director independently sustaining all of them. Steiger is as brilliant as you would expect: perfect in his reactions, especially in the superb scene where he returns home to find his pick-up has settled into the spare bedroom, and giving the feeling of a man *living* it out, not acting it out. Claire Bloom has never been so good. Judy Geeson will be lucky to find another part that will let her be so good again. Peggy Ashcroft, as Bloom's mother, a woman still reeling genteelly from the shock of her own broken marriage and the erosion of gracious living, is a perfect example of the way the film slots human insight into its appropriate social setting. The scene where Dame Peggy ticks off a list of stately-home plants, absurdly unsuited to her daughter's little suburban back plot, has undertones of a witless Ophelia distributing her own flowers of rue and forget-fulness. In a small part as a hotel keeper, Paul Rogers shines as brightly as his bar glasses.

Peter Hall has not only made his best film to date. He has made a film that will entertain every age group, reveal the young to the old without flattery or distortion, and catch the mood of the times better than many a more showy or solemn effort.

Evening Standard, 17 July 1969

Wrong. Or at least wrong where it most mattered to the makers of *Three into Two Won't Go*. The film fell utterly flat at the box-office in a way I still find inexplicable. Maybe it fell between the generations so far as its appeal was concerned. It wasn't a certified 'youth picture': indeed it wasn't even a flattering, sucking-up-to-the-kids 'youth picture'. Nor was it calculated to add to the comfort of the middle-ageing group of filmgoers who envied the rootlessness of the kids when they themselves were feeling the menopausal constraints.

The majority of the reviews didn't help, either: not that they were any worse than those Peter Hall was accustomed to receiving. Somehow his apprenticeship in the theatre and swift ascent to the top of its Establishment is held against him when he 'goes slumming' in the movie industry. He is 'read a lesson' for his presumptuousness, told he has no 'feel for film', rebuked for the 'theatrical quality' that film critics claim to find so overwhelming in the acting. All I can say is what I am already on record as saying in my review, and let it stand. When asked to recommend films representative of the 1960s, for screening at seminars, and so on, *Three into Two Won't Go* is always on my list, and it is the one that provokes most argument, though, to be honest, not always most admiration. (The other 'Sixties', recommendations, for anyone who is interested, are: *Live Now—Pay Later*; *The Servant*; *The Knack*; *Morgan, A Suitable Case for Treatment*; *Blow-Up*; *Yellow Submarine*; *If....*; and *Performance* (which was shot in 1968, though, for reasons made plain in *Hollywood, England*, not shown in London till 1971).

DADDY PAYS BEST/*Love Story*

The message that I took away, dry eyed, from *Love Story* is that wealth means never having to say you're sorry. (If, on the contrary, *you* thought that's what love means, my advice is to see the movie rather than read the poster.) *Love Story* is the bourgeois backlash we've been expecting against all those films about campus protest, tribal rock, civil rights, drug addiction and the whole hippy scene, absolutely none of which is so much as allowed to breathe on the young lovers (Ali MacGraw, Ryan O'Neal) lest it contaminate their romance. Not since Walt Disney made *Bambi*, has a courtship like it been seen on the screen.

Director Arthur Hiller's film kept reminding me of the junior-size version of *Un Homme et Une Femme*: every element of reality that might grate against the mood has been screened out of the finished commercial for love—every one, that is, except the solid bourgeois necessity of money.

The hero is a millionaire's son, Oliver Barrett IV, and the girl he meets on campus worships him in body, name and numeral but believes that the relative poverty of her own background rules out marriage. Which is odd indeed, as she's pretty liberated in everything else, especially her language. Very cunningly, the film uses a string of semi-obscenities, now presumably deemed fit for even the Royal ears at the premiere, including the girl's favourite expression 'bullshit', to give itself the air of anti-sentimentality when the goo-ing gets too sticky.

Oliver's father (Ray Milland) cuts him off without a cent. But being bundles of loveableness, the married couple survive several hard, decorative winters at Harvard, living off love the way Eskimos live off blubber, till he lands a job with a law firm in New York. Whereupon she falls ill, asking in her loveable way, 'Can we afford a taxi to the hospital?'—pretty superfluous enquiry, considering the rent they must be forking out for a tenth-floor apartment near the Park. Instead of opening his heart to Dad, the hero persuades Dad to open his chequebook to him and pay the medical bills. Like Oliver Barrett IV, the film has it both ways. It serves both Hymen and Mammon. It tells young lovers to cut free and follow their hearts, but not so free as to forget the way to the bank. The real give-away is not the well-publicised cosiness of the death-scene ('Hold me tight, Olly') but the severely practical decision the heroine makes to help her husband through college by teaching in a private school, where her married name has financial pull, rather than in a hard-up State school where it wouldn't fatten her pay-packet.

In the film's favour, it must be said that the acting is very bearable. Ryan O'Neal in particular keeps it going. He's got the bright-eyed, bushy-tailed charm of something in a cage, tame but watchable. Ray Milland plays the heavy papa with a restrained touch, doing the cutting-off like a stately Roman severing a vein. Ali MacGraw plays Camille with bullshit.

Evening Standard, 11 March 1971

I had breakfast with Professor Erich Segal a few months after this review: he was then in the limbo of the suddenly famous and wealthy and trying to arrange for his re-entry into the ionosphere of academic life. He was also on the jury at the Cannes Film Festival, which at that time scarcely seemed a prudent staging post to the groves of Academe—but then it was once, as he reminded me, a jury that included Jean Cocteau *de l'Académie*.

The breakfast hour turned out to be a cross between a literary seminar and a congressional committee hearing on the Mafia activities of film critics, at least those who practised the *ad hominem* school of journalism, taking apart the author as well as the work. Why should this be? 'For the same reason,' said the Professor with bitter, accusative tongue, 'that Goethe had to suffer for his big hit with *The Sorrows of Young Werther*.'

'Not that I compare myself to Goethe,' he continued, 'even though *Love Story* penetrated to Japan, which I doubt Goethe did in his lifetime. All I mean is that after an age of cynical disenchantment, which Norman Mailer and Philip Roth fed off, *Love Story* has ushered in the age of sentiment. The other part of its appeal is that, like the electronic age we live in, it gets quickly to the point. No long descriptions. The way Balzac used to write. Not,' he added, 'that I am comparing myself to Balzac.'

Films like *Love Story* are important, because while no one knows quite why they should turn out to be box-office phenomena, they do indicate one sure thing—the untapped, sometimes unsuspected amounts of money that a single film can return to its makers. The 'age of sentiment' didn't come in its wake: on the contrary, 1970–71 saw the last yippee of the kids who could have been supposed to feed off sentiment like ants off sugar; the psychedelic vision began to fall apart like rainbow-coloured tat; and a movie like *Gimme Shelter*, the Maysles Brothers' record of the Rolling Stones concert at Altamont which trapped a killing in its camera lens, showed the dark tide of the pop movement on the turn. From 1971 the cinema embarked on an explosion of unparalleled violence in movies like *Bloody Mama*, *The Grissom Gang*, *Straw Dogs*, and soon *The Godfather*, which enabled its backers to carry home buckets of money as well as blood. *Love Story* looked even more like an isolated aberration by the time the 'age of violence' was ushered in by filmmakers whose work slogan seemed to be 'Don't defuse it, detonate it: don't distance 'em from it, rub their noses in it.'

My own feeling is that it caught the 'youth' audience at just the right moment of radical exhaustion and campus despair. It sold balm for generational wounds, the way earlier films had sold consolation to ageing matrons. Instead of Paul Henreid and Bette Davis, we had the cuddly twosome of Ryan and Ali; and like many films a few years later, such as *The Way We*

Were, its audiences were encouraged to feed off movie memories the way the screenplay itself fed off other, earlier bits of Hollywood iconography. *Love Story* gave the kids a lollipop of nostalgia and encouraged them to suck on it: in other words, it showed the moviemakers how ruthlessly and profitably their audience could be manipulated; its success and its long-running success at that, gave the marketing teams the time and incentive to tool up a whole industry of selling techniques all aimed at *one* film, *one* experience, *one* event. *Love Story* was the experimental bench for perfecting the massive campaigns that were used to sell *The Godfather*, *The Exorcist*, and *Jaws* with their emphasis on eye-catching logos, merchandising spin-offs, saturation advertising and the pervasive sense of a phenomenon you must see since everybody else was doing so. Its author quite underestimated what he had done for the cinema. Balzac would have understood these things better: he would have left the sentiment to look after itself and plunged his hands straight into the money-bowl.

Lindsay Anderson's *If. . . .* made the most beautifully timed landing in world cinema in 1968. Out of the blue, it came: a film that pitched its anti-Establishment argument in an English public school, but totally unexpectedly spoke the language of the barricades everywhere in that year of revolution. What Cocteau's *Les Enfants Terribles* was to young people in the 1950s, *If. . . .*, with its regenerative rallying call to revolt, was to teenagers in the late-1960s. It was a film of emotional anarchy: the deed was its own justification. . . .

I admired the film, but I have chosen to reprint the review I gave its successor, *O, Lucky Man!* For if *If. . . .* was timely, the sad thing is that *O, Lucky Man!* was premature. It didn't seem so when it was being made: for the rebellion the earlier film celebrated had cooled off or been allowed to burn itself out, and, instead, the emphasis appeared to be inner- rather than outer-directed: aimed at changing oneself, not society, or at least changing society through oneself. Fatalism had replaced force. (Incidentally, some of the most crucial elements in the production of *O, Lucky Man!* drew on the prophesying techniques of I Ching for favourable omens.) Yet the sad result was a film that never found its audience at the time. Maybe the kids suspected the motives of big-budget movie companies: for though *If. . . .* had been financed by Paramount, it was an open secret that the company never liked it (and was even apprehensive of its power to stoke up violent rebellion) until it began to click in a big way. *O, Lucky Man!* had the full, generous, enthusiastic backing of Warner Bros—until that failed to win anything at the Cannes festival in 1973, and then everyone began backing off as the full weight of a movie company's salvage efforts fell on the unhappy talents who had created it. It was substantially shortened—which, of course, didn't add to its audience at all. And it now lies in neglect or nostalgic limbo.

It is predictable that it will one day re-emerge and be seen as the most prophetic statement about Britain in the 1970s that has so far been made in the cinema. For barely months after it was shown there began the still continuing series of public-corruption scandals that left no sector of British life—Parliament, local government, City institutions—immune from the sceptical attack that Anderson's film launched on *its* multiplicity of villains. It is the world of Stonehouse, Poulson, Millhench, *et alii*, which we see mirrored in *O, Lucky Man!* The society that threw up The Black Panther kidnapper-killer and dispatched the 'Dogs of War' off on their mercenary trafficking in Africa. The system that inspired the 'politics of envy' and the 'dialectic of violence'. I hope I am around when the film makes its comeback and finds its audience. This will have to do for now.

ROGUES' GALLERY/*O, Lucky Man!*

We last saw the rebel hero Mick Travis on the roof of his public school in *If...*', gunning down the combined Establishment of masters, parents, clerics, generals and old boys. The same name fits the hero of *O, Lucky Man!* But it is a different Mick Travis, even though the face in both cases belongs to Malcolm McDowell.

Inner change, not armed revolt is the subject of Lindsay Anderson's new film. It is about a rebel's experience in the outside world. It is not school beatings and sadistic prefects which motivate him into action by their pain and injustice—but the more corrupting effects of greed, gain and ambition. Anderson has moved over and on from the barricades of 1968. And Mick has moved with him. He is still the resilient underdog, but no longer the revolutionary dreamer. His sense of burning independence has been gentled by experience of the world into a hardy innocence which preserves him just as well in a Vanity Fair society that seduces, punishes, even experiments on him, but leaves him ultimately undefeated although more aware. Aware of what? We ask as the slow smile of enlightenment breaks over McDowell's face in the last few seconds of the film aided by a smack on the head from none other than Anderson, playing himself in the movie. Well, aware that some things have no answers, but that all things must be accepted—that inner liberation goes with a glimpse of ultimate reality. Not the Sten-gun, but the Zen lesson. Instead of clenched teeth, the dawning smile of transcendental acceptance of things as they are. With the smack on the head is created the spark of *satori*. This is the distance Anderson has brought us since *If....*

We march to the sound of a different drum, too. Not rebellion, but satirical comedy that looks at a contemporary, though not exclusively English society and bends reality just enough through the prism of its director's humour to show its essential madness.

Mick starts out as a trainee coffee salesman and lets luck lead him into an ever-expanding milieu that is recognisably real yet comes out subtly altered by the satirical scepticism of the writing and playing and direction. By its skilful incorporation of multifold events into the fate of a single character, the film can be justly termed 'epic'. Mick meets ruthless tycoons, hypocritical town worthies, venal policemen, Fascist mercenaries, two-faced PR men, sadistic judges, amoral scientists, sin-obsessed do-gooders, even intolerant down-and-outs whose response to the heartening speech about the Brotherhood of Man is to chase and stone our hero. Mick is that dangerous thing— dangerous for himself—a romantic in a sceptic's world. A world that is peopled and played by a cast who respond to Anderson's touch with repertory precision and enjoyment of role-swapping virtuosity. Multiple roles are filled by the same players: for though life changes, says Anderson, one keeps meeting essentially the same people on the journey through it. Thus Arthur Lowe is a pompous factory boss as well as a corrupt mayor and—best of all—the Black President of a Third World Republic eager to learn the worst lessons of the capitalist West. Rachel Roberts is a slinky PR lady, an Asian mistress and a demented house-proud Welsh woman who commits suicide tidily after doing the chores. If she recalls the character she plays in Anderson's *This Sporting Life*, that's not entirely accidental. The film is full of quotes from this and other movies—just as it's full of those improving quotes from the English poets that our schoolteachers administered to us like moral bromides, their ludicrous inappositeness now exploded by the realities of the adult world. What price Robert Browning when poverty sits in rags in the street?

Ralph Richardson, too, is a chameleon, appearing first as a gentle tailor, then as a ruthless, zombie-like financier, one of the un-dead of the City. He really wouldn't surprise one if he lifted off the top of his head along with his bowler hat as in a Toni Unger cartoon. In such a world, says Anderson, is it really unthinkable to show a mad scientist turning people into pigs to enable them to have a better chance of survival? Where torture is the norm, why shouldn't the cruel interrogation by electrodes be interrupted by the placid tea lady with her trolley of refreshments?

Anderson's apparently simple set-ups, aided by photographer Miroslav Ondricek's confident directness of style, are always leading one into today's complex moral enquiries. A bourgeoning simplicity best describes the film's feeling. The music and lyrics of Alan Price, cut directly into the film as he and his group comment on the action or prepare us for the next peak or dip in the fever graph of Mick's progress, are of enormous help in giving emphasis to the poetic heart of the film. And right there at the heart is McDowell. What a brilliant actor he is! He makes Mick innocent but not dumb, passive but not apathetic. The hard rind that defines those deceptively cherubic features of McDowell's extends to his whole characterisation and cuts Mick incisively into the action, even though it's the other characters who are creating it, so that even in repose he is eminently watchable. He and Anderson radiate such a sense of shared objectives and mutual pleasure that it would be hard to look at the director and his star and say who is the luckier man to have the other.

Evening Standard, 3 May 1973

I'M DISASTER, FLY ME/*Airport*

One of those nights when nothing seems to go right. You know the feeling? It's the worst blizzard in airport history. A Boeing 707 has done a perfect snow-plough into the main runway. The airport manager's wife (Dana Wynter) is throwing a divorce suit at her husband (Burt Lancaster). His devoted passenger-relations lady (Jean Seberg) is gallantly concealing her sorrow at having no man of her own to relate to. A ten million dollar damage suit for airport noise is winging over from the neighbourhood suburb. The airline's habitual little old lady stowaway (Helen Hayes) has made it on to the Rome-bound aircraft. Also aboard is a mad bomber (Van Heflin). And the captain (Dean Martin) has just found out that the stewardess (Jacqueline Bisset) is carrying his child. It's up, up and away with jet-opera—the airborne equivalent of soap-opera.

I must be honest and confess to enjoying most of its 136 minutes. For sheer contentment there is little to beat the sight of constant catastrophe happening to others. Whether it's a rich old bag (Jesse Royce Landis) being nabbed by the Customs (Lloyd Nolan) or simply some everyday event like a tail-plane breaking off. Very cunning, too, is the pitch that the film makes to an audience that's mainly matronly and best-seller fed—but it also puts hooks into anyone (and that's most of us) who's ever fastened a seat belt.

Granted that it glamorises transport, and puts in a commercial or two for Boeing. But its holding power is already being shown by the box-office returns in America, where it may well make producers break their vows about making only small-budget movies for and about youth. Filmmakers next year may not want to know anyone travelling economy class by motor-cycle. George Seaton wrote and directed *Airport*. There are times when he could have done with a tail wind. But the film's wax finish holds the eye and producer Ross Hunter applies it lavishly—the VIP lounge looks modelled on the Athenaeum club.

Veteran actress Helen Hayes slipping past security checks like a cheeky Mother Riley gladdens the heart of us passenger herds. And as well a subversion at ground level, another asset is suspense at a high altitude. A bomb at 30,000 feet generates more tension than one down below. The decompression turmoil its explosion causes in the cabin—a technically impressive piece of special effects—will make you keep your seat-belt forever fastened on future air trips. Acting? It's necessarily chairbound, but I commend the actor who plays a priest and in one unbroken movement crosses himself at the moment of crisis *and* slaps the face of a hysterical neighbour. Truly, God's right hand never sleeps.

Evening Standard, 23 April 1970

The huge success of *Airport*—by 1976 it was listed eleventh in *Variety*'s 'All-Time High Rental Champions' with a North American rental of 45 million dollars and world-wide receipts of possibly as much again—confirms the 'sequel syndrome' now locked so firmly into Hollywood's way of thinking and working. 'Think of a film: then double it,' became the established pattern around 1974–75, when 'event films' like *Airport*, *The Godfather*, *The French Connection*, *That's Entertainment* were all spawning their 'Part Two'—written thus rather than Part II, due to a certain public bewilderment over Roman numerals.

Disaster films in particular, which multiplied so fast that every box-office suddenly seemed to be crying 'Oh, calamity!' were the most profitable evidence of how thoroughly a trend established in the morning can become a rip-off almost before the sun sets. *Jaws*, *Juggernaut*, *Earthquake*, *Towering Inferno*, *Airport '75*, *The Hindenburg*, paradoxically proved that disaster was the safest investment—if *Airport* wasn't evidence enough, then *The Poseidon Adventure*, in 1972, about the ocean liner turning turtle, dispersed the doubts of the waverers searching for stories which resembled the worst nightmares of Lloyd's underwriters.

In an earlier section of this book, I've speculated on the way these lay disasters were replacing the old-style religious epics. The disasters, however, seldom sold the assurance of religion, even if they did hint at the existence of God (a vengeful, Old Testament, God I think we can identify Him as being) and the phenomenon remained of seeing the very medium that traditionally offered people a refuge from the outside world now undergoing a paroxysm of all-embracing catastrophes, each seeking to outdo the other in replicating the conditions of the outside world, even to the use of the 'Sensurround' sound process that sent a shudder through the cinema (and its patrons) when the earth opened in *Earthquake*. Maybe it was all easily explained as a return to basics. Story-telling in mainstream movies had been getting almost dauntingly complicated due to the elisions and ellipses now rampant in even popular genre-movies, like the secret-agent or the private-eye plots, or else to the personal and sometimes opaque visions of *auteur* directors. They had also got very bloody, particularly where they exploited the so-called urban crisis—which meant, in less exalted terms, the rogue cop, the Mafia boss, the mass killer. Give us a good clean calamity, seemed to be the prayer, something round which the stars can muster (and they come cheaper by the dozen, don't forget). Suddenly, catastrophe was the new numbers game. . . .

YOU'RE NEVER ALONE WITH CATASTROPHE

There was a time—are you old enough to remember it?—when people were allowed to enjoy personal catastrophes. It wasn't thought selfish then. Audiences would go along in their hundreds of thousands to see a character on the screen going through hell. 'Hell', of course, varied in location and intensity, but it was nearly always a personal hell. It might be Joan Crawford as a career mother seeing her children turning out spoilt and ungrateful; or Audrey Hepburn in a nun's wimple having to share the jungle clinic with Peter Finch ('Don't think for a minute, Sister, that your habit will protect you'); or Jean Gabin holed up in a Paris attic while *le jour se lève* and the police have to yawn through a long night of the wanted man's flashbacks.

All such hells were individual ones; they were laid on for us to luxuriate in. Every doom with its private bathroom of emotion. Now all this has changed; to enjoy a personal catastrophe these days is something that it takes courage to admit to, like owning a second home. Now we are living in the age of 'group jeopardy', which is the handy term that film and literary agents are employing to describe the currently fashionable themes and stories they trade in. Only things that menace all of us are considered worthy subjects of drama now. Quite honestly, I sometimes feel that if Sophocles were to come back today with an outline for *Oedipus Rex* he would be told to go away and think again. He that plays the king might be welcome enough, in theory. But would it be involving enough, in practice? Would there be *enough there* to make the plebs feel that, well . . . yes, this is really hitting us where we live emotionally? I mean one man and his mother . . . come on!

The tragedies we pay to be immersed in, totally immersed in, today are inevitably impeccable evidence of the democratic process at work. Personal tragedy was always aristocratic; mass catastrophe is invariably democratic. Death was always the great leveller, but these are boom times for him. They involve 'the group' in such colossal disasters that we feel we are participating in the catastrophic process the way that voters in a system of adult suffrage participate in the electoral process. Hijackings, sieges, earthquakes, shark infestations, all the acts of man or God that put the group in jeopardy are regarded as being really and truly where it is at today.

I saw the name David Riesman crop up recently. When I was an undergraduate it was his book *The Lonely Crowd* which we kept in our library carrel and from which we learned to see humanity as a tug-of-war between the people who were inner-directed and those who were other-directed. Nowadays, it seems, *everybody* is other-directed. The crowd has got bigger and no one is lonely. What has worked the change is the all-pervasive nature of the catastrophe which one can see reflected in those instant allegories of social change—the movies. Of course there were plenty of earlier movies about people in a group— the travellers in *Stagecoach*, the passengers in *Night Flight*, the guests in *Grand Hotel*, the diners in *Dinner at Eight*. All of them were more or less threatened by events well-known to mankind, and some known only to scriptwriters. But all such instances of group jeopardy pre- supposed a safe world to which the survivors would return. Now there is no safe world to return to, often simply no return. The whole accent of moral interest and almost the entire material of the physical drama is placed on the size of the disaster area. The inflation of the disaster appears to be just as uncontrollable as the inflation of the economy. Only last week the big sensation was an Underground train filled with New York commuters which was hijacked in *The Taking of Pelham*

One-Two-Three. But soon we shall be seeing *Black Sunday*, in which half-a-million people who have turned out to see a Sunday football game are held hostage by an overhead airship stuffed to the gills with high explosives.

Those were the good old days, weren't they? The days, I mean, when you could personally count the casualties.

Vogue, May 1976

FAREWELL TO THE CHIEF/Hollywood Democracy

Life isn't a cabaret, old chum, as Miss Minnelli declared it to be. Life is a movie script. This revelation God vouchsafed to his servant Alexander Walker at the Beverly Hills Hotel—a suitable place for God to be working—one Sunday morning in 1969 when I was eating brunch and growing irked because an individual several tables away was getting conspicuously more attention than I. 'Which movie actor is that?' I asked.

'That,' said the waiter, 'is the President of the United States.' After which, my service got slightly worse.

To me, Richard M. Nixon—for he it was—always looked not just like California's over-vaulting favourite son, but a Hollywood studio's over-paid character actor. A touch of the Fred MacMurray when at the piano; a little of Ben Johnson when glad-handing in the crowds; a whole lot of Broderick Crawford in that last amazing scene of farewell at the White House. When someone wrote that they half-expected the outgoing President to pull out a gun and end it all there and then in front of the cameras, I thought back to Crawford in *All the King's Men* with the dying line 'Tomorrow, the world' on his lips. And then I thought, No . . . no, that's not quite the right film. It wasn't a tragic scene. It was one of blackest comedy, Mr Nixon's rambling apologia in front of the White House staffers. (Even the chefs were there, summoned from the kitchens before they'd removed their aprons.) And the dialogue! 'What this country needs is good plumbers'—*that* after the Watergate break-in! I detected the hand of Ben Hecht or Charles MacArthur in the dialogue, of Billy Wilder or Preston Sturges in the direction.

Nothing that happened in the Watergate Affair ever surprised me. Not that I anticipated it, any better than anyone else. But it all happened exactly as a hundred humdrum Warner Bros 'B' pictures had laid it out for me over the last 30 years. After a childhood education in the Hollywood cinema's view of society, I expected City Hall to be corrupt . . . I expected a crusading newspaper to expose it. . . . I expected the arch-villain to give himself away by letting the public overhear him when he thought they weren't listening. (Remember *The Great Man*, remember *A Face in the Crowd*?)

The trouble is that life today no longer apes art: it apes bad art. Reality is proving an appalling enemy of fiction, outrunning it in the most melodramatic style. The whole world is looking like a Hollywood scenario. Even that word 'scenario' has become significantly popular, used even by people who never go to the pictures, usually when they're in court trying to explain away their actions ('The scenario of my actions that night, Your Honour. . . .'). Even the Woodward–Bernstein book *All the President's Men*, besides deliberately recalling the Robert Rossen movie *All the King's Men* in its title, looks to the movies to find a cover name for the reporters' informant. He is dubbed 'Deep Throat', after the porno movie. Throughout, the book is written like a movie scenario, too. 'June 17, 1972,' it starts. 'Nine o'clock, Saturday morning. Early for the telephone. Woodward fumbled for the receiver.' (The camera, one feels, moves in for a TIGHT CLOSE-UP.) Elsewhere the dialogue is sheer Warner Bros, 1930, give or take a slight liberality with Production Code taboos. 'Katie Graham's gonna get her tit caught in a big fat wringer,' says the Attorney-General, John Mitchell, venting his wrath on *The Washington Post*'s lady owner. ('Could we have that line again, Mr Cagney?')

Such a pity that the Woodward–Bernstein book hadn't had a third collaborator-investigator to co-author it. It's already got a blond WASP type (Woodward) and a dark Jewish type (Bernstein): what it lacks is an educated Black type to complete the obligatory ethnicity that every crime drama on TV or the cinema screen must nowadays possess if someone somewhere is not going to feel that his inviolable human rights have been offended. A bad oversight of the *Post*'s City Room: perhaps a sequel to the book will correct it.

A note, now, of regret. I am genuinely sorry to see Richard M. Nixon depart. I have inherited from the films a life-long affection for the villain, generally the most entertaining figure on the screen, especially if he poses as an honest man. One is wrong to speak of Nixon's presidency as a 'nightmare'. It was, rather, the glorious inversion of the American Dream, the turning upside down of the Horatio Alger story, the bloodless version of *The Godfather*—about the only things that *didn't* surface in the Watergate Affair were horses' heads in the bed. Even when his smile was broadest, Nixon carried around an air of sinister inevitability. It played marvellously against the grain of any scene he was in. While listeners at that final *au revoir* in the White House looked hunched against the coming storm, he talked like a garrulous orator at an Idaho picnic. He used the panoply of power like Little Caesar used the ritzy tailors, to pad out his importance— and I'm not sure if he wasn't better respected for it by all the other Little Caesars in Moscow and Peking than President Ford will ever be. As Nixon's helicopter lifted him off the White House lawn into exile, the *ex-deus in machina*, I thought of Gore Vidal's comment on Kennedy's death—that it gave Americans 'one of the first shy hints since Christianity declined that there may indeed be such a thing as fate and that tragedy is not merely a literary form of little relevance in the age of common man, but a continuing fact of the human condition, requiring that the overreacher be struck down and in his fall, we, the chorus, experience awe, and some pity.'

It is just what they were always trying to do in the writers' block in the Hollywood studios, and sometimes managing it. De Tocqueville gave me the theory of American democracy, Warner Brothers showed me the practice of it, and Richard Nixon starred in it.

Evening Standard, 16 August 1974

No, we now know that he didn't. Robert Redford and Dustin Hoffman starred in it. Even the real Bob Woodward and the real Carl Bernstein needn't bother standing up: that is the price they must pay for providing the celebrity that tilts the balance of events when newspaper realism is invaded by the entertainment values of the movie industry. Fortunately, the film turned out well. But I am reminded of a lengthy and remarkably candid account of the two movie stars soaking up newsroom authenticity which was published in *The Washington Post* on 11 April 1975, just about a year before the film came out. 'One day,' ran the piece, a composite effort by reporters Tom Shales, Tom Zito and Jeanette Smyth, 'high schoolers were touring the *Post* and spotted Robert Redford standing in an office. They rushed forward, pocket cameras clicking. "Wait," a reporter said to them. "Here's the real Bob Woodward. Don't you want a picture of him?"'

' "No," one youngster replied, and they rushed on.'

The best way of conveying the uncanny atmosphere of *All the President's Men* is to urge you to imagine Raymond Chandler's labyrinthine thriller *The Big Sleep* crossed with Gore Vidal's sophisticated novella, *Washington DC*.

This is a film with mystery, danger, suspense and all-pervasive corruption. It has all the paraphernalia of intrigue: bugged phones, cars prowling darkened city streets slick with rain, midnight meetings with unnamed informants in underground garages thick with shadows. It has a cast of heroes and villains and a good many people in between who are something of both. And for double measure it has not one, but two 'private eyes'—Bob Woodward and Carl Bernstein, the *Washington Post* reporters who, by dint of leg-work, phone-work and above all guess-work, followed the trail of political dirty-work that ultimately toppled President Nixon from office. A political detective story, then? Is that it? Yes—but something more still.

Detective stories have the sleuth searching for the answers he wants. For over half this film, the 'detectives' don't even know the questions they should be asking. The questions, of course, arising from that 'third-rate burglary' of Democratic Party head-quarters at the Water-gate Building in mid-June, 1972. Why should such a small-time crime warrant the money, news-space and reporters' time that the *Post* spends on it? That's what the paper's senior executives demand. 'I don't see *the story*,' rasps executive editor Ben Bradlee (impersonated with sleek authority by Jason Robards) for the tenth time. 'What are we supposed to be investigating?' That's the film's key-note. The earnest, dogged bafflement conveyed by Woodward (Robert Redford) and his newsroom buddy Bernstein (Dustin Hoffman). Men who smell something rotten in the State, but can't produce a body to explain the odour of fear, menace and tension polluting the political air. We follow their enquiries step by painstaking step—that's really where the film lies, that's its strength and its uniqueness. In this couple's tenacity is to be found the truth. It is a Washington paperchase followed by men with the dawning disbelief that it is leading them to the very office of the President.

As the reporter's detective goes back in time—uncovering the 'slush fund' set up by the Committee to Re-Elect the President (CREEP), the 'Mexican laundry' in Florida for washing the dirty money, the sabotage corps run by H. R. Haldeman, Nixon's chief of staff, to blacken rival Presidential candidates' reputations—we watch on the television screens and in the newspaper headlines the onward march of the very political figures, Nixon, Agnew, Mitchell, etc., whom the revelations will destroy. Thus a tight frame of fatefulness clamps events in place; and director Alan J. Pakula extracts from the unpromising material of interviews and conferences a dynamic sense of retribution in the making. He squeezes each scene for its seed of revelation. He very nearly gives away the Press' trade secrets in showing how the two reporters, when interviewing reluctant witnesses, adopt the most sympathetic personalities to coax out facts and confirm hunches. Every interview is a mini-drama of subtle implications. With the nervous lady book-keeper for the 'slush fund', Hoffman is like a big brother, offering a shoulder to weep on; with a Florida lawyer, he is crisp, quipping, man-to-man and leaning on edition times; with a repentant Nixon official, our boys are like father confessors; with Donald Segretti, the West Coast 'dirty trickster', the attitude becomes one of tolerant buddy-buddy campus conspirators.

The burden of the face-to-face encounters falls on Hoffman. But Redford had his moments, too, particularly when Woodward goes on his midnight errands to liaise with the still pseudonymous 'Deep Throat', probably an FBI or CIA agent with a grudge against Nixon, who keeps the reporters on the tracks without actually telling them the name of the destination. Played by Hal Holbrook with vocal brilliance —for he's almost invisible in the darkness—he is a voice from the graveyard of buried secrets. His few scenes register as the most nervy and ambiguous in the whole film. His taunting sarcasm as the reporters blunder has almost sexual undertones to it: the reproof of the older man to his errant lover.

Putting film stars into reporters' shoes has led to some inevitable glamorising. Redford as the controlled, blond WASP Woodward is at times an almost edible confection; Hoffman as the excitable, Jewish Bernstein is compactly sexy to an almost huggable degree. This Woodward looks as if he would only come for the story; but this Bernstein suggests he might stay on afterwards for something more flavoursome. Yet this is the extent to which the personalities are opened for our inspection. While they finally get to know all about 'the President's men', we're being told next-to-nothing about 'the Post's men'. Only rarely is anything they say or do in their pursuit related to their off-the-job personalities. 'I'm a Republican,' says an an interviewer at one point. 'So am I,' Woodward lets slip out, while Bernstein barely suppresses the snort of a contemptuous liberal. But such a moment is so rare in the film as almost to be an intrusion into their privacy rather than an illumination of their characters. Showing them only as functioning Pressmen makes for a certain coldness at the movie's heart. The *Post*'s executives are allowed more individual quirks and displays of temperament; the points-scoring atmosphere of daily editorial conferences has rarely been so well caught on the screen.

It is a brilliantly designed film. White light without shadows and deep-focus photography turn the *Post*'s editorial floor into a place of exposure that contrasts with the lurking gloom that veils the official face of Washington's government offices. When Gordon Willis' camera pulls up, up, up into the dome of the Library of Congress, the two reporters poring through the chores of their researches far beneath seem like tiny spiders in a concentric web of reading desks. The atmosphere of a paranoid network of deception and concealment is locked into concrete shapes and images.

The movie stops well before Nixon is fingered and brought to justice. It does not matter. The indictment has been drawn up: the conviction now belongs to the Law, not the Press. The cannon fire greeting the President's inaugural ceremony in 1973 cross-fades into the chatter of Telex machines, relaying the future lists of resignations, convictions, sentences—and pardons. The plotters have been brought down by the plodders. It is not often that the cinema today presents a morality play of such breathtaking conclusiveness and authority. But then it is not every day that the pressure of the Press puts a President out of office. It is a matter of relief, as well as professional pride, to report that the movie is the worthy equal of the media.

Evening Standard, 19 April 1976

WATERGATE WESTERN/*Posse*

Posse is the kind of film that raises more questions than it answers. Questions like 'Why was it made at all?' 'How can it have been set up?' 'What was the back-room dialogue like?'

—Paramount will bankroll a Kirk Douglas movie, if he'll produce, star and direct.

—Can Kirk carry that big a load any longer?

—Sure, if it's a Western. Set Kirk on a horse and the animal will carry him. Look at Duke Wayne. Put Duke in the saddle or the driver's seat and he's good for another 20 years. You should know old stars never die, they simply end up with horsepower under their tail.

—A Western . . . I begin to like it. But what sort of Western? A pacifist Western? A race Western? A psychological Western? A law-and-order Western? Jeez, I hanker for the days when we just made Western Westerns.

—Call it a Watergate Western—good for '76, huh? Presidential election year. Get it out quick into the nabe houses before Redford and Hoffman get their show on the road with *All the President's Men*. Does that grab you?

—But definitely. . . ! Say, what's a Watergate Western?

—Set it in Texas, not California. That'll take those Ronnie Reagan people off our backs for a start. They might think we wanted to do the dirty on Ronnie before the primaries. As I see it, Kirk plays a Nixon character, U.S. Marshal Howard Nightingale—mean s.o.b., but he gets things done. Does them his way. As the movie opens, he's running for Senator.

—You just lost me. The kids don't want politics these days. Sex, fine. Violence, great. But politics, that's no cure for cancer.

—Who said anything about politics? Kirk may be running for office, but he's gunning for a badman. He's going to get elected when he brings the guy in, dead or alive.

—Dead, I hope.

—Not so quick. Bruce Dern wants to play the badman.

—He was great in *The Great Gatsby*. About the only thing that was.

—He'll be even better in *Posse*. Brucie is a cool killer. Shoots the local sheriff the way every kid with a cycle would love to gun down the traffic cop. *In-stan-TAN-eous!* Bruce's front teeth are the most ferocious things since *Jaws*.

—*Jaws* . . . Jeez, I wish we'd made that one. But how do you think Kirk will take to that kind of set-up?

—Kirk's got the marshal's badge and the moustache and the right to the final cut of the picture. What more does Kirk want?

—You know Kirk, he may want more.

—He gets the film's big build-up. Man of integrity, total honesty, one of the best servants this country has ever known—all that horseshit. But gradually we come to suspect he's in the game for the loot, just like Dern—only worse. It's not just money he wants: it's power. He'll use Dern to get himself elected to the Senate and, after that, maybe he'll go for the Big One.

—The White House?

—We don't actually say so in the movie. But Kirk isn't carting that photographer along with the posse to make tin-types for his scrapbook. Manipulation of the media, 'managed news', get the contemporary ring?

—You know, this movie could have significance. Oscar material.
—Maybe Marlon would come through with an endorsement. After all, there's an Injun Joe in it who the bad guys will hire but the railroad bosses won't. Marlon is deep into that sort of discrimination. And we can certainly count on Paul and Joanne.
—Uh-uh! No way! The Newmans are still sore over how Paramount handled their *WUSA* movie.
—The Newmans are very genuine people as well as film stars. But listen to this. . . . In this film the man who really knows the score is—a newspaper editor. He gets Kirk's number on the first edition. We'll make him a kind of Ben Bradlee of the prairie belt, running a one-horse *Washington Post*, minus one arm and one leg which he's lost in the wars serving under a militarist who got to be general.
—The Vietnam connection?
—On the ball! Well, Kirk gets the man who's been terrorising the town. One of those *High Noon* dumps—you know, not a soul under the age of 50 and all the tradesmen handling their guns as if they'd scald their hands. Just the kind of schmucks to send Kirk to Congress on a 'Clean Up America' ticket.
—And do they?
—Looks like it, till Dern escapes, turns the tables and shows Kirk up for what he is—just one more crypto-fascist on the make. He even subverts Kirk's posse—buys their loyalties with the 30,000 dollars they've grabbed from the townsfolk when they've seen how their own boss is feathering his political nest. They all ride out of town for more train hold-ups, leaving Kirk looking pretty sick and thinking he's not even likely to get much for his political memoirs.
—Wait a minute, wait a minute. . . . You mean we let the *bad guys* win? This Dern character, hasn't he a reputation as a train-robber and cold-blooded killer? Are you suggesting that *we* suggest he's somehow morally better than the Kirk Douglas character who only wanted to become President?
—Look, anyone who wants to become President has just *got* to be a rascal. That's the post-Watergate message, man. And I'm sure Kirk and all of us would regard it as a very enlightened *and box-office* message to be associated with. One I'm sure Kirk will be happy to go along with.
—You make it all sound like a good day's work. I'm impressed.
—Look, every day above ground in Hollywood is a good day.

Evening Standard, 31 July 1975

What he did for the future in *2001 : A Space Odyssey*, Stanley Kubrick in *Barry Lyndon* has done for the past. He has projected us into an era of amazing strangeness. He takes the men and women from an age we can usually only view in museums and art galleries and places them suddenly, almost tangibly *there*—moving in their costumes, talking in their speech patterns, cleaving to their virtues and vices—especially their vices—in all their eighteenth-century realism. *Barry Lyndon* doesn't breathe history—for 'history' is what we look back on. It breathes actuality—the thing we feel as we look around us. Kubrick's favourite camera movement in the film is a slow, delicious, sensuous pulling back from a detail to reveal a panorama. It is the act of a man marvelling at the view of 200 years ago, recreated in a detail never before matched on a screen.

The film is no high-definition 'romp' of the kind, *Tom Jones* was. Kubrick has had the *chutzpah*, the nerve, to take stars like O'Neal and Berenson and use them as mere strands in a tapestry. His film is bursting with incident, but it allows its meaning to emerge from the total sum of events, and not be pegged on to any single one of them. Though he has invented incidents not in Thackeray's novel, he has observed the form of that book, which was published in instalments each of which made a moral point rather than a narrative one about the rise and fall of its hero. 'Worldly success' is the theme, if anything is, but it's a theme that's turned inside out, for all the romantic setting, to show the shabby, unromantic lining of manners and morals. Few films by other directors—certainly none by an American—have revealed how a society works at its many levels to aid and then ulti-mately to repulse the gentleman-scoundrel who wants to gain wealth and rank by means of marriage and bribery.

Barry Lyndon (O'Neal) is first revealed among the Irish gentry—of whom he's a minor sprig—as a gullible teenager brought up on a code of love and honour, but finding only deceit and mercenary motives when he fights a duel with a wilting English officer (Leonard Rossiter) over a teasing first love (Gay Hamilton) who proves excep-tionally faithless. A highwayman (Arthur O'Sullivan) crosses his route and relieves him of his guineas with pernickety precision; and the British army, then in alliance with Frederick the Great's Prussia, puts a redcoat on his back. Kubrick shows, as he did in an earlier film, that the 'paths of glory' lead only to hysteria and death in a muddy ditch. In the first of the film's meticulously staged set-pieces, the camera tracks into battle as line upon line of musketeers unloose their shot at the opposing troops till the nerve of one or other side is shattered in the sheer collapse of human bodies. Wars, we are reminded, are as often decided by the turn-tail panic of the enemy as the total supremacy of the victors.

To save his own neck, Barry masquerades as an English officer in a uniform filched off a tree while its owner is swearing a Rousseau-esque vow of sentimental affection for another officer while the pair of them stand up to their waists in the river at morning ablutions. A subtle Prussian captain (Hardy Kruger) finds him out and Barry enlists as a police spy reporting on a shady Chevalier (Patrick Magee) who is rooking the rakes of Europe at the card tables.

In these scenes all the consummate technical mastery of Kubrick and his photographer, John Alcott, creates an 'indoor world' of faces on which you can read by the light of hot tallow candles their greed, mendacity and constipation. Using an industrial lens of ultra-fast sensitivity, the camerawork regains the capacity to expose eighteenth-century life in its own hot, flickering illumination—the faces appear to be melting, you can feel the finery clogged with powder and sweat. Marisa Berenson plays the Countess of Lyndon as the very emanation of this world. A marble-white face under a galleon-sail of hair, breasts worn nearly naked at the dinner table, the cushiony voluptuousness of the woman whose soft life has stifled orgasm and whose response on finding herself betrayed by Barry as soon as he has married her is to retire to a warm bath and be read to in French.

The film's two stars have a minimum of dialogue. Indeed, the subsidiary parts are better supplied with lines, like Lady Lyndon's invalid husband (Frank Middlemass) expiring amidst an explosion of pills and a fulmination against her infidelities, or Milady's chaplain, the Rev. Runt (Murray Melvin) sourly sermonising at the wedding ceremony. But the stars' performances reside in their reactions. Looks take the place of words and tell us more about an era that Kubrick asks us to feel through our senses quite as much as our ears. His choice of music is as brilliantly eclectic as ever—Vivaldi, Handel, Frederick the Great's own compositions, an Irish traditional group called The Chieftains—the story for long stretches floats on nothing but the music.

The last quarter shows Barry losing his only child—a moment of unexpected tenderness for such a director, with the face of the dying infant swaddled in a snowdrift of sheets—and the hero's growing rivalry with his stepson, Viscount Bullingdon (Leon Vitali). This leads to a duel scene in an out-building that is the best of its kind ever filmed. Doves coo and flutter phlegmatically around the tensed-up men with pistols; and the combatants go through the etiquette of killing each other as if they were making the responses at a wedding ('Aare you ready to receive Mr Lyndon's fire, Lord Bullingdon?') while the vomit that sheer fear brings to the lips only awakens the embarrassed consternation, not the compassion, of the seconds at such an appalling, ungentlemanly *faux-pas*.

Lies, snubs, patronising remarks, subtle slurs on his pretensions to rank, sidelong looks at his claims on class: these are all Barry collects, while the notion that worldly success equals contentment is being eroded by the endless acquisition of debt which parts him from his wife's money and eventually even from her company. His end is less horrifying than Hogarth's 'rake', but no less heartless. In one of the last shots we see Lady Lyndon signing the annuity that has turned her absentee husband into a remittance man. The bill is dated 1789— the year of the French Revolution. The scene appears to freeze into a tableau and it is like a waxworks of a whole class signing its own death warrant.

Manifold talents have contributed to *Barry Lyndon*: Ken Adam's stunning rearrangement of reality in the production design; Roy Walker's art direction; the brilliant costumes of Ulla-Britt Söderlund (who did Jan Tröll's film *The Emigrants*) and Milena Canonero; Tony Lawson's editing that allows the story to move at its period pace and not at some frenetic filmmaker's attention-grabbing tempo. But when all is said and shown, *Barry Lyndon* remains Kubrick's sole vision, and a piece of cinema to marvel at.

Evening Standard, 11 December 1975

Seeing a Kubrick picture is like witnessing a ceremony. Its implications work their way into our minds long after the event itself. I've come to think this 'time lapse' phenomenon is an essential part of the response: it may well account for a couple of the well-known 'recantations' that have taken place, particularly among American critics, when they have been impelled to go back and judge again the film they damned the first time round.

Barry Lyndon certainly threw most Anglo-Saxon critics: perhaps the time we had to wait for the film, the better part of three years, screwed expectations up to the point of irritation. But expectations were also turned right round by the form the film took when we did see it. The cinema of 'swash-and-buckle', or 'picaresque romp', or 'historical romance' was something we were familiar with, could grapple with. But *Barry Lyndon* approached history as if those perversions of it had never been invented: indeed, as if the people in the film didn't know they were part of history, which is true of everyone really, but which we can only unself-consciously apply to ourselves in our own age. Very, very seldom today do we experience a moment that convinces us we are living in history: the most celebrated moment of this kind, which confirms its rarity, was Kennedy's assassination and it's become almost a cliché to say that everyone remembers where he was when he heard the news.

But Kubrick's film deals in behaviour, not in history. It is a rigorous exercise in the observance of life-styles at all levels in society—in European society, that is, not merely Anglo-Irish society. And not just society in its civilian dress, but society at war, since war was the great melting-pot of nationalities in the eighteenth century and all manner of life-styles became part of strategy and tactics. Kubrick concentrates one's attention on *what people do*: he frequently leaves us to divine the reasons for it. The much-criticised 'voice over' narration is a function of this; for by telling us what *will* happen, or even underlining what *is* happening, it relieves us of the normal response to events in films, which is to interpret the relationships and the connections between them for ourselves. We are forced to be observers, not interpreters—and of course Kubrick refrains from being a commentator as rigidly as he did in *2001: A Space Odyssey* which had only some 35 minutes of dialogue throughout its 141 minutes. And what we observe—a world of formal beauty counterpointed by a bleak, despairing biography of an *arriviste*—is so unlike what we have been conditioned to expect that we have to make a sizable effort of adjustment to it. It is easier for instant opinion to damn than adjust, unless there is a strong tradition concerned first with the form of things and prepared to seek the content later.

At least this is how I explain to myself the cool-to-frigid Anglo-American reviews of *Barry Lyndon* compared to the rapturous-to-beatific reception it got in all West European countries when it opened there in the late summer of 1976. The Continentals accepted intuitively that it was a film about 'forms' and responded to the beauty, the detail, the behavioural processes—the Anglo-Americans waited for the plot to develop, the characters to declare themselves, the theme to emerge. In one case, the result was rapture—in the other, a sort of rage. You couldn't say *Barry Lyndon* started a trend: you couldn't call it a timely film. It is *sui generis*. A landmark—as we shall grow to recognise.

A trend that deserves a lengthy study is Hollywood's cannibalism—the movies' habit of feeding on their own myths, finding material in their own past, holding up their own image to the public in either narcissistic or, more frequently, masochistic mood. About the middle of the 1970s this aspect was given the kinder description of 'nostalgia'. The reasons for it are easy to see and reside in the great success of films like *Summer of '42* and *The Last Picture Show* and *The Way We Were* which traded heavily in the anaesthetising influence of 'the years between' to produce a sense of sweet placebo in their audiences—either audiences which had grown up through those years or had been born just too late to experience them. But this wasn't the whole story.

The films also offered up myths that were based not on life as it actually was in those distant days, but on the view of life contained in movies that were made in those days. It was a case of one generation viewing the past through the moviemaker's viewfinder of a previous era. All the iconography of popular movies in the 1930–40 period can be discerned in a contemporary film like *The Way We Were* and assists the doubly-sweet feeling of nostalgic escapism that it generates. From this it was only a short step to digging up Hollywood's own archives—and not just the archives, but the once famous bodies that lay buried or cremated in the places of rest around Beverly Hills. I enjoyed the nostalgia cycle at first, but just as you could have too much of a good thing, I eventually couldn't help feeling that you could also have too much of a dead thing.

ENCORE/*That's Entertainment: Part Two*

The only thing Fred Astaire and Gene Kelly have to fear in *That's Entertainment: Part Two* is—Fred Astaire and Gene Kelly. Now aged 76 and 63 respectively, the pair have actually put on their dancing shoes again and it's inevitable that they court comparison with their younger, nimbler selves in the dozens of movie extracts that MGM have culled from the vaults for this jumbo celebration of Hollywood musicals, or, at least, those made within the boundaries of Culver City.

To our great relief and their greater glory, the two supreme dancers survive the comparison magnificently. Their 'shelf life' seems infinite. No sign at all of perished elastic in their legs as they enter sideways, so to speak, as if walking out of a clip of one old movie they did together and straight into this new one. In their grey suits and black bowler hats, armed with charm and proofed by sheer personality against the onset of greyer hair and thicker waists, they dance again for our pleasure and, obviously, for their own, too. Antic still, antique never! As well as heart-warming, it's a bit of history as well.

The rest of the film is pretty well all history. I like it better than the first *That's Entertainment*. With Astaire and Kelly the sole compères now, it hasn't the earlier film's air of patronising condescension when the stars did their gracious 'thing' for fellow-stars, some of whom they'd hardly met before they stood on the same film stage. The film also applauds the talents of writers, directors, photographers, lyric-writers and choreographers: it is thus far more democratic than the first. Kelly and Astaire drift in and out of some well-designed new numbers, all with a purpose to them. In one, the colours wittily disappear one by one as Kelly's lyric ranges through the spectrum till he's ultimately left in monochrome—which is the cue for ushering in the era of black-and-white movie musicals.

A lot of the old favourites are here: 'On the Avenue', 'Good Morning, Good Morning', 'We're a Couple of Swells', 'Make 'Em Laugh'; Kelly on roller-skates; Astaire in top hat; the incredibly long-stemmed Cyd Charisse proving the most perfect partner-in-arms either man could have. But there are plenty of surprises out of the barrel. Bing Crosby in *Going Hollywood* vamping Fifi d'Orsay with operatic soulfulness at a bar counter; Robert Taylor singing while grand pianos mushroom up through the floor around him; Jack Benny introducing a 1930 mini-musical 'quickie' that is unintentionally hilarious in its plethora of false steps and missed timings; Jimmy Durante hitting a high note and snorting, 'That note was given me by Bing Crosby and, boy, was he glad to get rid of it!'

Camp taste runs riot, of course, but it's mercifully un-guyed. No smart-alec nudges, just honest delight in the absurd and extravagant conventions of other days. Marge and Gower Champion, for instance, floating over a midnight blue field starred with glow-worms; Georges Gueteray sprinting up a staircase whose steps change colour at the touch of his toes; Eleanor Powell in *Born to Dance* marching and counter-marching on the gun-deck of an all-white battleship whose officers wear spangled tops and whose matelots blow trombones. A montage sequence flips enjoyably through every film buff's favourite moments: from Tarzan's first lesson in basic English to Gable's last goodbye to Scarlett O'Hara ('Frankly, my dear I don't give a damn'). The clowns make token appearances—Laurel and Hardy, the Marx

Brothers—and a reel of home movies shows Tracy and Hepburn in privately flirtatious mood. Inevitably some flop. Sinatra is a bit below par. A sequence devoted to MGM's long-running love-affair with Paris, France, almost runs into the very same banalities of the Fitzpatrick travelogues which elsewhere are condemned out of their maker's own mouth.

But lapses are soon forgotten in the cornucopia of talent. My own special favourites: A number I'd never seen before starring a dancer I barely know—Bobby Van, simply kangaroo-hopping down one of those folksy Mid-West main streets and turning on the invention at every step. And all in one unbroken take whose timing is perfection. The other moment is Esther Williams in a pink one-piece with flying panels starting off on water-skis at the head of a flotilla of muscular males, zooming over the waves behind seven speedboats, before she rises vertically off the water on a trapeze dangling from a helicopter and then plunges back into her element from mid-air.

Saul Bass's opening titles are an inspired compendium of every Hollywood credit sequence convention you've ever seen—and for good measure Messrs Astaire and Kelly sing the cast-list at the end. The only name I think they've left out is that of Louis B. Mayer, one-time chief of MGM. The slaves are free at last!

Evening Standard, 20 May 1976

MEMORY IS BANKABLE

Like plenty of other words that have worn out their welcome, words like 'ecology', or 'unisex', or 'liberation', the mere mention of 'nostalgia' is enough to set one screaming. But the likelihood is that it will be here for some time yet. So long as other people continue to live off it, we shall have to learn to live with it.

How well one can live off it, I had brought home to me a few months ago in Las Vegas, in the MGM Grand Hotel, to be precise, that Pharaoh's pyramid which lately rose out of the Nevada desert enshrining the symbols, if not the soul, of the old dear dead MGM film empire, as well as generating some livelier artefacts in the shape of a continuous cash flow from its gaming rooms back to the Hollywood studios. In the bowels of the place lies what I suppose the archeologists would call the Inner Chamber. What the entrepreneurs call it is the Nostalgia Emporium, a collective memory-cell packed with the solid make-believe of palmier movie-making decades. At a glance, all Hollywood seems to be up for sale.

Here the dream merchants are well-named: they know the price of everything once deemed transient or perishable. Here you can find (and buy) such things as the gown worn by Rita Hayworth in *The Story on Page One*; the pilot and co-pilot's chair from *2001: A Space Odyssey* ('later used in MGM executive offices: 1,100 dollars the pair'); the pants that Leo Carillo wore as Pancho in *The Cisco Kid*; the barber's chair sat in by John Wayne in *The Man Who Shot Liberty Vallance*; thousands and thousands of books from the library department all marked with the MGM bookplate (I know MGM made *Ben-Hur*, but why did they need 18 editions of the book including Esperanto?); portfolios of watercolour designs (*Mutiny on the Bounty* a pricey 200 dollars, *Goodbye, Mr Chips* a knockdown 35); cases of macabre regalia from the Lon Chaney horror movies ('Please Ask for Assistance Before Trying On the Masks'); racks of period newspapers and magazines that once lent conviction to a Times Square set (*Vogue*'s Christmas 1935 issue, 20 dollars to you today); walls and walls of bar-room mirrors from some gangster-era speakeasy gilded with legends like 'Pabst on Tap' (the beer, one presumes, not the director, though in a place like this one cannot be quite sure: perhaps they have sarcophagi of mummified movie-makers for sale to discriminating buffs); and, appropriately enough, the shadow of Shangri-la's time-lessness can be made to fall across contemporary faces at the 'Antiquo-graph Stand,' where the camera photographs customers in tones of already faded sepia with the promise, 'We will make you older and prettier.'

The charm of such ephemera is insidious enough to have created its own movie cycle. Distance, it's been found by the studios, lends enrichment as well as enchantment to the viewfinder. But have you noticed the rather eerie change that has been creeping over the nostalgia-industry, as far as filmmakers are concerned? They are not only reproducing the past in the stories they pick and the stars they groom and gown in the styles of other days; they have more and more been reproducing their own past, *Hollywood*'s past—and Hollywood's own famous stars of the long-dead past. They have, like the invasion of the bodysnatchers, been *replicating* the warm flesh and blood that once bore celebrated names and carried corporate fortunes in their unique physiques, smiles, wisecracks or less definable allure.

We are very shortly going to see Clark Gable and Carole Lombard back together in a new movie, though these two have been dead for 15 and 34 years respectively: a couple of barely known look-alikes have been cast in the title roles of *Gable and Lombard*. The great W. C. Fields fares slightly better. Though it is 30 years since he gave up the ghost, and the bottle, at least he will have an actor of distinction, Red Steiger, to reincarnate him in the story of him and his mistress, *W. C. Fields and Me*. One cannot say with certitude when Rin-Tin-Tin ceased to be, for half-a-dozen stand-ins reputedly shared the name as well as the glory. But the hair of the dog that saved Fox has been transplanted into Michael Winner's new movie, *Won-Ton-Ton, the Dog that Saved Hollywood*. However, the dubious glory of the year's boldest body-snatching is surely earned by Ken Russell who has selected Rudolf Nureyev to masquerade as Rudolph Valentino in the fiftieth year of the Great Lover's demise. Add to all these a host of movies actually set in Hollywood and containing lightly-veiled or bare-faced replicas of the once-famous, such as *The Last Tycoon*, *Hearts of the West* (the old cowboy stars), *Nickelodeon* and *The Silent Movie* (the new Bogdanovich and the new Mel Brooks respectively).

There is a dread stench of cannibalism exuded by this particular corpus of nostalgia. Practically all the famous personalities who figure in it can still be seen in films they made in their own lifetimes. but apparently, it is not enough to reissue those films which, heaven knows, have presented their own sweet and authentic nostalgia over the years. Instead we have to replicate the bodies, we have to ask the living to step into the souls of the dead, and give what in nine cases out of ten will surely prove paltry and unworthy imitations of them. It is a truism that you can go once too often to the well for your inspiration: but what Hollywood is doing is going to the graveyard. This isn't nostalgia, it is necrophilia.

Vogue, 1 March 1976

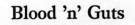

Blood 'n' Guts

Somewhat surprisingly—at first, anyhow—I found that most of the film reviews I'd chosen for this section came from one year, 1972. Undoubtedly this was when 'violence' peaked on the screen: I use the quotation marks (which I shall now abandon) simply to emphasise at the very first how many varieties and emphases there are to screen violence. Like the phrase 'the crime on our streets', the use of 'the violence in our cinemas' is a handy blanket condemnation for those who may, consciously or not, wish to put worse constraints on the freedom of citizens or artists.

Not all filmmakers, of course, are artists; and a fair number, perhaps the majority, know a good thing when they see it is popular. Violence is, always has been, that. But the new dimensions the screen gave it in the first years of this decade do reflect a more knowing, an altogether more dehumanised angle of scrutiny. *Bonnie and Clyde*, which I've referred to earlier, renovated the mythology of violence and gave it a lyrical spin-off in the example of a couple of classically doomed (and personable) young lovers. *The Wild Bunch* made the degree and realism of the slaughter, the 'medical materialism', into the major part of the fascination. From there it was but a short ride into the totalitarianism that goes with fashionable decadence and profitable exploitation. I think that, as usual, 'profit' may have more to do with the new 'ultraviolence' than any philosophical tenets; for it was when mainline movies had become so much a reflection of contemporary permissiveness that they were running into rating and censorship trouble, and could not be easily sold to television without extensive cuts and sometimes editing, that violence began to be upped as part of the replacement attraction. I've touched on this in an essay I wrote for *Encounter*.

Part of the fascination for me is seeing how violence adopts many exploitive disguises as well as some respectable suits of social allegory. Entertainment marches in step with social change and the swiftness of the escalation in social violence, from muggings to hijackings, from urban guerrillas who appear in the most sophisticated cities to mass murderers who expose the primitivism in our midst, has been an incitement to filmmakers. In its most depersonalised, yet not perhaps most disturbing, manifestation this has pushed the 'disaster' film into prominence and greater and greater profit. Particularly interesting is the way the 'law and order' lobby, who might have been among the first to condemn violence on the screen (and sometimes are, when it doesn't reinforce their prejudices) have gained the sometimes cynical backing of filmmakers hedging their bets by making the criminal into a cop, or vice versa, till the liberal conscience is reduced to whining in a corner and the vigilantes take over City Hall. The demeaning of the sophisticates is always part of the calculated appeal to the cavemen in the audience for these films.

What the effect of violence is on adults remains a matter of debate—and the debate will probably go on indefinitely, as the phenomenon crests and subsides, the way permissiveness has done, since it is very likely not an area of enquiry that can yield any conclusive or even useful answers. One curious feature of the debate is that while violence, in its blanket sense, is deplored as vigorously and sometimes as intolerantly as sex, in *its* blanket-and-sheets sense, there have been no excursions into court, in England anyhow, to prosecute a film on the grounds of violence. The illustration of sex hits at the roots of deeper taboos in society than even the depiction of pornographic violence. There are plenty of drawings on the walls of the Altamira caverns depicting violent actions that have taken place, or which the tribe with mouths to fill or enemies to repulse hopes will take place; but none, so far as I know, depicts the sex act that was necessary for the tribe's continuation. Violence on the cave walls of our darkened cinemas is still regarded as a rite of passage which establishes contact with our primal emotions.

This section and the next one should ideally be read together, for one follows from the other, and the *macho* heroes are very much representatives of the popular suffrage that's expressed through the box-office rather than the ballot-box. To find out about society, I would sooner trust the filmgoer than the party voter. Neither may offer ethical satisfaction: but I know which one approximates the more to awful contemporary reality.

FUTURE SHOCKWORK/*A Clockwork Orange*

What our nightmares have accustomed us to see in dreams, Stanley Kubrick's *A Clockwork Orange* shows us in broad daylight. It is one of the most unsettling films in the whole of cinema.

After it's gripped you by a bold, violent and clever story, an allegory of power and corruption couched in terms of a horror comic, the film expands into an infinity of terrifying implications for us and the times we live in. So many films have exploited the Permissive Society—this one is a landmark in the study of the Violent Society. Kubrick recounts his bovver-boy hero's exploits at a time not long from now. But he inserts into our minds, like the electrodes that give Alex the horrors in the brainwashing sequence, a sense of present fears made manifest; of a future that has invaded our consciousness before we are ready for it; of a primal past that our smooth skins and rational intelligence deceived us into believing had died out with the Ape Men. The urban landscape of *A Clockwork Orange* is recognisably our own. But it exists in a world that has lost its humanity. It has only a baroque eroticism, a proletarian ghastliness, an institutional callousness. Sexuality has been robbed of feeling; procreation has become just 'the old in-out, in-out'. Politics are totalitarian poles apart; there is no in-between ground for men of goodwill. Adults get by on tranquillisers, while society's vital energy is the monopoly of violent teenagers, king of whom is Alex (Malcolm McDowell).

Alex is a perverted Candide inspired by evil, not innocence. His face, in the film's unforgettable opening sequence, is that of a fallen angel; but when he rears up to bash one of his mutinous 'droogs' with a sword-stick, Kubrick's slow-motion camera delineates a prehistoric savagery—a replica of the King Ape and his lethal bone-club in *2001: A Space Odyssey*. He and his gang talk 'Nadsat', a boastful stream of slang that jubilantly conveys their zest for violence as well as a sense of future time and even the feeling of a mutation of the teenage species. This callous slang syntax with Russian roots ('horrorshow' for 'good', 'tolchock' for 'ounch') imported from Anthony Burgess' virtuoso novel which is composed almost entirely of it, works even better in the film than on the page: its words hit your ear one shuddering moment before you guess their meaning. The aural assault, which perversely gives the thugs some of the swagger of Mercutio's young bloods, accompanies their banter during the nightly sprees of 'the old ultra-violence'. But such violence as Kubrick depicts would be indefensible if the film's other powerful techniques did not confirm his honest intentions so successfully.

By using an amazing variety of music, from pop songs to the classics (or composer Walter Carlos' unearthly synthesised versions of them), Kubrick permits us to approach his scenes of violence with an altered consciousness. It's possible to view a savage gang fight like a balleto-mane once it is choreographed to Rossini's *Thieving Magpie*; or see a mugging turned into a surrealist soft-shoe shuffle once the not-so-soft boot is put in to the rhythm of *Singin' in the Rain*. Even a nude orgy between Alex and two mini-boppers is shot to fit the pace of a speeded-up *William Tell* overture—the sense of frivolous sex being perfectly contained in the batty pace of the multiple couplings. Music not only leads the dance, but motivates the retribution that falls on Alex after the police have got him for the killing of a prurient recluse (Miriam Karlin) with a piece of phallic sculpture—those that live by the sex-object shall die by it. To regain his liberty, he volunteers for shock therapy aimed at replacing his criminal will by conditioned docility, exchanging his pagan revelry for Christian guilt.

The fatal kink in this perfect plan, pioneered by the ruling totali-tarian party as part of its vote-catching law-and-order programme, emerges when Alex is accidentally alienated from the only bit of humane culture that has turned him on like a human being, the music of Beethoven. That a soulless nature like his dotes on 'the glorious *Ninth* by Ludwig Van', the most perfect hymn to human brotherhood, is the film's blackest joke. But Kubrick's icy cynicism is everywhere in it, though as an animating not a deadening force. Political oppor-tunism, for instance, could hardly be more hilariously conceptualised than at the climax when the Minister of the Interior (Anthony Sharp, like a benign Malcolm Muggeridge) literally spoonfeeds the con-valescent Alex into making a pact with the State—brute force in alliance with its respectable reflection.

Scene after scene of *A Clockwork Orange* is squeezed until the pip squeaks brilliantly: Alex's aversion-therapy treatment turning him into a human goose being force-fed to please society's palate the better; or the subsequent test he's put through by a pair of tempters, male and female, in an effort to re-kindle his violence or lust which resembles a kinky Berlin cabaret in the 1920s; or the reformed bovver-boys' last, sad odyssey, virtually a replay in reverse of the film's first half, which confronts him with the favourite Kubrick monster of the crippled intellectual (Patrick Magee), even sitting in Dr Strangelove's wheel-chair, whose love for 'the people, the common people' is as lethal in its radical-chic way as Alex's contempt for them.

Among a dozen masterly performances, Malcolm McDowell's Alex is that of a true star—a juvenile Satan whose vividly articulated gloating on his power status contains the same compulsive fascination for us as Milton's heroic villain in *Paradise Lost* who swore 'to do aught good never will be our task/But ever to do ill our sole delight'. In fact I believe his performance is what embodies the most unsettling fear in the film. The one that freezes people as they watch it, perhaps without actually knowing why. For Kubrick's hero represents the generation that has taken ultimate leave of its parents. He denies mankind's hope of its own posterity. The belief that our children will reproduce us is what has kept the human race going; but seeing *A Clockwork Orange*, one's faith is blasted. From it, one brings away the fear that what our children will do is—kill us.

Evening Standard, 13 January 1972

'Fear' is the word, I think, for what *A Clockwork Orange* slips into our consciousness by operating, as it does, so subtly, below the level of awareness. Kubrick has spoken of film as being 'a controlled dream'. This film in particular bears out that artistic commitment. I've dwelt in some detail, in *Stanley Kubrick Directs*, on its masque-like construction: I feel I should have dealt even more particularly with its ability to invade the stronghold of reason with its peculiar nightmare vision. We are operated on—though with far greater ethical and artistic purpose—rather as Alex in the film is operated on: his brain-washing is part and parcel of the cinema's techniques, though he is captive in addition to being passive.

In his case, however, violence is used in conjunction with pain to wean him off his propensity: in our case violence is used, in highly pleasurable surroundings, to expose us to the consequences of the world we have helped create. No wonder we don't like it. No wonder there has been a severe and continuing backlash against the film, though, quite honestly, its degree of actual violence is small compared with practically any standard exploitation film from America, and the violence is further stylised in ways designed to deny us pornographic gratification while not diminishing our horror.

It was all too easy, though, for certain anti-permissive groups in English public life to seize on the film and relate all social ills to it—apparently we had been without these afflictions till the moment *A Clockwork Orange* hit the screens. Now its very title is one of the 'trigger' phrases that provoke instant and usually unthinking reaction. By saying it, sometimes significantly narrowing the target even further by substituting the definite article 'the' for Burgess's indefinite 'a' in the title, such people convince themselves they can corral the corruption they sec around them. Remove the film and you remove the affliction: so runs the refrain. There is tribal magic here, too, whose potency Kubrick would well understand: but it is the kind that demands a sacrifice.

My own particular pleasure, reinforced each time I see the movie, is how each new Home Secretary we have in Britain gets more and more like the Minister of the Interior in his utterances. But then we have already seen *Dr Strangelove* give birth to Dr Kissinger.

HITCH IN TIME/*Frenzy*

Watching *Frenzy* makes you feel that for Alfred Hitchcock nothing has changed very much in England since 1939. I know you can see the new Hilton hotel in this film, read decimal prices, and the big issue is pollution—heartily satirised at the start by a corpse floating down the Thames right under the nose of some speechifying Government Minister. But otherwise it looks—even more, it sounds—as if Mr Chamberlain is still P.M. and Mrs Miniver rules over the country.

This is an England in which a squadron leader with the DFC has to take a job as a bartender; in which a killer with sadistic tastes has to apply to a matrimonial bureau under the name 'Mr Robinson' so as to gratify them; in which ladies still behave as if four-letter words had never passed their ears much less their lips; in which the term 'kinkiness' has apparently not yet been invented and the phrase 'certain peculiarities' has to do; in which old comrades give a hunted chappie a night's shelter with a loyal caw of 'Can't turn old Dicko over to the cops'; in which a Kensington hotel receptionist comes over all puritan at the very notion of an unmarried couple wanting a double-bedroom; in which the hotel porter vows that 'just thinking of the lusts of men makes me want to 'eave'; in which police sergeants play stooges to their superiors; in which their bosses, arriving at the scene of the crime ask for information with a 'Sergeant, would you do the honours?' as if it was all a matter of pouring the tea.

An air of seedy gentility drenches everyone, even the ladies' club where matronly members eat supper with their hats clamped on, and testifies to the continuing existence of a London that belongs to no one but Hitchcock who left it behind him when he emigrated to Hollywood in the last summer before the war. Now none of this would matter a bit—well, to be indulgent to a master filmmaker who's already carved his face on the cinema's Mount Rushmore, it wouldn't matter *much*—except for one thing. The grisliness of the murders is straight out of the permissive 1970s. They jar horribly, in a way I don't think was intended, on the nostalgic twaddle all around them. They are crude beyond belief, without the saving grace of wit, irony, suspense or even sheer naked shock.

In the first a middle-ageing woman is stripped, raped (at least I presume that's what befalls her since her killer keeps up throughout a chant of 'Lovely . . . lovely') and strangled while she recites the 91st Psalm. In the second 'set piece' the killer has to rummage through a bag of potatoes to retrieve his tie-pin (another sign of the 1930s, that) from a corpse whose *rigor mortis* has set in so stiffly that he is compelled to break open her fingers like sticks of barley sugar. The mixture of the gruesome and the genteel, which forms the characteristic recipe for the kind of 'English murder' Hitchcock was after, has curdled in the cooking.

Anthony Shaffer's screenplay would be funny as a send-up of the very detective fiction he spoofed so successfully in *Sleuth*. But that was on the stage. On the screen every scene is stagey beyond belief—there's even a complete little playlet shoved in without reason about the detective (Alec McCowen) being plagued by his wife's efforts at gourmet cooking. Since Barry Foster is revealed as the murderer before an hour has passed there was no point in throwing suspicion so implausibly (and awkwardly) on to Jon Finch. You can guess the unlikelihood of the plot from the fact that the killer stops to borrow a clothes-brush from a pull-in caff to get rid of the dust from the potato sack that's due to be dumped with its body not many miles away.

If you'd missed the name of the credits, you wouldn't guess *Frenzy* was the work of anyone but a beginner struggling against the odds of bad scripting and worse acting—but for one touch. This occurs when Anna Massey, as one of the victims, is lured upstairs to her death. But instead of showing it, Gil Taylor's camera begins a long, slow, beautifully unbroken retreat along the landing, down the stairs and out into the street while the sounds of London gradually filter in and then drown our horrible imaginings in a dispassionate roar of traffic.

Watching it, you might have told yourself that whoever directed that masterly moment might live to be a Hitchcock some day.

Evening Standard, 25 May 1972

Pictures like *Shaft's Big Score* are supposed to appeal to black consciousness. What I really think this one does is appeal to the black man's wallet. And I'd add that instead of fostering a sense of racial identity, it could be an object lesson in how to thwart it.

For it is simply a white man's fantasy that happens to be coloured black. The fact that both producer and writer are white and that MGM, which made it, isn't noticeably a stronghold of Black Power may have a lot to do with this. It's true that the director Gordon Parks *is* black. He once made a much better movie called *The Learning Tree*, about the experience of growing up black, that ran into accusations of Uncle Tom-ism; and Richard Roundtree, who plays Shaft, is black, too. But there the colour consciousness begins and ends. John Shaft is less Black Power than a black playboy. Like James Bond, he's not for revolution: he's for status and the *status-quo*. As long as he wakes up with a black chick in his bed—'I think I could lay a hand on her,' he tells a telephone caller who's asking after the same bedmate— and so long as he's got his car, his pad, and his high velocity rifle (a bigger weapon than 'Whitey' Bond, you'll note) then his 'people' have it made.

He's hired to recover the payroll of a murdered black who was running a gambling racket behind a respectable insurance front and the money is said to be destined for 'child welfare in Harlem'—that's as near as anyone gets to a big social issue, and it's a nice safe one, like the profits from the jewel robbery in that other 'black' movie *Cool Breeze*, which were to be used for founding a black bank. (Hurrah for black capitalism! A stake in the economy soon cools racial hotheads.)

Almost everywhere else in *Shaft's Big Score* the colour question is avoided. The police captain who bawls our hero out is black—so that's all right—whereas if he'd been white, like the policeman in *The French Connection*, which was scripted by the same writer (though it's hard to believe), then the liberals would be screaming, 'See how rotten they are to the blacks.' It's also true that a white police lieutenant has a racial chip on his shoulder, but all he's used for in the film is going out for coffee. 'Make mine black,' says Shaft. That's telling them, man! The villains, pigmentation-wise, are a well-balanced lot, too. The black mob is led by Moses Gunn and are marginally less exotic than the white crowd led by Joseph Lascolo playing a 'Godfather' who lives amidst a hand-bound library in a penthouse and slips on a silk dressing-gown to play the woodwind. What the blacks lack in class, they make up in brawn. The ever-resourceful MGM Press fact sheet tells me that among the henchmen is 'one of Muhammad Ali's trainers'.

Ultimately such a film stands or falls on whether it's 'entertainment' and on this score, *Shaft* collapses. Most of it is so slowly paced you could not only pour yourself out a drink between the lines of dialogue, but add ice, too. The plot is a limp carbon copy of films that were themselves carbon copies of the Bonds. Where it could have scored points for the quality of its 'blackness', it forfeits them by trying to appeal to every shade of skin and opinion and offend none. Result: it comes out a dull grey. If I've been hard on it, it's because it is among the earliest of a flood of movies about the blacks that are on their way over from America. And I think it's important to stress the difference not just between the good and bad films, but between the films that have grown, however unsettlingly, out of a true experience of what it is like to be black and the rest that have been put together after a worn-out pattern with but one thought in mind—simply to suck up to the black box-office.

Evening Standard, 10 August 1972

BUSINESS AS USUAL/*The Godfather*

I suppose 'blood' is the chief element in *The Godfather*. Not only the amount of it one sees on the screen, but the blood ties between the members of the Mafia family—and the blood that the family spills in defence of its unity, in the protection of its power and in laying down the law, the Mafia law, in American society. Often the two go rivetingly together, with a vividness that conveys the unforgettable sense of shock.

The film begins and ends with two holy rituals—a wedding and a baptism—that are interleaved with violence. And this conflict between the sacred and the profane runs right through Francis Ford Coppola's dynastic story of the fall of the 'Godfather', Don Vito Corleone (Marlon Brando), and the rise of his son Michael Corleone (Al Pacino).

Outside in the blinding sunlight of his garden, the Don gives his daughter's hand in marriage. Inside the gloom of the house, between the banquet's courses, he holds court and agrees to perform acts of vengeance for supplicant fellow-Italians who find the American law offers them no redress for the private wrongs done to their business or their honour. Thus the film drives home the first of its cynical truths: that in this day and age, when the machinery of the Law often delays justice or even perverts it, it is attractive to turn to an organisation like the Mafia which metes out revenge, a kind of 'wild justice', in return for total obedience.

At the end of the film, Michael, the new 'Godfather', attends the christening of his godson while his henchmen move out among the members of a rival Mafia gang and slay them in one of the most chilling bloodbaths to be seen on the screen. Michael's vows to renounce Satan and all his works alternate crudely but stunningly with the delivery of an enemy's soul to its Maker by the quick pressure of a trigger finger. This sense of ritual is what permeates *The Godfather* and gives structure to the sprawling plot, a feeling of epic continuance to what could have been just a random series of gangster atrocities. Running nearly three hours without an interval, it sets down roots in society: it shows organised crime to be the passport to the American Dream which the immigrant Sicilian 'godfather' wrote out for himself. In one central sequence when Michael has to flee to Sicily to escape a vendetta—becoming an immigrant in reverse—the film sums up succinctly through his courtship of an Italian girl, the code of honour, revenge and instant 'justice' which the immigrant boats carried to America. Only a film as long and as essentially serious as this one could have afforded such a vital analysis of Mafia 'morality'. It explains the inexorable logic by which Michael, the college-educated son, is drawn into the family business of organised crime. And just because it is a *business*, the film's violence assumes a peculiar justification.

It isn't the prodding, titillating, 'come and enjoy it' of violence. It is dispensed with awesome impersonalness—'as per contract', you might say—to people who expect it. 'There's anothing personal in this,' becomes the gruesome prelude to a liquidation, but it's only stating the truth. This is business efficiency in operation.

Such an ethos as it makes for itself has enabled *The Godfather* to include a multitude of violent episodes. The garroting of a henchman while his gun hand is pinioned to the bar counter by a stiletto; the vendetta that blows holes in Sonny (James Caan), the short-tempered son, in broad daylight; the revenge that Michael takes on a crooked police chief (Sterling Hayden) and his Mafia paymaster over coffee at a *trattoria*; the strangling of a brother-in-law mercifully masked from us by the car windshield until his threshing legs, in agonised reflex, shatter the laminated glass. Yes, I suppose it is life and death both heightened and glamorised: in real life the Mafia chiefs lead lives of restraint and watchfulness, always under threat of a police harassment that is conspicuously absent from this film. But its efficiency, like that of the Mafia machine, is impressive enough to make one forget this.

So are the performances, especially Marlon Brando's. His 'God-father' is introduced in the first shot with his back to us. Gradually the circling camera reveals a transplanted volcano—a volcano that's grown old over the years, yet retains its brooding power to erupt. The eyes are nearly sightless—they look through, not at, a person—the head sits like a meteorite on the shoulders, the voice is a quiet wheeze as if someone were continually trying to get a car engine started. It takes five minutes for one to get one's bearing on this conception—then it is hypnotic. Oddly enough—perhaps not so odd, when one stops to think—this man doesn't seem inwardly wicked, but simply a man made by his times as the monster was made by Frankenstein. In his magnificent down-beat death scene, when he wedges a slice of orange peel between his teeth and plays the bogeyman to his grandson, the actor's ability even suggests the *frailty* of evil, rather than its 'banality'.

But Brando isn't the whole film. If he delivers the goods, then Al Pacino is the bonus. It is Pacino's coldly effective style which makes plausible the transition of the boy from a 'respectable' member of the family to the new head of it, coldly proclaiming that it's 'business as usual', as he moves the headquarters west from New York to the new casino empire of Las Vegas. With its attention to period—even the colour tones look like those of the 1940s—and its sureness in every detail, *The Godfather* shows there is still life in the massive production engineering that made Hollywood studios the wonder of the entertainment world in their great days.

Evening Standard, 24 August 1972

I find I can forgive Hitchcock his trendy miscalculation over introducing 1970s violence into a 1930s ambience in *Frenzy*; I will argue a case for *The Godfather*'s presentation of violence as 'big business'; I am able to see that black consciousness must have its fantasies, and if these are as undesirably violent as Whitey's, then that is part of the price paid for equality.

But the *Manson* film, reviewed below, seems to me still the awesome ultimate in mindless exploitation. That there is a serious film to be made about Manson, no one doubts. He is Hollywood's own King Kong come true. He might have appeared anywhere in the length and breadth of the United States: the fact that he and his ghastly acolytes made their sorties over the Hollywood hills, and were just a short automobile drive from Beverly Hills, seems a grotesquely appropriate example of life aping fantasy. (Life no longer, or very seldom, apes art for reasons that are not hard to see: it apes bad art more frequently.) Manson was in many ways a retribution figure to the movie colony; the reception that his crimes got was intensified by the fact that the victims (their precise status, which was lowly in most cases, got confused early and permanently with the gilded setting of the crime) were people in a vastly pampered and highly privileged and usually well-protected condition of life. Manson embodied that latent hatred of the stars which can unleash such a crippling backlash when the public tires of them or they start to slide down the success ladder and become more desperate caricatures of their own fantasy appeal. He summed up the affectless violence then the hallmark of many movies in a way that left blood on the doorstep of many a Hollywood home.

It happened that I was with one of the old-time Hollywood stars, having lunch with her in London at just about the time the first reports of the Sharon Tate killing (as it was soon known, thus characteristically concentrating on the one legitimate, if minor movie figure in the bloodbath) was breaking in the English morning newspapers. She was obviously overcome by more than natural repugnance: it seemed that her way of life, her way of professional existence, had been the object of the outrage. She was right.

I have since watched the Manson fear permeating the Hollywood movies, for there is absolutely nothing the film world will not use for its profit. The final holocaust of *Beyond the Valley of the Dolls*, though highly risible in its effects, is also directly derivative from the real-life horror. The latest emanation of Manson is in a novel written, not accidentally, by a Hollywood actor and producer, Tom Tryon. *Crowned Heads* contains a *novella* called 'Willie' in which a grand-old-man of Hollywood finds his luxurious and narcissistic retreat shattered by youthful barbarians. He ends up nailed to the cross in his private chapel. It is a story that could be called 'Clifton Webb Meets Charles Manson' and strikes one as a symptom of the very movie decadence it purports to condemn. But then Manson was a symptom of Hollywood, in whose recent product he might well go uncondemned.

IN AT THE KILL/*Manson*

Sensational crimes that rate headlines round the world have one thing in common: they make money for those entrepreneurs quick enough and businesslike enough to cash in on the public's revulsion or prurience. A particularly ugly relic of the Sharon Tate murders of 1969 has just surfaced at the Venice Film Festival, presented in a section called 'Documents of Our Time'. It is a full-length movie called *Manson* and sub-titled *Family Ritual*

Although I rate as nil its chances of obtaining a censorship certificate in Britain—and rather higher its chances of drawing the attention of the Director of Public Prosecutions if it goes into a cinema club—I think it worth relating some of the more printable details to show with what ruthless calculation a human being's fate is turned into someone else's profit.

Manson doesn't re-create the actual slaying of Mrs Roman Polanski and her friends by the drugged or mesmerised 'slaves' of the Californian drop-out Charles Manson. The most we are shown are shots of the inscriptions left by the killers with the blood of their victims on the walls, doors and refrigerator of the Hollywood home—as well as a pathetic shot of the double grave in which are buried Sharon Tate and the baby she was carrying at the time. But this is virtually all we are spared. What the film ekes out its running-time with is the first-person testimony by those members of Manson's commune who quit before the slayings or else didn't participate in them, often for reasons no more moral than the fact that there was no room in the cars that took the others to the Tate house. Their jail-cell companions also speak fluently. Particularly appalling are the three drop-out girls, shorn to Peter Pan hair-cuts and caressing rifles and machetes as if they were love-objects, who speak to us with unshaken conviction in their erstwhile Messiah and still propagate his philosophy that 'anybody can kill anybody'. We see the vest that Manson's hippy harem embroidered for him with pictures of their pornographic fantasies and further bedecked with 'scalps' in the shape of the long locks that the girls cut off their heads when they left their middle-class homes, campuses or safe jobs to live like animals with their Master and feed out of trash cans, though only on greens, since they were all vegetarians.

Manson's disciples describe their random procreation—umbilical cords being tied off with guitar strings once the babies have been delivered—and dwell on necrophiliac perversions, such as having intercourse with a suicide, which are probably by now their own personally elaborated fantasies stimulated by the media interviewers' gathering of material. As well as the glorification of murder, there is the justification of it hurled out at the audience by the Mansonites on the grounds that such people as the Polanskis made films that were invitations to be killed and, in any case, they the killers are simply reflecting back on society the violent fantasies from the TV serials and commercial advertising on which they were weaned. The film has undoubtedly some socio-psychologically valid material. But how can it be justified on any but commercial grounds when it makes this available to us in a form of entertainment for general audiences, rendered even more marketable by glossy production values ranging from an insidiously mellow commentator, sounding like the robot HAL 9000 in the film *2001: A Space Odyssey*, to split-screen and double-image photography more appropriate to the TV presentation of folk-singers and pop-balladeers, and even to the inclusion of six or seven melting songs that punctuate the grisly recital and will soon, I suppose, be available on LP?

The glib interpretations offered—the Mansonites were all people with grudges against society: he had, like Hitler, an incomplete personality—are not enough to justify this stylish wallowing in other people's blood. I do indeed wonder at the world I live in when I see a billboard advertising this film sited exactly across the road from the Festival Palace on the Lido where Roman Polanski's own movies were once acclaimed and honoured. Quite clearly, death is not the last thing one has to fear.

Evening Standard, 30 August 1972

BODIES COUNT/*The Stone Killer*

The bargain this column offers today is how to get in on the fastest-growth trend in current movies. I mean, of course, the 'cop as criminal' film. And I herewith present a do-it-yourself assembly kit based on Michael Winner's latest prefabrication, *The Stone Killer*.

First of all, you must give the impression that your hero is a cop. But as early as possible in the film, contrive to separate him from his badge, his uniform, indeed the particular police force he's belonged to. In short, 'bust' him. The purpose of this is that he can now play dirty, as dirty anyhow as the criminals, giving the impression that this is how cops must play if society as we know it is to be saved. This will please the 'law and order' brigade, who are basically people who have lost faith in legal 'law and order' and prefer vigilante 'law and order'. But also it will not turn off the people who simply want the thrill of violence, from whichever quarter it comes. Remember one thing, though: genuine liberals, like film critics whom they sometimes resemble, may feel queasy, so have on hand a liberal mouthpiece to voice their reservations. This can be any senior cop/mayor/DA, anyone who goes by the rule-book. (It can be intimated however that what he's *really* thinking about are his pension rights.)

Leave nothing to chance. A snappy slogan on the posters will save you pages of dialogue in the script. The following examples are offered as patterns:

'You didn't assign Dirty Harry, you turned him loose.' (*Dirty Harry*)
'He's a busted cop, his gun unlicensed, his methods unlawful, his story incredible.' (*McQ*)
'Take away his badge and he'd top the ten most wanted list.'
(*The Stone Killer*)

In the opening minutes, have your man shoot someone. Anyone will do, provided he is armed/young/long-haired/coloured (this last is optional). In Charles Bronson's case in *The Stone Killer*, it's a Puerto Rican fleeing from justice. 'He was scared,' say the film's liberals, in mitigation. 'Sure he was scared,' raps Bronson, 'but he was dangerous.' This is the tone you should aim for, aphoristic and rabid. Another example? As a suspect drug-peddler is slammed up against a wall and clobbered: 'You're a connection and you're black and this ain't a tolerant society.' And for reflective moments, such as when your police car is being stoned by blacks, try advising the rookie cop riding gunshot beside you: 'You might as well get used to it, you're part of the white power structure—the enemy.'

Remember above all else that the cop in such movies isn't there to heal society's wounds—he's there to inflict them.

Now to less important things—like the plot. The body count is really what matters, not the story, and trying to sort things out intelligibly may simply slow your man's fire-power. But if a plot *is* thought necessary, take your pick from films that are already so popular that any charge of plagiarism is easily disposed of. Top of this league is the Mafia Plot. *The Stone Killer* involves its hero in a plot to foil a leading Mafia Don's attempt at the wholesale slaughter of his rivals. And Bronson follows the blood-trail through the Los Angeles underworld of professional 'hit' men. Do not neglect a chance like this to cover the field. Include as many popular figures as you can in this rogues' gallery: all-powerful Mafia bosses, Negro militants, homosexual assassins, dope pushers. . . . Stage scenes in the men's lavatory where possible: this adds audaciousness to your script (Are there no limits a director like Winner recognises!) and if possible try to comment on the times we live in in other ways, too.

In *The Stone Killer*, for instance, all the assassins are ex-GIs—and you can guess on which war-front they learned their socially useful arts. 'Vietnam doesn't make heroes, but it makes a generation like this,' Bronson philosophises. Give yourself a mark for historical hindsight, but don't dwell on it unduly—there are *more exciting* things to do. Like the car chase. This you must have. And *The Stone Killer* has one—police car versus motor-cycle—that sums up all this brand of film's contempt for innocent bystanders as the vehicles crash their way through property and people regardless of anything or anyone but their own mindless confrontation.

Do you need something more? Are you thinking of something, say, like a message? Then how about the parable Bronson spins at the end of the film? How the carnage he's participated in so invulnerably, not to mention criminally (no, do *not* mention that: you are nearly home by now), reminds him of what the gladiators used to call out to the Christians in Roman times. And what was that? Namely, that they'd got just five minutes more before entering the arena. Says Mr Bronson, looking straight at us: 'You got five minutes, Christians.'

Actually, filmgoers and Christians, you got 96 minutes of this vicious stuff; and I'm sure its director will measure the importance of what he's got to say by the number of column inches I have devoted to it. After all, that's the kind of calculation that's gone into the making of the film; and I know that, at some point, quantity is supposed to turn into quality. I'm still waiting.

Evening Standard, 21 February 1974

GAME, SET AND MASSACRE/*Rollerball*

Rollerball presents itself as a movie with a moral for the future. But it strikes me as more of a metaphor for much of present-day entertainment. It is spectacular and violent, compulsively watchable but innately repugnant, doing very well what it has the muscle to do, which is to produce a horrifying view of man's inhumanity, but distinctly out of its league when it tries to flex its brain cells.

The rollerball game itself is one, we're told, that will be played world-wide in the near future to replace the wars which will have gone out of fashion—how this will happen we're not told—once the globe has been conquered by giant industrial corporations in the name of peace and commerce. Though the movie is extremely hazy about the nature of these enlightened tyrannies, I imagine they're on the lines of the huge business conglomerates that not long ago took over many of the Hollywood studios in the name of fun-and-games and profit. To keep the people entertained (and therefore non-rebellious) these rulers have invented rollerball, a game that pulls in all the thuggish elements, everything that's foul and downright beastly about such spectator sports as ice-hockey, cycle racing, roller-skating derbies and American-style football.

It is played on an indoor track by padded gladiators with spiked gauntlets whose aim is to maim and even kill each other in pursuit of an armoured ball fired from a torpedo tube. Immense efforts (and almost everything in the movie that passes for cerebral thought) have been lavished on giving such games the barbaric touches that gratify the spectators. In just the same way, the cinema audiences watching *Rollerball* are egged on to respond with visceral delight to the sight of James Caan, supreme rollerball champion, carving up the competition. There's a strong feeling about the film that the screen is a mirror in which the cinema masses will see the reflection of their own lusts.

The man behind the games, rather reminiscent of a movie mogul running the film studio, is a sardonic luminary played by John House-man in the manner of the Harvard Law professor he incarnated so acidly in *The Paper Chase*. Bread and circuses is not the only motive behind rollerball, he explains to Caan. It's also meant to teach the masses through the example of the bloodied gladiators in the arena, that there's no profit in individual effort, no use trying to come out on top of the heap. In short, the old principle of Hollywood studio-rule by the men in the front office, slapping down their pampered but servile employees, still pertains. Just as a film studio boss used to slap down an uppity star by slipping him a bad picture to be in, Houseman tries to eliminate the superstar by laying on a rollerball game that's dirtier than usual. All the rules are suspended: every last man on the teams has to die.

Now it needs very little thought—though apparently more than Norman Jewison's film can muster—to detect that the whole rollerball premise of the ruling class in the film is based upon a logical fault as wide as the Grand Canyon. For given any kind of competitive sport, *someone* is sure to emerge as the star—and stay put in the crowd's affections. If conformity is the name of the game, then the rulers in *Rollerball* are playing the wrong game.

Why this thought never struck them may well be explained by the glimpse we get of their off-duty hours, spent giving deadly dull cocktail parties in featureless modern interiors, the men wearing Cardin-esque suits, the women in Greek tunics and looking slightly frostbitten, and everyone putting in the time by looking at themselves on wall-size television screens. This is exactly the way that film folk entertain themselves during the long boring evenings with their own status-groups in the drawing rooms of Bel Air and Beverly Hills. At every point, *Rollerball* looks like a film that filmmakers have made in their own mindless, narcissistic image.

But the really disturbing implications of its muddled pretensions come right at the end. Once again Caan has come out top dog. But he's done so by ruthlessly maiming or killing everyone in his way on the rollerball track. When he salutes his checkmated masters on the rostrum he leaves a wake of mangled bodies behind him: in other words, the road to individual achievement lies over the corpses of the rest of humanity. Instead of a Spartacus, a gladiator leading the revolt against the rulers of a slave state, Caan has remained the Aryan superman abiding by the rules of the game. There could scarcely be a more insidious example of that self-same 'triumph of the will' which the Nazis understood so well and fostered so sedulously in their propaganda. It's not even as if Caan were protrayed in an ironic light, as a dupe of 'the system'. The accent of interest is placed squarely on equating murder with manhood, on suggesting that the one sanctifies the other. There is something deeply, dreadfully horrifying about the ingrained anti-intellectualism in *Rollerball*. Even the scene where reason, or at least liberalism, might have made its comment on the rollerball society is reduced to clumsy farce when Ralph Richardson, playing a scientist in charge of a computer that is the last repository of the world's knowledge, is made to clown around like a nutty professor. Seeking to ape Kubrick's brilliantly designed collison of moods as in *Dr Strangelove*, this movie only commits a calamitous misjudgment.

It is scarcely less deplorable, even if less surprising, to find a film that relies on sustained and repeated violence for any success it achieves being given an 'AA' Certificate by the censors instead of the clearly appropriate 'X' rating. If the new film censor comes over with the old line so beloved by his predecessors about cracking down harder on violence than sex, we shall now all know what reply to give—
rollerballs!

Evening Standard, 4 September 1975

I think the characteristic of filmmakers using the *angst* engendered by their own art, or their working conditions, as a more or less conscious element in constructing their films is commoner than we suspect.

I've already speculated on *The Exorcist* as the fantasy of a screenwriter anxious to protect his precious brainchild of a script from being 'possessed' by all the inimical forces that bedevil working in films. To some extent, I feel the same about Antonioni's *Blow-Up*. On the surface it is a mystery: has there been a crime or not? Beneath the surface one feels an on-going meditation by the director on his own art: 'Does filmmaking connect with reality? Have I lost my bearings in fantasy? Am I pointing my camera at the things that matter?'

Something in the film usually gives us a clue to this process, generally some reference, overt or not, to filmmaking. For instance, it's hardly accidental that Alan J. Pakula's paranoia thriller about organised political assassination was called *The Parallax View*. 'Parallax' is the discrepancy between what the camera lens sees and what the cameraman sees when his eye is to the viewfinder. It is also the name of the vast, faceless corporation in the film that recruits potential assassins. Either way, the word fits very well into the 'reality' of Hollywood where artists are constantly having to make 'adjustments' in the way they view things as part and parcel of the necessity for survival, or, at least, freedom; and where the chief threat can also come from conglomerates who, as in the film, use the screen as a means of 'screen-testing' potential new material. The movie capital's endemic mood of mistrust and betrayal, the constant crisis that accompanies achievement, the lack of stable bearings that's experienced by all but the most ruthless and self-confident: these are the realities of the Hollywood scene, frequently hidden under the two-faced life-style of the place, that find their way into the ingredients of movies which appear to be telling another quite different kind of story on the surface.

For instance, Joseph L. Mankiewicz's puzzling and underrated film *The Honey Pot* is instantly explicable if one recognises its modern updating of Ben Jonson's *Volpone* as an allegory of all the fantasy, double-dealing and deceit of the movie scene, in which Mankiewicz had just spent a couple of *years* directing *Cleopatra*. Rex Harrison's Volpone was your contemporary film producer, a Korda-figure, forever pulling last-reel triumph out of near-certain disaster (at a price), and his parasite Mosca had become a secretary who literally had to write the dialogue for his master before the wheeler-dealer could function. Close study of the three females in his entourage will suggest strong resemblances to actresses whom Mankiewicz worked with and suffered from in previous pictures. At the end, it's revealed that the man's whole prosperous life-style has been baseless: he is bankrupt. Even the furnishings in his palazzo have been rented from Cinecitta. The film looked as if it had been written, produced and directed by Mankiewicz as a catharsis to his *Cleopatra* trauma. But even more disquieting is Arthur Penn's *Night Moves*.

Ostensibly a private-eye story, it is signposted to the point of desperation with omens of its anti-hero's plight, very much resembling that of a film director who has lost control of his project and is steadily evading rather than solving his problems. As in *The Exorcist*, the stock figures of movie-land loom up in the detective's haunted search, which actually turns into flight— a promiscuous starlet, a movie stunt man, references (as Philip French's encyclopaedic memory detected) to Humphrey Bogart characters now absorbed into another context, and, finally, the motor-launch named 'The Point of View', which is the commonest camera direction occurring in film scripts. As the private-eye-cum-film director ends the film marooned in it and going round and round in circles, the difficulties of communication, always at risk in filmmaking, now appear acute. Chess is the (rather pretentious) motif used in Penn's film to invoke the ultimate stalemate: but 'the cinema' could just as well serve as his metaphorical point of reference. *Night Moves* may well refer to chessboard moves: isn't it even more apposite, though, to think of it as 'night movies', the commonest kind of 'home entertainment' among the Hollywood set?

DEATH SENTENCES

Holmes bent over this grotesque frieze for some minutes and then suddenly sprang to his feet with an exclamation of surprise and dismay. His face was haggard with anxiety.

'We have let this affair go far enough,' he said.

The Dancing Men

About five years ago a change came over the character of death on the cinema screen. What came into being has been called 'medical materialism', a phrase I owe to Dr Jonathan Miller. By this he meant that death, which had hitherto been a fairly ritualised affair, was turning into an anatomy lesson, or, rather, an autopsy. Previously, the gun barked, the victim jack-knifed, a token bloodstain welled up on his shirt front, another public enemy lay down and died. The damage was more sartorial than arterial; the censor's work was correspondingly simplified, since although deserving justice had been seen to be done, there really was no mess to speak of or to view.

It is curious, considering the high place that *cineverite* techniques occupy in the screen's approach to life, that the film which probably did more than any other to change its approach to death has been overlooked, in spite of being seen by more people the world over than maybe any other American movie in history. Let me momentarily conceal the event it recorded, as well as the names of the parties at the centre of it, and quote instead from a synopsis written some time afterwards, but very like a 'continuity script' which is put together from the completely edited film:

'The (car) continues to slow down. The interior is a place of horror. The last bullet has torn through (his) cerebellum, the lower part of his brain. Leaning towards her husband (she) has seen a piece of his skull detach itself. At first there is no blood. And then, in the very next instant, there is nothing but blood spattering him. . . . Gobs of blood as thick as a man's hand are soaking the floor of the back seat, (his) clothes are steeped in it, the roses are drenched, (his) body is lurching soundlessly towards his wife, and Motor Cycle Police Officer Hargis, two feet from her, is doused in the face by a red sheet. To Kellerman it appears that the air is full of moist sawdust.'*

Those who have read William Manchester's landmark piece of investigative reporting, *The Death of a President*, will hardly need to be told by now that what this describes is the assassination of President Kennedy in Dallas in November 1963.

But what makes it relevant to this enquiry into the contemporary cinema's approach to death is the way that Manchester duplicates the effect of a camera's eye seeing in slow motion, and therefore giving itself *time* to see, the bloody havoc accompanying the onset of sudden and extremely public death. As well as the eye-witnesses he names, Manchester had indeed the supplementary evidence of a camera's eye—the one with the famous Zoomar lens being wielded by Abe Zapruder, the garment manufacturer and amateur cinematographer

* William Manchester, *The Death of a President*, p. 196.

who happened to be filming the Presidential motorcade at the precise moment of the assassination. In the 8·3 seconds which it took the colour film to register it on 152 frames, the most notorious piece of 'medical materialism' in history was recorded to be relayed throughout the world during one of the most deeply shared periods of grief in centuries.

It is odd how this reproduction of an event dramatically heightens it. As the narrator in Stanley Kubrick's *A Clockwork Orange* says, 'The colours of the real world only seem really real when you viddy them on the screen. . . .' Not that the Zapruder film recorded the anatomical detail of the Manchester 'scenario', although once the posthumous event is treated to an 'action replay'—as it was, countless times in the course of the subsequent enquiries, lay and official—one seems to be seeing it broken down into the fractions of time in a slow-motion version. Over the years it has assumed an iconographic vividness well-nigh irresistible to any filmmaker disposed to draw his inspiration from an historical and moral shock of this magnitude. So one is not at all surprised to find this confirmed in an Arthur Penn interview in *Les Cahiers du Cinema*, four years after Kennedy's assassination, in which the director of *Bonnie and Clyde* explicitly refers to the earlier event when speaking of the fusillade of 87 bullets fired into the eponymous hero and heroine at the end of his film. 'We put on the bullet holes,' says Penn, 'and there's even a piece of Warren's (Beatty's) head that comes off, like that famous photograph of Kennedy.'* In fact if one turns to the screenplay of *Bonnie and Clyde*, written by David Newman and Robert Benton, what one finds is an eerie echo of the precise, present-tense tone of the Manchester 'scenario' which came out in the same year as the film, 1967:

'We see alternately the bodies of CLYDE and BONNIE twisting, shaking, horribly distorted; much of the action is now in slow-motion. CLYDE is on the ground, his body arching and rolling from the impact of the bullets. BONNIE is still in her seat; her body jerking and swaying as the bullets thud relentlessly into her and the framework of the car.

EXTERIOR. THE CAR ON THE VERGE

BONNIE's body slews out sideways, head first. A final burst and her head and shoulders droop down on to the running board. CLYDE's body rolls over and over on the ground and then lies still. The firing stops.†

* *Les Cahiers du Cinema* (December 1967) Arthur Penn interviewed by André Labarthe and Jean-Louis Comolli.
† *The Bonnie and Clyde Book* compiled and edited by Sandra Wake and Nicola Hayden, pp. 162-4.

The reason Penn used a slow-motion technique at this point in the film was to obtain what he called the effect of a 'spasm of death', and a most sophisticated technique it was. It involved no fewer than four cameras shooting at 24, 48, 72 and 96 frames a second, 'so that I could cut to get the shock and at the same time the ballet of death. There's a moment in death when the body no longer functions, when it becomes an object and has a certain kind of detached, ugly beauty.'

Now anyone who talks of the 'beauty' of death is treading in a very grey area of aesthetics; yet can anyone doubt that Penn acquitted himself responsibly in *Bonnie and Clyde*? Freely admitting to the fascination he found in rendering the kinetic effects of violence, which is what makes it so dangerously appealing where most spectators of events real or imaginary are concerned, he nevertheless saves himself from the charge of mortuary gloating by what one can only call an act of charity towards the victims. While slow motion gives us the time to see them die by protracting the moment of death into an eternity, it nevertheless withholds the full destructive force of the medical materialism which 87 bullets ripping into two people would have conveyed to us. They would have been literally torn apart. What really horrifies us is the 'overkill' nature of the lawmen, almost believing that their victims bore charmed lives and must be filled with their own weight of lead. All the same, their outlines are intact as they lie there, like effigies. What Penn has done is extinguish the life, but preserve the legend.

When we next saw slow-motion used to record the violent rhythms of death, it was in a far more materialistic cause. Sam Peckinpah's film *The Wild Bunch* also derived from the Kennedy assassination, more precisely from the debate on the role of the gun in American life which, in the aftermath of this event and the deaths of Robert Kennedy and Martin Luther King, looked like ushering in far tighter curbs on the sale and ownership of firearms in a society traditionally based on a man's right to bear and use them. Peckinpah's film celebrated the power of the gun by showing it in action, which meant showing the bloody destruction contained in one split second. Blood spurts like a drinking fountain from a burst artery in the opening massacre, a body bumps up off the ground like a rubber toy, dust rises in slow-motion, a limb trails out at a ghastly angle as if in a state of weightlessness and the corpse settles down with a spasm that has the effect in slow-motion of a small avalanche. *The Wild Bunch* always keeps returning to the gun. It is the hero, if anything is, far more so than the human beings, a bunch of ageing cowboys feeling their obsolesence, whereas their guns will go marching on into the new century, coming out in ever-improved models. The brand-new machine-gun that goes off like a fractious baby in the arms of the ignorant peon cuddling it is a quantum leap into totalitarian destructiveness.

But what is the film saying to us? This is more difficult to answer and even after a prudent second viewing, I am driven to conclude that it *says* nothing for the very reason that it *shows* everything. The end doesn't simply justify the means, as it always does in a Peckinpah film; the end *is* the means in the way that (remember?) the medium is the message.

Now this should have put us on our guard. I know that some people were; but to me, reviewing the film at the time, its bloody excesses seemed justified as a response to the contemporary wave of revulsion against violence. I am far less certain of this now—especially after Peckinpah's *Straw Dogs*, which I shall return to. In any case there were other omens we should have read in the cinema's attitude to the new violence. As Pauline Kael put it once, 'immediately something enters mass culture, it travels fast.' Which in this case meant not only the new presentation of death, but the film industry's hope of new life for itself. What we're apt to forget is that it isn't really a creative industry: it is an imitative one in which only a few creative people are tolerated at any one time. Commercial opportunism which can present an honest face to the world by the opportunities it gives an artist frequently shows a truer and cruder side in the way it later sells his work. The lyrical spell of *Bonnie and Clyde*, presented as 'Lovers' on the posters at the film's opening, swiftly dissolved into a keener pitch for the audience's emotions once they moved into the hinterland of suburban cinemas and became 'Killers'.

Over the last few years one has witnessed a whole arsenal of death-dealing weapons coming to dominate the cinema posters, in Britain anyhow, as the central, selling feature of the film being advertised: they irresistibly recall the swollen organs of potency commonplace in every porn book. (A prospective Ph.D. would find richly rewarding territory to research in the psychopathology of cinema advertising.) Of course every true craftsman is vulnerable to exploitation by the very trade that gives him work; but the film industry's sense of where the appeal lies is shown to be fairly accurate by the box-office success being enjoyed to a phenomenal degree by this quantum leap into human physical destruction and violent death. A frieze of death has stretched across the screen since *Bonnie and Clyde* and *The Wild Bunch* initiated the 'action autopsy' approach to it or, in Joseph Morgenstern's phrase, tried 'to explore the nature of life with the aesthetics of death'. To follow the trail of bloodstains makes for a profoundly disquieting experience. And when the perplexed Watson reaches the point where he cries, 'There are no more bloodstains,' one must sympathise with the inevitable reply from Holmes, 'Yes, that is the most disquieting thing of all.'

I don't think it was accidental that the curve of violence in films began its steep rise just about the time one would expect the new Hollywood films, which had profited from the 1965–66 revision in the Production Code to deal with sex more and more candidly, began to face the problem of their subsequent sale to television. Sex undressed is patently sex; violence, on the other hand, can be dressed up as many other things. Moreover, the motion-picture code, reflecting the taboos of the early Legion of Decency, and the Roman Catholic Church, as well as truisms at the centre of the American historical experience, was basically more tolerant towards the depiction of violence than sex. One has also to reckon with a number of filmmakers, men whose forte lay in the harsh-grained action film, now finding that the dangerous but exciting tide of fashion was running with them and even propelling their ingrained aggressions along almost faster than they could keep up with it. The world's escalating violence finds its most vivid reflection in the movies; which is not to say that the movies necessarily predispose us to add to the violence. But as the power of certain films proves so strong that we tend to conceptualise real events in their terms, I think that it may predispose us to tolerate violence, or at least its latest form when it is succeeded by some new and awful escalation. The imitative pressures of the film industry drive its filmmakers to let themselves rip on a spiralling ascent into new levels of death and destruction until it 'peaks' in some explosive display of psychopathy.

For film censors, this creates increasingly difficult problems. One of the recent crises, according to many commentators, came near to dislodging the new British incumbent at the censorship board, Mr Stephen Murphy, who learned in his first few painful months in office that he was caught between two irreconcilable duties—protecting the public from the excesses of the filmmakers and at the same time shielding the filmmakers from the intolerance of the public. Central to this crisis was the new character of death on the screen.

I am not going to allude in any detail to the two films over which the debate raged, *Straw Dogs* and *A Clockwork Orange*, for they have already been examined in articles and correspondence in *Encounter*. But as the person largely responsible for initiating the letter signed by 13 prominent film critics and published in *The Times* at the end of 1971,

I may perhaps be allowed to fill in some of the less well-defined aspects of the controversy where they are relevant to this theme. This is all the more necessary since a belief has grown up, at least amongst those who don't read letters to the Press all that carefully, that the British film critics in the main wanted to see *Straw Dogs* banned. In fact we did deplore its almost psychopathic obsession with violence: but this is not the same as demanding its suppression. I believe none of the signatories would have supported this, especially as we were protesting in the very same letter against the censor's own suppression of the Warhol/Morrissey film *Trash*, to which he had denied a certificate. Now the British film censors have always protested that they are more concerned with violence in films than with sex—the reverse of the American attitude—yet many of us felt that here was a case of one film being penalised because it dealt with aberrant forms of sex, while the other was passed for public viewing in spite of its manic degree of bloody violence—and even sexual violence. At the time of the protest to *The Times* none of us was aware of the prior history of *Straw Dogs* at the hands of the British censor: not that it would have modified anyone's attitude, I think, and conceivably it might have hardened some people's, had we known of it.

In brief, Mr Murphy had viewed the film, which Sam Peckinpah had shot in Britain, when it was in its final rough-cut, an unofficial procedure sometimes resorted to by his predecessor, John Trevelyan, when it was a question of 'tricky' material requiring a 'helpful' indication of attitude on the censor's part before he or his examiners were asked to pass it officially. Mr Murphy advised the producer and distributor that he did not feel able to pass it in its then rough-cut state. When it was officially submitted to him some weeks later, he was gratified to find his advice had been heeded. The shot of a man's guts being blown out of him by a double-barrelled shotgun had gone; the protracted rape scene in which two youths assaulted the hero's wife had been broken up by cuts to the absent husband on a duck shoot; and the double rape had been shortened, though the unintentional effect of this was to make it appear as if the unfortunate girl, caught the wrong side up after the 'conventional' assault on her, was now being buggered as well! Even in its surviving form, the rape was one of the most protracted and calculated acts of sexual violence I and others had up to then seen on the screen, the girl being beaten into submission and then having her scanty clothing ripped off her to the accompaniment of the noise of tearing material, which showed how well Peckinpah knew the emotive value of the sound as well as the sight of violence.

But it was the climacteric of violence when Dustin Hoffman is forced to abandon his pacifist stance against the wild bunch of assailants, and suddenly turn himself into a somewhat unlikely vest-pocket Hercules, which revealed the ferocious extent of the film's anti-humanism. Bodies were filled with buckshot, beaten insensible with iron bars; one man accidentally blew off his own foot and was left gawping at a close-up of the shattered stump; and the *specialité* of this particular *maison* came when the last assailant, alive or conscious, choked to death with his head caught in the toothed jaws of a game-keeper's mantrap.

There was a difference, though, compared to *The Wild Bunch* whose slow-motion technique also found its way into the mayhem. This film said something as well as showed it—namely, that a man needed to be put in touch with his primal instincts before he could call himself a Man. Peckinpah had come out of hiding with this one. Instead of bidding an elegiac valedictory of *The Wild Bunch* and giving a helpless shrug at the continuing role of the gun, he appeared as the champion of the Superman and gave his blessing to the machismo ethic which equates violence with virility, and suffering with manliness. '*The knock at the door meant the birth of a man and the death of seven others,*' was the film's publicity slogan in Britain. I am not sure if the same shameless advertisement for the totalitarian ethic prevailed in America: but I am told by the British distributor that it was the director's own invention. It was odd that with this staring him in the face from every hoarding, the British censor stoutly maintained his own reading of the film's last spoken line when Hoffman echoes the words of the pathetic village idiot who says he doesn't know the way home. The censor's interpretation of this gnomic aside is that it shows how far he has lost his moral bearings. On a more prosaic level, it could equally mean that he has no intention of hitting the trail back to his tramp of a wife. What indignation the British critics' attack on *Straw Dogs* aroused from some of the non-signatories to *The Times* letter came from sources where film criticism of a peculiarly narrow and sterile type confined itself to matters of style and technique. It was entirely appropriate as a response to Peckinpah's picture. 'Like' was reviewing 'like' without experiencing any need to consider the inter-vening matters of intention or morality.

It is also a matter of record that Stanley Kubrick's *A Clockwork Orange* was caught up in the moral backlash unleashed by some of the non-professional interest groups, notably the Festival of Light's divinely guided *illuminati* and the egregiously recruited members of Lord Longford's anti-pornography committee. These investigators discovered, embarrassingly late in the day, that violence was now the 'in' thing. To his credit, the censor had passed the Kubrick film uncut before the deluge: it is to be hoped that his courage would have withstood the subsequent outcry.

A Clockwork Orange is a useful reminder that in this enquiry we must pay more regard to intention than to content measured in quantitive terms. Though Kubrick's film has its violent sequences (not so many, however, as the outcry might lead us to expect), it is a film that is really about choice, not violence. While Peckinpah asserts that a man only becomes a man when he kills, Kubrick is saying that a man ceases to be a man if he cannot choose. Better that he should have the right to choose, even if it is the right to sin, than that his moral functioning should be replaced by the programmed mechanism of the State. What violence there is in the film is not of the medically materialistic kind. Very little physical injury is depicted, though much is suggested, and what there is gets 'distanced' from the audience by the 'ballet' of the gang fight and the 'vaudeville' of the assault-and-rape to the melody of *Singin' in the Rain*. I happened to be present while Kubrick shot the death of the Cat Woman, brained by the sculptured phallus, and it was a matter of lengthy deliberation by him not to let any physical injury be seen. This was to preserve the logic of the scene's nightmare dimension. For it's well known that in dreaming the mind's censor tends to exclude this sort of anatomical gruesomeness which would otherwise jerk the dreamer awake by his own too horrible imaginings. Kubrick's regard for the quality of the story as a 'controlled dream' made him take the same precautions.

But as one moves along the bloodstained trail to *The Godfather*, one enters some extremely dark territory. By late August 1972, when Francis Ford Coppola's film opened in Britain, the censor had finally screwed himself to the sticking place where he was now prepared to pass the Warhol/Morrissey movie, *Trash*, which had languished for many a year, with an 'X' Certificate but also with substantial cuts. (An 'X' in Britain excludes any person under 18 years of age.) He reached a decision over *The Godfather* with far less moral wrestling, giving it an 'X' Certificate, too, but insisting on the smallest imaginable cut, namely a nine-second trim towards the end of the scene where Sonny has run into the vendetta at the toll-gate and been slaughtered by the rival Mafia. The censor thought it objectionable to show one of the gang kicking the inert body: on the old British principle, I suppose, that you should never kick a man when he's down, even if he's dead.

Now the feast of death that *The Godfather* provides is so well known that I may perhaps be spared from running through the obits. I only observe that the garrottings, assassinations and serial slayings have their appeal deftly enhanced by the care that's taken never to repeat the slaughter twice in quite the same way. This is the principle of pornography, too. In contrast, what the censor advised should be cut out of *Trash*, in order to give it an 'X' Certificate, was almost entirely sexual and included a fellatio scene (shortened) and a moment when a beer bottle is put to a highly unusual use to obtain an orgasm (though as the self-pleasurer was a male-in-drag, it remains a mystery what arcane technique the censor was ascribing to him/her). The interpretation is irresistible—that the censor deplores violence, but he cuts sex.

For anyone operating on this double standard, *The Godfather* is a gift. In spite of being one of the most continuously violent films ever made, it contains absolutely no permissive sex scene—none at all. This has escaped general notice, perhaps by its very obviousness. It was brought home to me by the satisfaction with which a rather staid friend, who had frequently deplored the growing permissiveness of the movies, expressed his pleasure that here at last was a film to which he could take his wife without embarrassment. No distressing full frontals, you see, at least not where sex was concerned. I think he might have been more appalled, or maybe his wife would have been, if one of the early victims whose gun hand is skewered to the bar while his throat is garrotted, had been in a state of nudity at the time.

A film cannot be estimated to earn 150 million dollars world-wide without the layman's opinion of what is decent for him and his wife to see being shared by the majority of those who will go and see *The Godfather*. Indeed the audience reaction is interesting. I saw the film several times, having had to take along friends from backward countries, lands where *The Godfather* hadn't yet played, and on each occasion the audience sat dumbly through the plethora of Mafia killings. When they did react audibly it was on only one occasion, a low collective whistle of shock at the end when the 'godson' deliberately lies to his wife. Seeing death at its most anatomically violent on the screen had apparently lost its power to repel: lying to your wife, on the other hand, is still something that gets home to the heart of the *petit-bourgeoisie*. Nothing else has so sharply indicated to me how the tolerance level of violence is rising.

I don't ascribe the fact that the film fails to shock or outrage to the nice, safe feeling it paradoxically generates—keeping death inside the family, so to speak. Of course these Mafia bosses are 'golden oldies'— the slaughter of '46 out of the summer of '42. But distance lending security to the viewer doesn't satisfactorily explain its appeal. As I see it, we are witnessing a far more frightening phenomenon than the deaths on the screen: we are witnessing nothing less than the deaths of people's humanity. We have been so raped by violence that we are like the daughter heeding her mother's injunction as she leaves on a dubious date: if you can't resist it, lie back and enjoy it. And even this residual pleasure is losing its savour. It is drying up the way the emotions are put on the screen. Death no longer has any humanity, so it can offer no purgative satisfaction. Not even our pity is solicited. Man-made monsters once had hearts, which broke even as they crushed their makers. Now all they exhibit is the coolness of the successful psychopath—no emotions whatsoever. In contrast, there is scarcely a gangster film out of the 1930s which hadn't some particle of humanity embedded in it, besides the slugs of rivals for the South Side 'empire', even if it was only misguided mother-love for Jimmy Cagney.

In the second half of *The Godfather* an extraordinary change overcomes Al Pacino, which is relevant to this point. At the start of the film it is almost as if Paramount were making him into a 1940s *Love Story* figure, with his air of diminished cuddliness as he nibbles at his courtship on the fringe of the family. When he takes over power (and the story) he reverts to a much earlier decade than the 1940s: he affects the glossy, brushed-back hairstyle and closefitting wardrobe of the 1930s. He appears as a stereotype companion of Humphrey Bogart and George Raft—except in one vital respect. The movie still assigns to him the arid, passionless, mechanistic ethos which is its own attitude to all human life in the 1970s. Its nostalgia only goes back so far. When it comes to killing, it is bang up to date.

The Mechanic may look like a freelance *Godfather*, operating exogamously against any target he is paid to eliminate. In Michael Winner's film, as in *The Godfather*, one is overwhelmed by the same emotionally drained attitude to death. But whereas the 'godson' reminds his girlfriend that 'everybody kills today, the Army, the Government, Big Business,' the professional assassin in *The Mechanic* takes this acceptance of the world as it is to its logical conclusion and propagandises that anybody has the right to kill anybody. The same refrain was heard from the acolytes of Charles Manson: it is language being used as an instrument of murder. *The Mechanic*, in fact, takes it a stage beyond Manson. Charles Bronson's assassin doesn't kill for the thrill of it all; to him, it is simply 'the Job', carried out dispassionately upon receipt of a registered envelope of instructions. Whom he kills, much less why, we are never told. What does it matter, since the act of killing is all that counts? We have come a long way in the few years from the pathetic dimension of the massacre in which Bonnie and Clyde died, and by doing so made us care, to the almost bloodless killings of *The Mechanic* in which we don't know who dies and couldn't care less. These are literally 'clean' killings. The only scene in which I can recall blood actually flowing and lingered over is the one in which the jilted girlfriend of the mechanic's young male apprentice severs her wrists with a razor blade as the two men sit looking on. Her pitiful gesture is an attempt to move at least one of them into emotional involvement with her; they simply regard her suicide as the test of how 'cool' they can remain. Such men are smooth operators; but their essence is their refusal to sympathise, to become involved. It is the black side of Kennedy's avowal of 'grace under pressure'—'coolness under stress'. The essay on *The White Negro* which Norman Mailer wrote in 1957 praising the 'psychopathic brilliance' of the hip style that models itself on the black experience has been brought to life in *The Mechanic*—if 'life' is the word for a mode of existence dedicated to keeping on top by extinguishing all human feelings and maintaining one's mechanistic responses in trim for the taking of human life.

In an earlier script, I am told, the liaison between both men in *The Mechanic* was homosexual as well as homocidal. Even that emotion has been siphoned out of them, leaving only their mutual boast that in a society which is actually no better than they are, the psychopath is king.

Even this is not the film's most ominous feature. The way it has been *accepted* is highly disquieting. Far from being given a British 'X' Certificate, putting it on the same shelf beside *The Godfather*, it has drawn a straight 'AA' Certificate, a much milder rating allowing 14-year-old children to see it. This view is presumably based on the belief that in its externals it differs little from a standard gangster drama of the 1930s. There could scarcely be a more dangerous mis-reading of its essential significance. In it, as in other films, we are being asked to accept the ascendancy of the psychopath, the man who knows no fears, has no doubts, experiences no guilt, feels no humanity, but simply acts in the only way he believes gives meaning to a society in which the rejection of restraints has become endemic. He kills.

From the addition of medical materialism to its repertoire, the cinema has passed on to the celebration of moral anarchy. And it has us staring at the panorama as ambiguously as the Mechanic himself stares at the reproduction of the Bosch painting known alternatively as *Earthly Pleasures* or as *Lust*, depicting a carnival of hideous fantasies, which hangs on his living-room wall. Is it a foretaste of Hell that he draws from it? Or is it fresh inspiration? And is there any difference?

The bloodstains we've been following have given out: in the moral void in which much of the contemporary screen exists and flourishes, the only guide from now on is our own fears.

Encounter, March 1973

Macho and Ms

Toward the end of 1976, the rising fees of superstars seemed to be taking the trajectory of a Moon-shot. Huge sums, unthinkable only a few years before in the crisis of 1969–71 which brought much of Hollywood to the verge of bankruptcy, were now being paid to a dozen or so performers whose presence in a picture was box-office collateral of an equally kingly kind. This was possible because movies that succeeded did so now beyond the dreams of speculators—at least the dreams that speculators had had the day before. By the beginning of 1976, *Jaws* was the all-time, box-office champion with nearly 103 million dollars; next came *The Godfather* with more than 85 million, then *The Exorcist* with 79 million and *The Sting* with more than 72 million. There seemed no end.

There certainly was none to the fees that stars now demanded for their help in piling up such Midas-like fortunes. A million dollars a picture, plus a percentage of the gross, held good for perhaps only a few months, until word spread that one or other of the superstars, had winkled 1,500,000 dollars out of the producers, then 2,000,000 dollars—and even more. These were truly the bionic men of the movies. Their wishes became the laws of movie-making. The Hollywood syndrome of 'I want'—FADE OUT—FADE IN—'I got' turned into daily reality where money was concerned and virtually every 'big, important picture' that got made was first offered to one or more of these stars to whom I gave the collective title of 'Million Dollar Men', while aware how inflation was already making a mockery of that label. It was a bargaining power almost no female stars possessed. In spite of the Hollywood chapter of Women's Lib, there was no sex equality when it came to the pay cheques made out to the likes of Robert Redford, Clint Eastwood, Marlon Brando, Charles Bronson, Jack Nicholson, Al Pacino, Dustin Hoffman, James Caan, Steve McQueen, and a few others. Maybe Barbra Streisand could command a million dollars, if the movie was a musical and her unique talents could transfuse the show and lift it into a box-office spiral. But she was the exception.

It will be evident from many of the foregoing reviews, and the commentaries on some of them, that women are not at premium prices for star parts because they are not at the centre of experiences which the public seek at the box-office. The themes which make fortunes, and permit the stars to charge up their talents accordingly, are unquestionably male-dominated ones. They focus on the corrupt policeman and the Mafia Don, on the open road and the urban hell, on the *macho* ethic that commands a man to prove himself by winning merit badges for pain inflicted or suffering endured, on the rapist and the vengeance seeker, on the cameraderie of buddies on horseback or bike-saddle, on the loner who lives in Edge City or the go-getters with the thrust of jet-engines behind their psychopathic ambitions, on the hard men who take short-cuts through the law's delay, on their victims who are the walking wounded of life's psychodramas.

For better or worse—probably for worse—the screen at the end of 1976 reflected a man's world of ritualised primitivism and patterned irrationality. And at the centre of that world were the multi-million dollar stars, some of them enshrining the age's few redeeming features, others embodying the ugliest trends in society today, all of them exerting a powerful, sometimes baleful fascination for the millions who still go to the movies. I thought it timely to examine a select handful of these men in more detail than reviewing their films normally allows— and also to enquire why the Women's Lib movement, so influential where much of the rest of the media was concerned, had so far failed to throw up its own platoons of like number and financial muscle in the cinema.

EARLY AMERICAN BOY/Robert Redford

Robert Redford, just on 40, is well on the way to becoming the Howard Hughes of film stardom. Given his way—and more and more, he is— he would prefer to be seen and heard in one place only, and that's on a cinema screen. There, all that makes Redford the superstar he is can be controlled and nurtured; all that makes him vulnerable can be concealed.

In London earlier this year to promote his own company's production of *All the President's Men*, he put out the order: no interviews with individual newspapers. Only a 'seminar' on pre-selected issues in the film: as pompous a decree in its way as that of the Pop stars who aggrandise their own self-importance by billing a one-night stand as being 'in concert'. Moreover, Redford's aides insisted, no one must photograph the star without permission: the truth is that his face has sometimes a pudgy appearance in the wrong light. He *did* speak to a group of editors, but they came from campus newspapers, not Fleet Street. Students with the future in their hands still presumably had the integrity which a recent 'bad experience' with the very same *Washington Post* that his film celebrated—it had published a less than kind account of him and Dustin Hoffman soaking up 'colour' in the newsroom for the film—may have made him doubt that the working Press possessed. They could bring down a President—*okay!* But could they report a film star accurately? While in London he did one interview on television, a medium that usually gives the interviewee most of the say, and used most of the half-hour not to talk about the film but about the need to conserve our environment. His views on ecology are articulate, if commonplace: what was much more revealing was the opportunity he took to sell his image of himself. Not as a movie star, but as a conservationist.

For Robert Redford is a materialist who has assiduously cultivated the stance of an idealist. The public believes that the roles he plays in film after film are part of the reality of the man—this is the potent interplay that creates the great stars. But the reality has much more to do with the way the man has used his worldly assets, the material rewards of power and stardom, to create a life-style that more and more takes him out of this world. In particular, out of the Hollywood world. 'I look upon going to Hollywood,' he once said, 'as a mission behind enemy lines. You parachute in, set up the explosion, then fly out before it goes off.' Fly out—but where? In Redford's case, to Sundance, his private kingdom of 4,300 acres set 6,000 feet up in the Rocky Mountains of Utah, a natural ski area where a select 15 or so families, mostly Redford's friends, relatives or business associates, like film-maker Sydney Pollack who has directed four Redford movies, have built their own *House and Garden*-type of cabins from local rocks and timber, often with their own hands.

Redford wakes up under huge triangular windows soaring aloft like Viking prows and bringing in the purity of Sundance's snowpeaks to rooms filled with Red Indian handicrafts, tribal blankets, snowshoes, saddles, hides stripped from animals that have foundered in natural disasters, not fallen to the hunter's gun. Because of his athletic, blond, boyish good looks, Redford is generally called the All-American Boy; a truer name for him would be the Early American Boy. In his mind's eye at Sundance, the buffalo, caribou and grizzly bears are still roaming the terrain he used in *Jeremiah Johnson*, the film closest to his heart—closer, even, than *Butch Cassidy*—because of its pioneering sense of people developing their capacities for survival through raw contact with life.

Asked about his early days as a college drop-out, Redford usually replies vaguely that he bummed around Europe, tried discouragingly to be a painter, and got his greatest thrill out of living rough on the barest of resources. To *Newsweek*'s Charles Michener, he vouchsafed one extraordinary detail: 'One night in France . . . I got warm by standing in a pile of manure.' Now that the handsome hobo-boy, surely more Jack Kerouac than Jack London, has become the moneyed homesteader of Sundance, he has more to keep him warm than organic muck. What Redford does not like to emphasise, if indeed he is aware of it, is that his way of conserving nature is actually an oasis for the favoured few; that his concern with reclaiming land is one way of keeping unwelcome folk from fouling his doorstep; that all the diurnal activities at Sundance, improving the soil, raising scholarships for Indians, re-stocking the trout streams, abating noise, planting forests— are actually the luxury mutation of a pioneering community. If one asks whose quality of life is improved, the answer must be 'the owners'. However, the impression that while others damn America, he is preserving her, is one that has fostered Redford's acceptance as a culture-hero among the all-important 'youth-audience' that made him a star. To kids who were demonstrating against Vietnam, against the economic resources 'wasted' on going to the Moon, against the sinister 'military-industrial conglomerate' that ran the Government, there was an ally in the film star who could look so young and say so boldly, 'The Space Age is not attractive to me,' or 'Nixon—I get sick to my stomach,' or 'I have shaken the hands of many politicians, but never met their eyes.'

Redford never fell into the trap of formulating his political credo, like Jane Fonda on the one wing or John Wayne on the other. He didn't need to. His looks, not his politics seemed to exemplify the best of America. Even his purchase of the Woodward–Bernstein book, *All the President's Men*, for a reported 450,000 dollars, was the gesture of a patriot, not a radical. Probably that of a romantic, too. Of *Butch Cassidy and the Sundance Kid*, he once said: 'On a gut level it appealed to me as a fairy-tale. It also fitted in with some of the things I had done in life.' *All the President's Men* was like a true fairy-tale; and it contained some of the things that a guardian of the American heritage might wish to do, such as destroy a President who was polluting it. As of August 1976, the film had notched up a 26 million dollar rental in North America alone and will surely make Redford and his company, Wildwood Enterprises—note how the 'virgin nature' ideal even permeates his big-business deals—into dollar millionaires. According to *Variety*'s list of 'All-Time Box-Office Champs', the North American rentals for such Redford successes as *The Way We Were, Butch Cassidy* and *The Sting* totalled respectively, 25, 45 and a whopping 72 million dollars by the end of 1975. To get the world-wide rentals, the rough multiplier is two. Remember that in addition to fees that have now escalated to a million dollars and more per picture, Redford's company owns substantial percentages of the take—and it will be appreciated how impressively he has converted star power into the kind of financial power that bankers must envy. He can be forgiven the relative disappointment of *The Great Gatsby*, which he blames on the hypersell the film received. It taught Redford a salutary lesson about over-exposure. 'I'm supposed to be doing something wonderful every second I'm alive,' he complains, adding that the adulatory masses 'see me as having the temperament of *The Sundance Kid*, the charm of *The Candidate*, the sense of humour of *The Sting*, and the wardrobe of *The Great Gatsby*.' By the studios who bankroll his films he is seen as possessing a rarer quality than all these. He is an artist 'with discipline'. Which means he gives no trouble, costs no one a fortune, knows that whatever the message, it is primarily *entertainment* he is selling. 'To the moneyman,' the American critic Pauline Kael has written, 'discipline means success-plus-a-belief-in-success.' Redford has that belief, in common with the pioneers he so earnestly strives to exemplify.

To explain the rest of his success, it would be easy to follow most writers and say it is because he is 'so outrageously adorable'. Easy, but not the whole truth. He is not aggressively sexy in a way that would get bad vibrations from competitive males in the audience envious of his style and looks. In fact his greatest box-office successes have been in films that don't pair him with another girl, but with another male star (Newman in *Butch Cassidy* or *The Sting*, Hoffman in *All the President's Men*) in a rootless, often jokey, buddy-buddy liaison, quite a-sexual of course. On this score, Redford is defensively square. Of sex, he's said: 'It's best natural.' When Alan J. Pakula was reading my review of the Watergate film he had directed, his eye hit my remark that the 'Deep Throat' character's taunting sarcasm when the two reporters make a blunder had almost sexual undertones to it: the reproof of an older man to his errant lover. 'My God,' Pakula said, 'I'm certainly glad Bob wasn't told *that* when we were shooting the scene!'

Redford's relations with women, to judge from reports, contain a fair measure of male chauvinism. Or so it seems. 'I enjoy girls who don't come on like Supergirl. The type that's vulnerable. I find vulnerability very attractive'—and, of course, no threat to *him*. When his wife Lola asserts herself . . . 'I tell her to back off. We argue, and eventually things work out.' Be wary, though, of calling this the response of a 'male chauvinist pig'. What forms Redford's relations with the other sex is probably the older pattern of the pioneer era he finds so seductive, when the functions of men and women had to be divided if both were to survive: he hunted, she stayed at home. When he says about his wife, whom he married when he was 21 and she 17, 'She puts out a consumer newsletter, that's her job in life . . . I'm an actor, that's my job,' it is surely the sentiments of the frontiersman he is echoing. A case of love me, love my life-style. On screen, though, a directly competitive approach appears imperative, to judge from some sharp-edged comebacks attributed to female co-stars, from Katharine Ross, the girl in *Butch Cassidy*, who said, 'It was spade-work all the way,' to Jane Fonda, who played a newly-wed in *Barefoot to the Park*, 'Secretly, I think Bob's afraid of women. He likes to tell them what to do. He likes them to be subservient to him. He treated me as if I were an extra or something.'

To a man of Redford's massive 'cool', such comments are not likely to be wounding. In his 40th year, he knows he has got it all together, taken the strain of superstardom, made an immense fortune, proved his muscle as a wheeler-dealer with the 'boss men' of Hollywood, kept his resplendent good looks, managed his image with ruthless efficiency, become the world's top-ranking leading man, the screen's most romantic fusion of dreams and reality. What can possibly be left to tempt him. . . ? Perhaps only the colossal arrogance of a male Garbo—walking away from it all, to the Kingdom of Sundance, or even deeper into the interior. 'Are you *really* Robert Redford?' I heard an excited girl crying at the Cannes Film Festival. Came the tight-lipped reply, 'Only when I'm alone.'

MERCHANT OF DEATH/Charles Bronson

The jewel on the lady's silk evening gown looked as if it had come from Cartier's novelty counter: it was the size and shape of a beetle, with expensively enamelled wing-cases and rubies for a head. Charles Bronson, down in Cannes for the film festival, wouldn't have given it a second glance, if the heat of the wearer's body hadn't stimulated a set of tiny black legs into action. Slowly, blindly, its freedom limited by a thin gold halter, stupefied by its semi-precious encrustation, the 'living jewel' began crawling around the lady's bosom. She laughed. Bronson did not. I filed away the scene for when the time came to consider the man who is now the most popular killer in films.

I suppose Bronson's show of repugnance could be attributed by some to humanitarian motives, but I am not among them. 'I'm not in the movies for social reform,' he's made a point of saying—nor for the protection of wild life. No star in fact holds human life cheaper on the screen today. In films like *Death Wish*, Bronson as New York's self-appointed vigilante made killing into a kind of public sanitation pro-gramme, ridding the streets of their undesirables, and thereby won a stand-up ovation in the cinemas from every victim of the urban crisis who believed that 'law and order' flowed out of the muzzle of a gun. No: Bronson the 'hard man' wasn't revolted by the sight of a lady who kept a £5,000 cockroach in her jewel-box and fed it nightly on powdered wood. What this decadent little trinket probably affronted was Bronson the puritan, the shockable, up-tight *petit-bourgeois* who has wrapped his film roles and life-style round himself as if they were protective pagan rites. It is hard to credit that at heart Bronson is a man of censorious prudishness, that if you scratch Attila the Hun you find a 'square'.

Here is a man whose idea of relaxing is hurling knives at moving targets, hammering a punch-bag, riding his 17 motor-bikes and cultivating a torso (part of an otherwise average physique) as over-muscled as any disciple of Yukio Mishima, the self-admiring Japanese fascist who took his own life in a gory ritual suicide in 1970. An almost chronic concern with masculinity and reiterated warnings about his own aggressiveness mark Bronson's utterances. His publicists have a well-rehearsed trick of warning interviewers that 'he's really a nice guy—but watch out! It just might happen that he could erupt and kill you.' To tamed newsmen, further cowed by such Distant Early Warning signs, Bronson certainly looks dangerous. But he knows that one scowl is worth a thousand words. Doesn't he apply the lesson himself on the screen, where he never says 'Yes' if a nod will do? If he's temperamental, it's only to the superstitious extent of believing that interviewers who have something of his own *macho* physique—which note-taking and typewriting rarely encourages—will give him more favourable write-ups than the weak-kneed types.

The other refrain Bronson keeps up is the hardship he's been through on the way up—and here he's on more genuine ground. He was ninth in a family of 15 children born to a Russo-Lithuanian immigrant coalminer called Buchinsky—a name Bronson used on the screen up to 1953. After a childhood so impoverished that he had to go to school dressed in a sister's cast-off frock, he himself dug coal out of the

Pennsylvania mines. He's applied the same technique to the movies, which he now looks on as 'Scooptown', a sort of open-cast mining area, except that the fuel you dig out is called money and it comes in millions of dollars, not ton-loads. Making a film for Bronson is like working a shift in the pits. At 54, like a man inured by past hardship—which he swears is responsible for his present success—he is driven to work the maximum number of shifts before his day ends. Because he makes more films than anyone else, at 1,500,000 dollars a time, he is the biggest screen-earner in the world, owns a 40-room Bel Air mansion, a farm in Vermont, a villa in France, with ranks of butlers, cooks, nannies, tutors (for his family and that of his second wife Jill Ireland) secretaries and bodyguards, just to mention the domestic retainers. If he has a fear, it is the understandable one of going 'soft'. Even when he talks of his new film, *The White Buffalo*, it is in terms of hardship sought and suffered. 'We were 14,000 feet up . . . had to take our oxygen from bottles . . . lit a fire in the snow . . . it melted a hole ten feet deep without reaching bedrock.' Bronson's face goes so strikingly with its owner's story of hard times that it validates them and makes further character-drawing superfluous. 'With Redford, Nicholson and the rest, you also need a story,' says one film producer. 'With Bronson, you're half-way home already.' He never wears make-up: that might be considered 'soft'. Anyway, what can it add to a face that already brings descriptive writers up to lyrical pitch with their comparisons of it to 'a rock quarry', or 'a crushed beer can', or 'a scalp-hunter with the vocabulary of a totem pole'?

But Bronson probably wouldn't owe his stardom to his face—and eventually to the more metaphysical assets of personifying the equally ugly face of society—if it hadn't been for the switch in audience tastes which happened at the end of the 1960s. Filmgoers started giving their loyalties to character actors like Hoffman, Nicholson, Elliott Gould or George C. Scott who assumed the persona of stars without losing their rough-cast kinship with the fans. 'We're hiring the uglies now,' crowed David Picker, then production chief at United Artists. The 'hard men' were coming in, propelled by a rip tide of escalating world violence and also by coarse-grained but powerful directors like Sam Peckinpah and Robert Aldrich whose emphasis on the good, the bad and the ugly in human life was in ascending order of their popularity at the box-office.

Bronson appeared in *The Magnificent Seven, The Great Escape, The Dirty Dozen*: the titles alone reflect the decay of individual chivalry and the hero's quantum leap into violence as a solution to a man's problems, and often the verification of his own manhood. Lee Marvin,

Telly Savalas, George Kennedy, Lee Van Cleef, Donald Sutherland, Charles Bronson: all were brutal, functional, often 'ugly' role-fillers who viewed women as expendable, sentiment as shameful, violence as inevitable. What cut Bronson out of the pack was a 'spaghetti Western' directed by Sergio Leone, *Once Upon a Time in the West*. Though a flop in America, its mix of Latin ruthlessness, *machismo* sadism and equation of honour with virility made it and Bronson a phenomenal hit in Europe. I have often thought that his slow-fuse style, which makes it hard to take one's eyes off him less one miss the moment of explosion, was formed by having to do nothing on screen in such a film while Ennio Morricone's sourly suspenseful score did the work for him by suggesting everything about him. It took only *Death Wish* to transplant this mesmerising nihilism to a modern American setting and Bronson became the focus of a terrifying large section of frustrated citizens goaded by the slow, often muddle-headed reaction of the Law into wanting to see violence fought with violence. In this film and others like *The Valachi Papers*, *The Mechanic*, and *The Stone Killer*, the real emotions aren't anywhere visible on the screen or in Bronson's performance. They are out there among the audience looking at the films, whooping with joy at seeing their present-day ills being 'cured' by gunfire on the public streets.

Bronson, naturally, doesn't see it in such disquieting terms. A man who once said, 'I used to walk down the street in a straight line and knock down anything that was in my way' now uses a more sophisticated line of persuasion on anyone who stands in the way of the box-office. 'My films aren't violent films: they're *action* films.' Is it hardly surprising, either, that such a guru finds sex more embarrassing than, Uh, 'action'? 'Violence in pictures is a public affair,' says Bronson, 'but sex is very private.' How fortunate his career is in a position where he can resist it. Sex scenes have always made him uneasy: he once rewrote a scene in *The Valachi Papers* so that he wouldn't have to share a bed with two prostitutes. And indeed he should resist them, for when he has done a sex scene, he does it crudely and badly, as anyone can see in *From Noon Till Three*, where perhaps it was the presence of his wife as his co-star which emboldened him to attempt love-making at all. In earlier films he's refused to appear nude or make bedroom love-play, lest it shock his family if they saw him in the raw or else had the equivalent of a 'primal scene' springing out at them from *The Late, Late Movie* on TV in a year or two's time. 'I've got to have some moral standards for my children to value,' Bronson says: an affirmation worthy of the civic-minded, non-promiscuous killer of the best sort, one who makes a distinction between 'clean' killing and 'dirty' sex, who's got an answer when his children ask 'Did you really kill all those men, Dad?' but draws the line at doing anything to prompt the family circle to enquire, 'Did you really screw all those women!'

Support your local vigilante: he'll keep your streets clean, and your minds, too! Many people ask for nothing more. While they ask, Bronson acts: all bang-bang, no kiss-kiss.

COOL CRUSADER/Jack Nicholson

For Jack Nicholson, overnight stardom took 14 years. One minute, he wasn't a name that registered. The next, he was the one genuinely touching, comic character in *Easy Rider*, in 1969, doing his slow-burn look round the American landscape and sighing, 'This used to be one helluva good country.' I remember thinking: Is he so good because he's the one guy in the film who articulates well enough to be understood?—then being ashamed of my doubts. Nicholson was good: he is good.

He knows it, too, though he defers to the man whom he calls 'the one on the hill'. This 'one' is Marlon Brando. And the hill is part of Mulholland Drive, on an eminence above Hollywood where he and Brando share an entrance road and a fence over which they did that famous deal whereby one said to the other, 'Would you like to make a quick million dollars?' and both finished up with that amount each in *The Missouri Breaks*. That's good-neighbour policy, Hollywood-style. Other plots of land in this well-protected compound belong to Warren Beatty and Robert Towne, the screenwriter of Nicholson's two big hits, *The Last Detail* and *Chinatown*. This peer group of respected equals represents a vital part of what Jack Nicholson wants from life and work.

'Jack,' says one of his friends, 'is very loyal, never forgets the people he comes up with, lets them put up at his home between jobs . . . the ever-open host.' True: but Jack also craves *acceptance* as well as company. His idea of acting well is to 'please the peer group'. To hear, for example, the laughter of U.S. Navy regulars savouring the big, life-loving, rule-busting seaman he played in *The Last Detail* and saying, 'That's the way it is, that's really it!' Nicholson ties his friends to him with the little secret knots that peer groups use to promote their own interdependency. Nicknames figure large in the gang. His sometime girlfriend Angelica Huston is (or was) 'Toolman', Candice Bergen is 'Bug', Mike Nichols, who directed him in *Carnal Knowledge*, is 'Big Nick', Peter Fonda is 'The Bike', Art Garfunkel is 'Art the

Garf', Warren Beatty, his co-star in *The Fortune*, is 'Master B', and so on down to a Mercedes he drives which is the colour of a Bing cherry and with which he plays a game called 'Making Bing Dance'—i.e., bumping up and down on the upholstery. When he was in London in 1973 he made time to buy gifts for the Group (and its groupies): a silver belt, a maxi-skirt, a scarlet kaftan for a girl who didn't own a coat, a see-through black blouse, a psychedelic sweater and (for himself) red-and-yellow ringed socks: it was the kind of shopping list a lonely sailor might make in port to bring closer the friends he'd return to some day: Nicholson has a whiff of this wistfulness hanging around him.

Rapport with him is easy and spontaneous: he puts no barriers up, unlike Robert Redford who one feels has to be broken out of his sanitary wrapping like the bathroom fittings in the ritzier American hotel suites. It's a surprise—or would be, if it weren't so commonplace with film stars—to find he's no more than average height (and looks smaller) with thinning hair and small, highly mobile features. The face is only a generation or two away from Cork, Ireland, where there are many like it, right down to that dazzlingly clear-cut, yard-wide smile which can give Nicholson the instant sunniness or sexual menace which makes him both attractive-looking—and dangerous. Push the ethnic origins a bit farther and one can connect his air of extreme relaxedness with the archetypal Irish 'Mick' leaning on his shovel and passing the time of day with the world except . . . except that Nicholson has an additional spaced-out look. The kind to be observed on many experimenters with marijuana or LSD (which Nicholson acknowledges he used to take) who have kicked the habit, but retained that dry, contented, monotone voice which still issues from Nicholson's lips like the smoke from a joint that's been held in the inhaler's lungs while it works its fantasies in his brain. For the scene round the camp-fire in *Easy Rider*, he smoked over 150 joints and played it stoned, but straight—it's the self-communing quality of someone who's high but still making sense which gives the moment its magic.

Easy Rider was the perfect film to start Nicholson's star rising. On the one hand, it was a certified 'youth picture', relevant to the inarticulate, alienated, travelling kids of the 'Woodstock Nation'. On the other, Nicholson was no kid. He was a ripe old 32, and thus mature enough to win friends among the age group that was uneasily aware of its own squareness and envious of youngsters who had found their own grass-roots identity in the greening of America. Nicholson had a foothold in both generations—and also a hit movie that cost 300,000 dollars and went on to make a worldwide 35 million. This irresistible combination—new face, 'event film'—made Hollywood positively fawn on him and ask, 'Where *were* you all the time, Jack?' The answer, as so often, was right there in Hollywood—in MGM's mail-room at first, working as a 30-dollar a week clerk, and then as a boy (well, boy-ish) member of American International Pictures' youth-oriented stock-company who included players like Peter Fonda and Dennis Hopper and director-producers like Roger Corman. In his first year he earned 1,400 dollars ('Which, in Hollywood, is like nothing at all') playing either a clean-cut kid or a mass killer, the two poles of American life. Occasionally he wrote screenplays, for such drug-cult rave-ups as *The Trip* (banned for years by the British censor) or *Head*, which starred the Monkees.

It was a mind-blowing period and suggests why, ten years later, Nicholson flew so sublimely into the *Cuckoo's Nest*. Both this film, which won him an Oscar in 1976, and the film *Drive, He Said*, which he himself directed in 1970, are tales of subversive drop-outs whose own heightened awareness impels them to throw open the doors of other people's perception and release a flood of primitivism into society which it's presumed will be life-enhancing, at least by the disciples of the decade's head guru, Ronnie Laing. In the one film, it's lunatics who are liberated; in the other, it's the reptiles in the campus laboratory. Now Bedlam and Eden are twin states of mind to the habitual acid-head: Nicholson's cool, almost recuperative state of relaxedness suggests he may have looked into both in his time and is now thankful to have made the return trip in such good shape.

'Whenever I play a character, I draw on my own experience,' he says. On his own intuition, too. Though he went to a California branch of the Method School, he is refreshingly pragmatic about how he gets his effects. Any aid to imagination will do. 'If it works, *that's* the Method.' As the roles have grown older with him, the kids have continued their loyalty even though his own rebellion has cooled off. It has not all been an easy ride, however. He played an ageing woman-iser in *Carnal Knowledge*, keeping a score card on his 'hits' and finding in the end it added up to nothing; but the film's bleakness didn't burnish his star rating. Then he failed to land *The Great Gatsby* role, though he was the studio's first choice, because, it was said, he asked too much money; and he made a flying visit to London to try for the lead in *Day of the Jackal*, but Edward Fox got in first. Then came *Chinatown*.

'More than any other film, *Chinatown* made Jack's career,' says its producer, Robert Evans, adding, 'It found him a character actor, it left him a star.' It did more. If *Easy Rider* suggested a man criss-crossing America in search of an identity, then *Chinatown* felt as if he had found one, in the person of J. J. Gites, private-eye, a bruised romantic in the Chandler mould. Nicholson kept a lot of the sharp suits he got to wear in the part and also—say close friends—some of the quizzical, don't-trust-appearances attitudes that went with them. The part of the Los Angeles' loner in the film was assembled out of the seedy glamour of movie tradition going back to Dick Powell, Alan Ladd and Bogart, all of them, like Nicholson, small-statured men transformed into giants of integrity by their snap-brim hats and wrap-round trench-coats.

Nicholson hasn't had to suffer Brando's lacerating experience of Hollywood, and movies to him are above all else *glamorous*. 'Glamour was what they contributed to society,' he says, 'I'm a big fan of it.' Which more than anything else explains his gregarious penchant for doing the glad-handing rounds at Cannes, for working within the Hollywood 'system', for savouring the glamour of Oscar Night, and now, at last, the ultimate acceptance of his peer group that comes from winning the award. It is not vanity, not narcissism that drives him on. A film for Nicholson is a glamour trip, not an ego one. What other star would have let his director stick a nose-plaster on him for half the film as Polanski did in *Chinatown*; or had what remained of his hair frizzed out to make him as much as possible like the Fourth Stooge in a period comedy like *The Fortune*, while his co-star Warren Beatty stubbornly clung to the semblance of a smart operator? With Nicholson acting is a matter of 'taking a chance', of finding out where he is vulnerable, and then using it as a way of changing how he feels and thinks about himself. His performances are all of separate people, all different. In this, he's unlike the classic Hollywood stars of the 1930s: but in another he *is* like Cooper or Tracy or Stewart or Fonda.

He shows that a screen hero can still be a force for good. People feel there's a degree of essential optimism in a Jack Nicholson character. He holds out the hope that society still has a place for the individual. A tenuous hope, I grant you—but all the more precious for that.

WHITE INDIAN/Marlon Brando

He is a belligerent 52, and at one of the last weigh-ins was 18 stone. To find peace these days, he needs a whole private atoll in the Pacific. When producers call him and he senses in their voices the fear he induces in people—forget it! It's a wasted call. Would you offer a peace treaty to a man bent on declaring war?

Marlon Brando's relationship with the industry that feeds him between 1,500,000 and 2,000,000 dollars a film, and enables him to support three households and two women, is one of creative hostility. Pictures, even ones as expensive as they make now, can be made or broken as artistic entities by this man's daily reading of his barometric pressure; and it's probably not reassuring for the money-men to read that he once said, 'You have to upset yourself: unless you do, you can't act.' Brando's 'upsets' in the past have been on the heroic scale: so, sometimes at least, has the bill to be faced by others. One employer was left near to tears, lamenting, 'I do not think *any* artist should be so difficult. I think of Bach and all his kids, and still getting *his* work done!' Other superstars may manage movies, produce movies, direct movies: Brando *imposes* himself on them, a state of benign majesty if all is well, a state of anarchy if it isn't. Bertolucci, who directed him in *Last Tango in Paris*, recalls he was 'an angel as a man, as an actor a monster.'

Of course other film stars have a similar need to dominate a scene, to test a director and find his breaking-point in advance; but only an operation as inherently manic as filmmaking, with its volatile combination of ego, art and money, could so long sustain a star who is a combination of Tamburlaine and St Sebastian—a conqueror and a martyr, a despot who inflicts pain and a masochist who enjoys receiving it, too.

'He does not mind bruising his soul.' Kenneth Tynan wrote this in 1950, of great actors generally, but it still hasn't been bettered as a capsule description of Brando's genius—except that part of the hurt in his present-day life and career comes from bruising mind, body and soul. Not all of it is self-inflicted. When he flew off to Hollywood in 1950, leaving Broadway and the stage forever, like one of the Lost Boys in *Peter Pan* setting course for a Never-Never Land, he imported the first new style of acting that the movie colony had received since talking pictures. The Method. He was a 'why' actor in a 'who' scene, always demanding to know, What's my motive? The time and money it frequently took him—and dozens of talented rivals or quick imitators— in finding out the answer was hostile grit in the well-oiled production machine that had up to then clanked out entertaining, often brilliant pieces of personality-acting. Brando was honoured, so long as his movies made money, but never forgiven for being not just better than, but different from the subservient industry folk around him.

'An actor calling the shots!' thought the front-office machine, which in those days had still the teeth, legal and financial, to chew up actors at the first sign of rebellion. 'I just wanted to act: they wanted to sell me,' Brando said years later, like Caesar writing an epitaph on the Punic Wars.

It was a symptom of his genius that he grew bored easily. I have stood, concealed and incognito on more than one Brando film, and watched him quickly and physically tire of the effects with which he had originally freshened up some dull bit of direction. A complex man doesn't always need a complex cause to help explain him: it may have been something as simple as the space between the takes, the time it took just waiting for the director to call 'Action', that eroded his creative patience and gave him even more encouragement to take over and *make* things happen whatever the consequences—it's the fractiousness of the bored child that one sometimes senses in his vicinity. He once said, 'I get excited about something, but it never lasts more than seven minutes. Seven minutes exactly. That's my limit.' So he told Truman Capote in 1966 when he was making *Sayonara*. Unfortunately we don't know how much of that famous Capote interview, entitled 'The Duke in His Domain', is Brando revealing all, or simply putting Capote on. But bored people are dangerous people. They experiment. Frequently they find what they like: which is even more dangerous. In Brando's case, assisted by those random periods of psycho-analysis he's had over 15 years to help keep himself among the world's 'walking wounded', his discovery was a deep masochistic pleasure in scenes where he could wallow in suffering. A case of, 'I suffer, therefore I am.' A beating-up in *On the Waterfront*, a burning in *Mutiny on the Bounty*, a self-flagellation in *One-Eyed Jacks*, the whole autodestruct mechanism going subtly but terribly into action in *Last Tango in Paris* where the heights of acting were located in the depths of human degradation. He was like one of the Francis Bacon paintings which the Bertolucci film used so emblematically: he showed in his face the suffering in his guts.

No one else on the screen has this lacerating force. It is remarkable, isn't it, that so violently private a person—one of the few stars who really does land punches on nosy newsmen—should expose himself spiritually, if not physically in *Last Tango in Paris*, where in one painful monologue after another he stripped the veils off 40 years of his life, a kind of True Confession serial that mingled the boyhood and manhood memories of Marlon Brando with the fictional figures he has played in a dozen films over his Hollywood career? If there was any connection between him and the darker, kinkier tastes of the character in the film, we can only speculate. Undoubtedly, though, there is a morbid glamour to Brando—and more than a measure of self-disgust. I feel that when I see him mugging his way through a film, that's when he's taking it out on himself—for what? Perhaps for the position of artistic whoring that the film industry can reduce some of its brightest and best—of having to work for the money because their life style or their dependency demands it. 'I somehow always feel violated,' Brando has said, adding, 'Everyone in America and most of the world is a hooker of some kind or another.'

This refrain started being aired in his interviews—he is approachable, but only just—around about the time his box-office power was being dissipated in one flop after another after another—the wasteland of the 1960s when Brando, in his 40s, might have been considered in the prime of his art. In this dreary fag-end of movie stardom, still linked by contracts to major studios that forced junk on him, there developed that almost demonic need to escape—literally, physically escape from Hollywood. It is not just in his choice of partners that this pull to the foreign and the exotic shows itself: he married Tarita, the Polynesian girl from the *Bounty* film, had two children by her and one by Movita, and then a son by Anna Kashfi, an actress who still claims Asian-Indian descent though her family is Welsh-Irish. He also found a home outside America, on Tetiaora, a 400-acre Pacific atoll. There he spends half the year, under thatch with a modicum of comforts, recuperating that bruised soul of his.

Another symptom of his manifest dislike of Hollywood is his espousal of causes that are militantly critical of the American (and therefore Hollywood) ethos: Civil Rights, Black Power groups and especially (and now dominantly) the American Indians. The Indians suit his anti-Hollywood stance beautifully, since the motion-picture industry 'has been as responsible as any for degrading the Indian and making a mockery of his character.' He sent Sasheen Littlefeather on his behalf to 'refuse' the Oscar awarded him for *The Godfather*; and he takes interviewers to task with schoolmasterly sarcasm if those who have come to quiz him on the latest Method manifestation don't know such imperative pieces of historical fact as what happened to the Apaches in 1830 or what the *per capita* income of the Sioux is in 1976. Brando's ethnic liberalism is obviously sincere; but this doesn't make its expression entirely free of wounded resentment at the condition to which he himself has been reduced. An actor is pretty much like an Indian, runs the sub-text of his complaint. All those 400 treaties that the Paleface broke with the Redskins are like the contracts that the studios offered their stars, then sold out on. When he says, 'We just excised the Indians from the human race,' he is obviously over-stating the case; yet to have been a star in Hollywood in the 1950s must have felt like that at times, particularly if one had the pride of one's own uniqueness to cherish and felt it being daily insulted. Resentment is a two-edged weapon: it can quicken perception, it can also blur reality. Both forces seem at work today under Brando's war-paint. He may feel a spiritual kinship with Sitting Bull: but towards the great, deceiving hordes of Hollywood, he is a wounded bull. His co-workers on one highly 'disturbed' film once made up a piece of doggerel that's instructive on this score:

> Brando, his heart,
> It bleeds for the masses,
> But the people he works with,
> He kicks in the asses.

Despite the fact that all his intense caring for such causes doesn't influence events one iota, Brando will probably go on 'upsetting' himself on their behalf. 'He is all instinct,' Bertolucci has said. It is a dilemma he will find hard to resolve. Though he seeks out roles in films that can be made, somewhat tortuously, to reflect social issues as he sees them, he keeps on demanding his actor's close-ups. His sympathies may be with the outcasts, but he can never really alter his own pre-eminence as an artist.

In 1957, Norman Mailer wrote a celebrated essay called 'The White Negro', about the new breed of white urban hipster who tuned into the black man's painful experience in order to investigate the nature of his own frustration and what would satisfy it. Marlon Brando has used his own sense of outcast-ness in the same way 'to give voice to the character and quality of his existence, to his rage and the infinite variations of joy, lust, languor, growl, cramp, pinch, scream and despair of his orgasm.' Brando is today's White Indian.

AVENGING ANGEL/Clint Eastwood

The man lunching opposite me in Le Bistro restaurant, Beverly Hills, rose to leave and kept on rising . . . up, up, up, till he reached his own impressive ceiling, six feet four inches from the carpet. It was only then I recognised Clint Eastwood. Perhaps because his hands had been filled with a knife and fork, not six-guns.

Eastwood is 45: his favourite weapon is a digit lower, a Magnum 44. Remember him turning it against us, the audience, before *Magnum Force* began and saying, 'The world's most powerful hand-gun. It will blow your head into little pieces. What you've got to do is ask yourself are you feeling lucky today.' It was a message from the sponsor of some of the screen's heaviest violence today. It was also the statement of a new kind of heroism. Here was a hero who shot *first*. A hero for our times, when no man has a commitment to anyone but himself: a man completely in control of himself and his world: and thus reflecting, to the power of a million dollars and more per film, the unvoiced longings of a mass public who feel that Henry Kissinger, speaking softly and carrying a big stick, gets results as far as he goes, but could do with the back-up force of Clint Eastwood who carries a gun and doesn't speak at all.

You don't, however, have to belong to the Gun Clubs of America Inc. to admire Clint Eastwood. He is so darned graceful and good-looking. In contrast to Charles Bronson, who has the stunted strength of a bonzai tree, Eastwood is one of those redwoods rooted in the American heritage, almost protected by Act of Congress. A youth spent sweating in pulp-paper mills, at open blast furnaces, on bull-dozers (excavating swimming pools for film stars) put that muscle on his frame which is daily maintained in better running order than even the Ferrari he will let none but himself drive. The cheeks make unexpected hollows, the eyes are deep-set forcing a spectator to peer in—he has the 'stretched parchment' look that sometimes goes with organic food diets (Eastwood seldom drinks, never smokes off-screen, and begins the day on grapefruit juice and white raisins). The long luxuriant hair completes an undeniably romantic look. He claims a gentleness of manner off-screen. Even his new home in the lovely verdant country of California's Carmel area is built so as not to hurt the feelings of a tree growing up through the living-room.

So how on earth has this paradigm of manly chivalry, this Camelot stalwart whom King Arthur could have safely left with his wife—how on earth has he won a screen reputation as the undertaker's friend, a merchant of death who may look as if he's ridden out of Zane Grey but was taking his moral map readings from the Marquis de Sade? Certainly, as a concerned parent might say, he didn't get that reputation at home. He'd been shooting off his mouth more often than his guns over the six years he appeared as Rowdy Yates in some 300 episodes of *Rawhide*, when he was offered 15,000 dollars and a paid trip to Europe in 1964 to appear in a 'spaghetti Western'. Although *A Fistful of Dollars* was a Spanish-Italian-German co-production that desperately wanted to masquerade as the authentic-looking Hollywood oater (to the extent that its director Sergio Leone sported the screen pseudonym of 'Bob Robertson') its native Latin traditions of sadism, vengefulness and utter ruthlessness proved too strong. It forced Eastwood into a mould that suited foreign audiences who had long grown scornful of American ideals. He was an avenging angel whom Goya might have painted. Being called The Man With No Name, and having no background, he was an instant myth-figure. He had almost no dialogue, either. This saved money on the dubbing, and Eastwood learned that silence actually contributed to the character, concentrating it. Henceforth, he puts his bullets where his mouth had been.

The poncho he wore in *Fistful* and two other *Dollar* sequels was almost a holy vestment, protecting him from the flying lead; today it hangs, unwashed but marvelled over, upon the wall of The Hog's Breath restaurant, an expensive eating-place he part-owns and uses as his California HQ. But what really established the *Dollar* character was his attitude to life. It was simple—'Kill'. The film depicted a Wild West where the Age of Overkill had arrived long before the H-bomb; the bodies were piled up in numbers that would have robbed the James Brothers of breath as well as ammunition. In a world viewed as totally corrupt, the Eastwood hero could afford no mercy, no honour, no humour, no trust. Crowds were invited to sit back and enjoy the philosophy of both superman and nihilist—and that's just what they did. In less time than it took to pull the triggers of both guns—he is naturally ambidextrous, so things didn't drag—Eastwood was bigger box-office in Italy than even Mary Poppins. Due to copyright difficulties —the Italians had forgotten to buy certain film rights—the three 'spaghetti Westerns' didn't hit America till after 1967. Then they did so in a punch that was like walking into Muhammad Ali. But the big pay-off didn't come till Eastwood discovered—as Bronson was to do in *Death Wish* a few years later—an All-American container for the Latin obsession with revenge and sadism. The container was *Dirty Harry*, the rogue cop who had only himself to rely on. 'You Didn't Assign Dirty Harry,' ran the advertising slogan, 'You Turned Him Loose.' From this moment there was no doubt that Eastwood's box-office power was inseparable from his gun-power. Virtually all the cinema posters for this kind of movie flourish pistols in the public's face— even *The Eiger Sanction* showed him scaling Switzerland's 3,970-metre mountain with a gun in his free hand.

Such illustrations don't quite evoke the shudders the way Bronson's paranoid battery of firearms does. Partly because Eastwood looks Byronic as well as bionic. Partly because his avowedly Right-wing movies are more subtle and hence more insidious variations on the good old liberal myths about man's essential goodness. *Coogan's Bluff*, for example, about a country cop having to take on the Big City as well as its underworld slickers, is really an up-dated *Mr Deeds Goes to Town*, with a hick who turns out to be a hip marksman in place of Gary Cooper's hayseed who turned out to be a shrewd philanthropist. Liberals understandably felt affronted and fearful of a policeman invested with the power to take direct action without reference to (and often in disobedience of) the law book. Eastwood refuses to be drawn into the controversy of *Dirty Harry*'s confrontation politics. 'I'm a political nothing,' he says, emphasising his nihilism rather than his neutrality. If pressed, he may add, 'Isn't a cop who knows how to use a gun better than a private citizen with a headache?'—a clear reference to Bronson's vigilante tactics in *Death Wish*. If asked whether it wouldn't be a good thing to ban guns in America, he replies easily that, 'No, it would be a better thing to register them.' He is a wonderful PR man for the gun lobby which, even before the death of one President fades from memory, still heads Congress off at the pass every time stricter gun laws are advocated. To his off-screen life, Eastwood applies the same strict control that he does on screen in more flamboyant fashion. He has been married to his wife Maggie for more than 20 years. The fact that they waited 14 years before having their first child may suggest the extent of his self-discipline—'By then we knew we could get along well enough to last,' he explains.

In 1968 he extended control over his career by forming his own production company, Malpaso, which means a 'bad step' in Spanish, an ironical reference to a business adviser who had told him that going to Europe to make *A Fistful of Dollars* was just that. But in business, as in fatherhood, Eastwood is careful of his steps. Nowadays he directs films as well as starring in them and though his latest *The Outlaw Josey Wales*, shows him brandishing two Civil War pistols, his mouth bawling defiance at us, the story it tells of a man with a name but now no home suggests a more humane strain in the Eastwood hero. He may be coming to terms with life rather than death. So be it, anyhow, until Dirty Harry returns to the screen in the recently completed *The Enforcer*, where, it may be feared, as Pauline Kael said in one of her reviews, it will again no longer be 'the romantic world in which the hero, fortunately, is the best shot: instead, the best shot is the hero.' Eastwood no longer represents merely the triumph of the good. The world is not so simple nowadays. In a phrase that derives from the tradition that nourished his fame, his is the triumph of the good, the bad and the ugly.

Evening Standard, 27 September–1 October 1976

Even as these pieces were appearing in the *Evening Standard*, it seemed that a reaction was starting against the prices being asked by the superstars. *Variety* on 22 September 1976 carried the front-page banner headline, 'H'WOOD SKIRTS MALE STAR DEMANDS', which, when translated from this weekly's characteristic (and often witty) telegraphese referred to the fact that in some cases where male actors were too expensive, the roles they should have filled were being re-written so that lower-priced female stars could play them. *Variety* quoted the case of Louise Fletcher, who had won the Oscar for best actress in *One Flew Over the Cuckoo's Nest*. Her latest co-starring role with Richard Burton in the sequel to *The Exorcist*, entitled *The Heretic*, had originally been written for a man, but the studio apparently could not, or was unwilling to, meet the asking price of the male stars to whom it was offered, since a hefty slice of the budget was already assigned to meet Richard Burton's fee. So the role of the male psychiatrist had a skirt wrapped round it—and Louise Fletcher became eligible. Other examples of such sex changes were quoted. I am sceptical whether the male-into-female technique would be applied to a really top-notch leading role in which a male star was essential; but if women at last begin to reverse the male dominance of the last ten years or so, it may be because the men have now begun to price themselves out of perhaps not the market, but certainly the good graces of the producers whose relationship with stars, of whatever sex, is always one of alternating love and hate. But in 1976 I detected little other evidence of women moving to the top.

MISSING LEGIONS

It is still International Women's Year, isn't it? I mean, I'm not too late to have my say, am I? One cannot be certain with an event that has been less well publicised than, say, 'Plant a Tree for '73'. One would think from where I sit, in the cinema, I would have the best possible view of just such a consciousness-raising event as International Women's Year. But not at all . . . The truth is that in 1975 it has been harder than ever to find women playing the sort of prominent, important movie roles which the Beverly Hills Ladies Auxiliary have been insisting are essential if oppressed people such as women are ever to be permitted to write their own sex's history. Where are all the stars that Women's Lib seemed ready to procreate so recently, if possible without the intermediacy of man? Most of them, I am sorry to say, stillborn, gone Ms-ing.

Part of the trouble, of course, is that in a sexist-dominated industry like the movies, no one will yet allow the women to write scripts, never mind history. It all looked ready to change a year ago, just when I met Eleanor Perry. She had written the screenplay of *Diary of a Mad Housewife* and she came on strong like the 1970s version of the Blessed Dorothy Arzner, matron saint of feminist cineastes and the only woman director of the 1930s, so they say, who undermined 'the patriarchal ideology' that was Hollywood then (as now). (The Blessed Dorothy later went on to make Pepsi commercials for Joan Crawford's company: and a body of feminist scholars is even now at work analysing these for the evidence they may offer relating to 'soft drinks from a woman's point of view'.)

Eleanor Perry vowed to me that all this was changing. Women's Lib was taking over the movies in fact as well as aspiration. At daily Press conferences at the Cannes Film Festival, she used to make directors dry-lipped with her searching interrogation ('Does the last shot of your film imply that you regard women as basically treacherous?') and she played the activist for real, too, spearheading a flying squad of Liberationists armed with red-paint aerosols to obliterate a poster for the film *Roma* on which Fellini's male fantasy had over-endowed the wolf that mothered Romulus and Remus with three female breasts. At that time, even two would have been provocation enough.

And then this year I saw the new Women's Lib film that Mrs Perry had scripted, a Western called *The Man Who Loved Cat Dancing*. It had Burt Reynolds riding into the Badlands with Sarah Miles over his saddle. It was about as liberated as *The Sheik*, but without as memorable a line as Valentino's rebuke to his lovely captive when she asks why he has abducted her—'Are you not woman enough to know?' Now *that's* what I call consciousness-raising! Eleanor Perry swears that a man 'got' at her picture. But the fact remains that only one movie so far in International Women's Year has had a woman as its star, Ellen Burstyn, who used her power to determine what the character she played in *Alice Doesn't Live Here Any More* said, did and stood for. And even liberated Alice ends up not living her own life, but helping some man out with his.

All of which illustrates the problem of combining traditional stardom with being a torch-bearer for revolutionary feminism. I am sure the dominant male chauvinists of Hollywood do not want to see the two things wedded indissolubly together on the screen; but I am not convinced, either, that the great majority of filmgoers actually *want* to see it. The reaction to stars who play the militant feminist between roles, and sometimes in them, too, has been anything but universally welcoming and rewarding. It is all very well to muster your militancy and assail the major-league chat shows, or use the promotional tour for your latest movie to assert that 'women are trapped in the male discourse', or that 'the United States is an exploitive patriarchy', or simply that the best way out of it all is 'open-hearted, open-minded, open marriage'. But the fact remains that the great majority of filmgoers are still work-a-day, stay-at-home women who keep their liberation fantasies, if they have any, a secret from the PTA and do not regard the half-dozen or so feminist film actresses traipsing around the sexist battle points like agit-prop 'groupies' as attractive links between themselves and the basic impulses to which the cinema has historically catered.

I am not defending the hostility of a section of woman-kind who believe that the headlined claims made by these privileged spokes-persons for their own sex are overtly self-assertive, and who suspect that in many ways they are professionally self-serving as well. I am only identifying this as one strong cause for the absence from the screen of all those militant new stars and themes which the Women's Lib movement was ready to sponsor. Militant film stars work by subversion, when they work at all, not by the kind of full-frontal attack that makes men see them as threats to their virility and women as a reproach to their submissiveness. The non-conformist feminist often makes news. She seldom makes box-office.

Vogue, 15 September 1975

JANE'S ALL THE WORLD'S POLITICS

I wasn't really surprised the other day to find myself thinking, 'Can Jane Fonda survive without a war?' For there she was in front of me, in person, a 'Barbie Doll' in a helmet of hair and a skinny pullover, and she was saying, 'I cried every day I was in Vietnam.'

Useless to tell oneself that the face was totally unstained by tears or travel weariness. I mean, would you look at a Raphael painting and ask why the angels in it do not cut their bare feet on the sharp rocks? Some things are matters of faith, not fact.

The Fonda voice, splashes on, child-like in its tenacious naïveté, through the shallows of revolutionary politics and liberation movements and U.S. imperialism. It is hypnotic, in a way. After a time, all one begins to see is the Fonda mouth, that little bit of Henry sticking obstinately on to his daughter's rebellious face; and, quite honestly, the sight of this All-American feature so insistently bad-mouthing American intentions is an image that appears more treasonable than anything which is actually heard coming out of it. The audience loves it, of course. She has a name, so they listen; they assent to what she speaks before she has even spoken it; they anticipate what she is going to say the way that the fans' lips are locked into the dialogue of Bette Davis or Ingrid Bergman in the famous endings of films like *Now Voyager* and *Casablanca*. Indeed if she didn't describe herself as an activist, if she hadn't interviewed Lo Duc Tho, if she were not actually there to be seen in the film she has brought all this distance to show us, actually walking along the seventeenth parallel and saying to a North Vietnamese, 'What don't you like about the Americans? Go on, be honest,' you know what she would irresistibly remind one of? A film star, that's what.

I cannot pinpoint exactly when film stars like Jane Fonda began to turn the world into their scenario and grab themselves more of the action than any producer would think it good for them to have. Hollywood has always bred discontented children. But they used to vent their discontentment against the system that made them, and so often humiliated them, by running up the budget on a whim, or bitching their directors, or courting suspension. When the system collapsed, there was only one thing the stars could do—join the fans. So the stars turned themselves into superfans, aping their life-styles, espousing their causes, and generally committing themselves (filming permitting) to carry on the fans' war against capitalism or imperialism or militarism. It was a much more exciting scene, I can tell you, than those poky little showdowns with Louis B. Mayer; and all those fascinating liberal '-isms' had far more class than the traditional old '-ism' that Dorothy Parker had said was the only one Hollywood really understood, and that was plagiarism.

Of this new class of star, Jane Fonda has become, by youth and favour, the natural cheer-leader. Just as Patty Hearst announced her conversion from insouciant affluence to committed anarchy by posing with a gun in front of a seven-headed cobra symbol, just like a film star on a movie poster, so Jane Fonda has seized the same chance for a heroic rebirth as a Vietnam activist from being simply a Vadim sex-symbol. 'My love has expanded as a result of my experiences to embrace all people,' said Miss Hearst on one of her tape-recordings issued on the Symbionese Liberation Front label. Miss Fonda's love has expanded, too, though more selectively. In East Germany recently to show one of her films, she embraced her Socialist hosts, the Palestine Liberation Organisation, the whole of the Third World, and all of the North Vietnamese. Some armful! But no room in it, apparently, for the Americans.

Her film, by the way, is called *An Introduction to the Enemy*, and she made it with her husband Tom Hayden, the 'Chicago Seven' Hayden, whom she married in a free-form wedding outside Hollywood, both of them making their vows to a backing of Vietnamese songs. The film is pretty free-form, too—free as anyone's home movie, as Jane roves around Vietnam turning the world of international politics into her scene. You cannot honestly say it is as wild a trip as, say, that famous Star-Studded Evening with Angela Davis, another specialist in the dialogue of her nation's guilt that is almost a form of rape upon the body politic since the defiance of the language is combined with such seductive femininity. But the camera follows Jane patiently, and once, when a Vietnamese gets blown up by a mine half a mile away, it flies on to her face as if her reaction-shot to American imperialism contained the real reality. But then Hollywood habits are hard ones to kick. 'Follow the money', they used to instruct the cameramen when the star was in a crowd scene: it takes a little longer to remember to 'follow the enemy'. Moreover, the impression of a star making a series of personal appearance stops on the anti-war circuit isn't diminished by the visit Jane pays to a Hanoi film studios—I said old habits are hard to kick—and the enquiry she makes of a Vietnamese performer: 'I'm very interested to know why you decided to become an actress.' They appear a modest and tactful people, this enemy. No one asks Miss Fonda why *she* ever decided to become an activist.

Vogue, 1 March 1975

FRONTAL ATTACK/*A Doll's House*

Joseph Losey's is the first version of *A Doll's House* in which the sub-plot, involving the embittered clerk blackmailing the heroine, actually comes off more memorably than the latter's feminist militancy and marital liberation. Edward Fox, playing this extraordinary character, contrives to make him of primary interest in the film. And David Mercer's Ibsenite screenplay, by transferring all the rusty exposition from the body of it to a prologue set beside a wintry skating rink eight years before the play begins, rivets our attention as Fox, a haggard ghost of his role in *The Day of the Jackal*, is jilted by the girl he loves, played by Delphine Seyrig as a smart, heartless variation of her role as the amorous countess in the *Jackal*. When both characters then appear in the film proper, our sympathies, interest and anticipation have been engaged and stretched much more securely than they are by the more dramatically vital relationship between Jane Fonda as Nora and David Warner as her husband.

Fonda falls so far short of what is required that one simply gives up measuring her performance by Claire Bloom's exacting standards in the Patrick Garland film. The cheer-leader for Women's Lib would need a step-ladder to get within reaching distance of Ibsen's liberated woman. Voice, face and upbringing are all against her. Her tongue is untutored for roles that call for a period awareness and not just the projection of a star personality. Her air of hurt resentment anticipates the blow before it has landed. Her performance suggests that under the same roof as Nora there was an American *au pair* girl living in and helping out with the children and chance callers. Never for a moment does she take command as a plausible nineteenth-century Norwegian housewife imprisoned by her own wifely submissiveness and society's double sex-standards. What it shows, I am afraid, is that roles of Nora's complexity are not mastered on the battlefields of Vietnam. Fonda has turned the world of politics into her theatre: now the legitimate theatre, as it were, is hitting back.

Just to take one example of the injury that ideology has done the film. Originally, Fonda played the last scene, where Nora leaves her husband, as if she were using a public-address system giving out the Women's Lib message; then, according to Joseph Losey, at his judicious advice in the post-production stages, she modulated her vocal attack, but of course could not re-model her facial movements. The result: an audio-visual compromise at the crucial point where one needed a single-minded purposefulness.

David Warner isn't happily cast, either. There are moments, especially at the soirée, where Nora's husband looks a lecher as well as a male chauvinist: hardly Ibsen's intention. There is accordingly no pity and small understanding to which the man can lay claim when his wife bangs the door on him. Trevor Howard, as dying Dr Rank, the walking infection of a sick society, effectively holds on to life as he would hold on to the last drink. But whereas Howard totters on the graveside, Ralph Richardson in the Garland film is already being gnawed by the worms.

The Losey film has been opened out from a chamber drama to almost a topographical landscape, though I don't agree with the facile view that including sleigh-rides and roof-top views dissipates the claustrophobia. The snow is a tangible symbol of the white lie lived by Nora, which the wintry element reflects back at her. If only Jane Fonda didn't create a social void as she walks through it.

Evening Standard, 17 May and 5 July 1973

OLD-FASHIONED GIRL/*The Man Who Loved Cat Dancing*

There are times when I come away from a film half-expecting a Women's Libber to cross-examine me angrily about whether it lives up to her expectations of all a film should be—a film, for instance, like *The Man Who Loved Cat Dancing*.

Women's Libber: Just like the sexists who rule Hollywood to call a film by such a title. Who is the male chauvinist and why is he dancing while women work?

Critic: He is Burt Reynolds, ex-Cavalry officer turned train robber. And he doesn't dance once. Cat Dancing is the name of his first wife, a beloved Indian squaw.

W.L: A doubly-oppressed woman. Is she Sarah Miles?

C: No. Cat Dancing is dead before the film opens. Sarah Miles is a white lady who's on the run from her husband.

W.L: With good reason, I don't doubt.

C: With no reason at all that the film explains, except that he's played by George Hamilton, which may be reason enough.

W.L: Doesn't he want to possess her just for sex? Isn't that why she's left him?

C: No, he has a highly idealised view of his wife.

W.L: Setting her on the shelf as an ornament, you mean. I suppose he views sex as just a type of hygiene. I know his kind. Tell me more about the Miles woman.

C: She is a lady. She canters into the film over the desert in the sort of riding habit that ladies usually wear for chasing foxes, not running away from husbands.

W.L: She has been well conditioned!

C: Maybe, but such a garment is a wonderful defence against impulsive rapists who would have to go three rounds with her before they could even lift her skirt.

W.L: The Reynolds man, I suppose, can't keep his hands off her.

C: On the contrary. He treats her with uncommon kindness . . .

W.L: A mere love object, you mean.

C: . . . rubbing mud on her face to protect her against sunburn, watering her at intervals, bedding her down—

W.L: Ha!

C: —without molestation, though he does tip her rather rudely out of the horse-blanket in the morning.

W.L: Doesn't she defend herself? Doesn't she go for any of the 12 parts of the body where men are most vulnerable to attack from a weak-bodied woman?

C: No. She says, 'Is that absolutely necessary?' But she says it the way that only a Heathfield-educated girl like Miss Miles could. In fact she sounds throughout like a Pony Club Girl Guide stranded among a bunch of Rover Scouts from the back streets.

W.L: She sounds to me a lamentably old-fashioned girl. Has she no modern notions, no liberated ideals?

C: Well, after she's been nearly raped—

W.L: I knew it, I knew it! By the Reynolds brute, of course!

C: —by the Redskins, as it happens. You seem unduly interested in the virility of this male film star.

W.L: I once saw him showing his all, or very nearly, on the centre-page spread of *Cosmopolitan*. I have to read such sexist publications if I'm to keep looking angry and aggressive.

C: You would probably calm down when you heard Miss Miles—

W.L: Ms Miles, *if* you please!

C: —when you heard Ms Miles saying to Burt Reynolds, 'I've been thinking about it a lot. I'd like to have your baby.'

W.L: 'Your' baby! '*Your*' baby! Is that what she says?

C: Well, after marriage to Mr Hamilton, who's pursuing her on horseback, she hasn't had much experience of bearing anybody's baby.

W.L: I begin to understand the child. Obviously a case of enforced frigidity. Inability to have a child, perhaps. There could even be a history of abortion—some men *wish* their marriage to be incomplete, you know. What reply does Reynolds make to her proposition?

C: He says, 'Have a baby? Here, in this wilderness?'

W.L: Thinking only of his own comfort, as usual!

C: But he smartens himself up from then on, shaves off his beard, takes her to a worked-out mining camp and soon she's cleaning and cooking and saying things like 'I thought I'd put too much salt in the stew,' and generally showing a natural instinct for home-making.

W.L: Women have no 'natural instinct for home-making'. Home-making is a male conspiracy in which they are trapped from puberty, or as soon as they can view the TV commercials, whichever is the earlier. Tell me, this film has now been running a long time . . . is this woman still, well, you know. . . ?

C: If I read you right, yes, she is. But the roughest member of the Reynolds gang puts an end to that when he suddenly appears and just as promptly rapes her.

W.L: I hope Reynolds shoots the brute between the eyes.

C: You'll be pleased to hear he does even better—he shoots him between the legs.

W.L: Well, you find allies in the most unlikely places. So what happens next?

C: The pursuing husband rides up, reins in, and says to his wife, 'I take it you're all right.' She shoots him, presumably for his under-statement. But just before that, he's shot Burt Reynolds.

W.L: So once again, a woman has to face life alone. How typical!

C: I'm afraid there are signs that his wound isn't lethal and Miles and Reynolds will soon be facing something or other together, though I doubt if it will be another film.

W.L: Well, if it is, I hope it will be a better one. From your account, even the Blessed Dorothy Arzner, Hollywood's only woman director of the 1930s, couldn't make much out of this one. Who is responsible for it?

C: It was written and co-produced by the Liberated Eleanor Perry, who wrote *The Diary of a Man Housewife* and, three years ago, sprayed an anti-feminist poster at the Cannes Film Festival with red paint. But I did hear a rumour that she had had difficulties with her co-pro-ducer Martin Poll, not to mention her director Richard Sarafian.

W.L: You see! What did I tell you! Let the men take charge and what do you get? A piece of male chauvinist propaganda like this with the message that if you treat women roughly enough, they'll come crawling. I tell you, we can't win, we women.

C: Maybe not, but you leave yourselves enough let-outs not to actually lose, either.

Evening Standard, 19 June 1975

One of the fronts that the Women's Lib movement has success-fully advanced on in the United States relates to society's view of the male rapist. A number of notable cases have been won in the courts recently, challenging the view that rape is a male prerogative and that women should not complain too loudly or ask the court's sympathy for an act in which they've probably found some pleasure themselves. But as rape has caught the headlines in the crusading tactics of its female opponents, it has appeared more and more on the screen in the context of stories that pay Lib service to the victim while continuing to exploit her plight for the box-office. This trend has run into the current fascination with *macho* reflexes, except that here it is not a case of a man proving his virility by taking it out on the next man, but of a woman restoring her self-respect by taking revenge on the rapist. Perhaps it is not entirely accidental that this type of films has flourished since the Italian filmmaker Dino De Laurentis transferred his production offices from Rome to Los Angeles. As the production company responsible for both *Death Wish* and *Lipstick* (to name only a few such films), he has successfully transferred to America the Latin ethos surrounding rape and revenge—or '*R*' and '*R*' as it is now known in the trade papers, a bleak transmutation of the welcome meaning such initials once had for Servicemen on leave from the battlefront, namely '*R*est and *R*ecuperation'.

KISS-PROOF/*Lipstick*

Many a middling movie is built on an idea far more interesting than has been worked out in the script. In *Lipstick*, the idea is this: A high-fashion model (Margaux Hemingway) whose photograph sells lipstick by the million across America is raped in her apartment and elects to take her rapist to court. Apparently 'only' 10,000 rape victims have the nerve to do this in California every year. But under cross-examination, the certainty of her case wavers and weakens. After all, is she not herself a 'commercial' for a kind of high-toned lasciviousness? Her face, its mouth invitingly ajar, is replicated provocatively on billboards and TV screens and the pages of the glossies. She admits that to achieve the photogenic 'arousal' look during camera sessions that are themselves a 'rape' of her identity, she thinks about acts not too different from those inflicted on her. What's on trial, in fact, is not so much a personable male (Chris Sarandon), but the commercial hypocrisy that exploits people as objects—and then goes into shock when people are treated as objects.

Of course, the producers of *Lipstick*, being themselves engaged in the field of commercial exploitation, don't exactly push the argument to limits that would get them the Marxist vote or even, quite frankly, the Women's Lib seal of approval. On second thoughts, though, I'm not so sure about the latter: for *Lipstick* is really the distaff side of *Death Wish*. It belongs to the currently 'in' trend of vendetta films. It says loudly and explicitly at the end, 'If law and order have failed you, take the law into your own hands and establish your own order.' Which in this case means Miss Hemingway (grand-daughter of Ernest, by the way) taking a hunting rifle in her hands and aiming at the acquitted rapist's balls. Mr James Ferman and Lord Harlech, our film censors, have trimmed the target area, since they don't wish people over 18 years of age in the interests of shock or pleasure to set eyes on what they and their examiners keep their eyes on in the way of business. Other cuts have been imposed on the indignities inflicted on the girl, though these have been made in Hollywood, following audience indignation at a preview, and in order to get the film an American censorship code rating that wouldn't put it out of bounds to people under 17. But it is still a graphic sequence that involves the girl being tied up with scarves, smeared with her own commercial product, and then sodomised.

The film is clinical to a degree, having taken advice from the U.S. National Organisation for the Prevention of Rape and Assault. All the more regrettable, then, that its own exploitation of the subject hasn't been curbed. It vitiates its points by the cynicism of the way it sets up its scenes; it manipulates filmgoers with a skill as mechanical as it is methodical; it plays on an audience's resentment of the pampered star-status of celebrities, so that the brutal rape scene derives a quota of fascination from letting the base instincts of the admass public loose on its idols. True to its title, *Lipstick* applies its argument without deepening it: it smears the issues without clarifying them.

Anne Bancroft plays a radical-lib attorney with a stiletto tongue; Mariel Hemingway, who is the star's kid sister, also plays the raped heroine's kid sister, and very well, too, even though putting a child on the witness stand to answer queries about *The Story of O*, and whether women actually like to be humiliated, is yet one more way in which the film panders to the audience's prurience. There remains Margaux Hemingway. That she's not a good actress is irrelevant: she doesn't need to be. She is what she is—a model whose own awkwardness before the camera in a fiction film at least ties in with the nervy panic of the leading character in an exposed court-room. *Lipstick* is one of those film-factory products, with all the vices and virtues of its calculated assembly, that sometimes hits a public nerve more accurately than the custom-crafted artefact. No better because of that: but none the less significant, either.

Evening Standard, 8 July 1976

The Lighter Side

Comedy I have found one of the hardest genres to review. Partly because one doesn't want to spoil the fun. But since much of the fun *is* the fun, it becomes a daunting task to pick and choose among the items that will convey the flavour and, one hopes, the unique quality of a comedian without leaving the reader feeling sated. Neil Simon's films are particularly hazardous. One begins taking down a gag or two: one soon finds that one is transcribing virtually the whole screenplay.

What I admire particularly, but see rarely, are comedians who can use their bodies and their environment, and not just their lips, to produce their effects. I have selected three of these, though I'm aware that in Woody Allen's case it will be objected on good grounds that he is a gag-liner. True, but his gags on the lips of others less endearingly shaped than he would not, I think, amuse me so inordinately. Tati, too, is scarcely the most elastic of comics, but it is the plastic sense of what is funny which he extracts from the all too mutable environment around his own solid unchanging form that makes me feel his films are lively ballets. As for Sellers, this review was written in the flush of delight after witnessing the very first appearance of Inspector Clouseau. The creation has not stayed the course in my affections for subsequent movies of The Pink Panther species. But at first sighting, I thought it had genius, and still do.

SLIP-STICK/*The Pink Panther*

The Pink Panther is the name of a diamond as big as a golf ball. But we can forget about that. Padding in pursuit of it is David Niven, a titled cracksman with a burglar's mask over his blue eyes. But we can also forget about him. Owning it is an exotic Eastern princess played by Claudia Cardinale who gets deliciously sozzled on champagne on a tiger-skin rug and has to be towed off by the tail, of the rug. But we can even forget about her. For putting everyone in the shade and bringing out the sun to beam on this Blake Edwards' comedy is Peter Sellers.

Once again I must go on record that Sellers is just about the subtlest and funniest clown on the screen at the moment. And this performance puts him into a select new class. He joins the ranks of the great silent comics who could raise accident-proneness to the level of a high art.

He plays a highly defective French detective who suffers accidents on a scale that would turn an insurance company corporatively pale. The world is not his oyster, but his banana skin. And not once, but three times in every scene, so it seems, he sets his foot flat on it and skids into pure acrobatic brilliance. All the belly-laughs come from what he does with his body. A far stiffer test of clowning than anything he can do with a gag line. And it's not just a case of the door that opens in his face and rebounds on his behind. Sellers turns every mishap into a hilarious but ultimately sad commentary on the married life of the little man doggedly in love with his disdainful wife (Capucine). Eager to be into bed with her, he tangles the tassle of his dressing-gown and has to step shame-facedly out of the robe. Gallantly trying to whirl an extra blanket over her, he muffs his cast and has to crawl humiliatingly into bed with it draped over him like a collapsed tent. Bending over her like Don Juan poised for conquest, he kisses the pillow at the exact moment he lets her slide off the slippery quilt between his knees. Even when their lips safely meet, his Robin Hood-style hat is left pendant on one of her hairpins. And when he pops from their bedroom into the bathroom for a sleeping-pill, Blake Edwards switches joyfully from a sight gag to a sound one. We see nothing. But we hear the hail-shower of spilling pills—then the resigned crunch-crunch of slippers walking over them.

Sellers is too much in love, too preoccupied in keeping his dignity, to see that Capucine is in league with Niven. The big fancy-dress ball at the end, before the police lock everyone up, generates an escalating zaniness with Sellers in a suit of armour, Colin Gordon (the man from Lloyd's) in cap and bells, Niven and his college-boy nephew (Robert Wagner) in identical gorilla suits, and even gendarmes in a zebra skin.

If *The Pink Panther* sometimes dozes off for stretches, the reason is to be found in the over-wordiness of the screenplay. Dull stuff for ears to listen to when eyes are impatient to get back to Sellers. Suddenly hen-toed when crossing cold tiles in his bare feet, and always pathetically intent on pretending that nothing untoward, nothing unplanned, nothing unexpected has happened to him, he never misses a trick, retains a gravity that suggests it is the rest of the world that is leaning at an angle to him, keeps his timing immaculately and even keeps us guessing wrong when we try to forecast the next accident that will befall him. Here is genius wearing its funniest face—a man who plays the clown straight.

Evening Standard, 9 January 1964

Playtime for Jacques Tati has been a five-year labour of love. That it's also been *a labour* is only intermittently evident. Considering it's the first comedy of intimate gags and miniaturised slapstick which has been made in 70mm on the superwide screen usually reserved for epics of War, Christianity or Outer Space, it's an unusually intelligent, ingenious, witty and wholly individual movie. Even the stereophonic sound inseparable from mammoth productions is used to titillating effect, since a lot of Tati's gags are aural as well as visual: they invite you to listen before you look.

Tati himself again appears as the pipe-clenching innocent-at-large—this time in the ultra-modern, inhuman world designed by man but basically at war with the way the people in it have to live, work, eat and enjoy themselves. It falls into four loosely-connected segments, the first being a kind of ballet set in the shining dustless wilderness of Orly Airport with concrete music supplied by the idiosyncratic sounds people make as they move about its Kafkaesque floor space. Nuns flip-flop soulfully along, a dust collector snoops on any passing specks, photographers strike acrobatic poses to capture pictures, a tycoon's cabin-baggage label spins like a propellor in his high-powered wake, a dropped umbrella sounds like a portcullis. . . .

Things begin to take over from human functions when Tati's business takes him to a skyscraper complex: the result is a nightmare sequence of disorientation. Pneumatic chairs honk and hiss when sat on. The eerie silence amplifies a nail file into a buzz-saw. Reflections in the plate glass take on more solidity than the persons reflected. Legs glide alarmingly apart on the ice-rink floor. There's a hilarious impression achieved by an extremely high-angled shot of how labour-saving lay-outs in fact multiply the work to be done. This is *Playtime*'s most successful stretch of comedy—everything stripped down to hygienic essentials, controlled to the last functional heel-squeak, as precisely edited and counterpointed as an animated cartoon.

The next most enjoyable sequence is more lavish and baroque, but also more of a hit-or-miss affair: it's the opening night at a plush restaurant that has prematurely invited in the guests before it has got out the builders. The chaos is piled on in particles of disaster. It starts with the dance-floor tiles sticking to the waiters' feet and ends with the collapse of the entire ceiling. In between, bar stools tilted too far back, decant their occupants on to the floor (the same stools stood on end serve as handy pens for inebriated guests); the gilt fretwork on the chair backs embosses its design on the men's lounge suits; the doorman goes on opening and shutting a massive brass handle after the glass door that it was attached to has been shattered into pieces—in fact the best comedy derives from the waiters' determination never to deviate from routine, although all hell is literally breaking loose. But the nimblest moment has Tati sticking a wet beer-mat on to a semi-circular serving hatch so that the chef peering out from underneath it instantly seems to be wearing a Napoleonic hat. The rest of the gags have ingenuity, this one has genius. The bold decision to use the huge screen is justified again and again. Not only for gags showing the length of corridor a man has to walk down in order to make contact with another, but also for accentuating the witty disproportion between a gag and its environment. Like a pocket cartoon occupying the whole page of a newspaper, the conspicuous waste is part of the effect. *Playtime* is a series of brilliant doodles by an artist who has earned the right to indulge himself on such a scale.

Evening Standard, 18 July 1968

RIP VAN WOODY/*Sleeper*

Woody Allen in his new comedy plays a man who enters hospital in 1973 for minor surgery—'Be on your feet in five days,' the doctor tells him. The doctor is 200 years out.

As a result of 'unexpected complications', Woody finds himself being woken up from his foil wrapping like a TV dinner in the world of 2173. Woozy from future shock, he can still recognise some bits of the old world. 'Norman Mailer, he donated his ego to the Harvard medical school . . . Charles de Gaulle, a great French chef, had his own TV programme . . . Billy Graham, he knew God personally, they used to go double-dating together.' 'And *this* man,' says the examining doctor, showing a picture of Nixon, 'we think he was a President, but we can't find any trace of him. It's as if the record had been totally erased.'

'Sleeper' is a term used in the movie business to denote an unex-pected box-office hit. Woody Allen's film is this all right, except that it was totally expected. He is quite simply the funniest verbal clown in pictures—a man whose talent for the gag line has matured into a fecund inventiveness for concept comedy, the comedy of situation and observation. Running over the surface of his own jokes like a pond-skater in spectacles, he keeps you constantly afraid you'll miss the next jest, they come so thick and—thank God!—they come so fast. Fleeing from the State police, he takes refuge among the tail-coated robot butlers who service the intelligentsia. He fights off a belligerent synthetic pudding which he's cooked up in the kitchen. He deposits the guests' coats in the cloakroom, only to find it's really an incinerator. To see him mimic the mannerisms of the automated servant—homosexual households have robots that mince—is a piece of perfection timing in itself.

In the middle of a bit of running slapstick, like his life-preserving suit that suddenly inflates itself, Allen can snap off a hilarious line of snide quips like detonating charges for the larger explosion of mirth. The situations often lead up to a single gag, but what an enjoyable approach road. The Volkswagen covered in a 200-year pall of dusty neglect that starts up at once . . . the Jewish robot tailors kitting him out in an instant suit ('So we can take it in . . .') . . . the giant fruit farm where Woody slips on the world's biggest banana skin.

Forced to go on the run with a girl (Diane Keaton 'who reminds me of a Trotskyite girl who became a Jesus Freaker and was arrested for selling connect-the-dots pornographic books'), he ends up being brainwashed into working for the State machine (threading giant tape-recorders) and finally impersonating a famous surgeon whose task it is to clone the Leader, a terrorist bomb victim, from the only piece of him that's survived—his nose. There are scenes one can see haven't quite come off—you can also see how ruthlessly Woody has shortened them when they don't. But they're rare. It is a comedy with a brain behind it ('my second favourite organ', as Woody would say) and it ticks over like a Rolls-Royce clock.

Evening Standard, 2 May 1974

Shock Waves

It was round about the second half of the 1960s that one noticed pornography in its diluted form beginning to show up in popular entertainment. By then inhibitions had been loosened along with the 30-year-old 'morality code' that enforced the observance of a multitude of taboos on the film producers. But I really think the social acceptability of soft porn owes more to its steady diffusion through the voyeuristic pages of the men's magazines and the fashion pages of the women's.

The latter phenomenon particularly interested me. After all, one *expects* the men's market represented by *Playboy, Penthouse* and their crasser imitators to start plumbing the once-private depths of sex, and particularly aberrant sex, as soon as it has been demonstrated that the laws against pornography in many countries are uncertain and full of loopholes, or that juries are reluctant to convict in the absence of generally accepted standards of morality. But it was of more interest to watch photography that used to be considered as simply an aid to selling garments gradually turning into a means of sexual arousal. A sort of 'deviant chic'. One picture sequence I remember in a high-style glossy showed a woman being alternately nuzzled and beaten by a man while the clothes on her back moved ever more extravagantly up the price range till the acme of modishness as well as masochism was reached with blows raining down on her 140-dollar cat-suit. Before it went out of business in 1975, the English women's monthly, *Nova*, was featuring photo-spreads and cover illustrations modelled, with only a delicate semblance of parody, on the kinkier examples of machismo, power and domination. The issue of January 1972, for example, displayed on its cover a masked blonde in fishnets, black suspenders and matching foundation garment who pensively regarded the buyer, or voyeur, as she pursed her lower lip on a huge coiled and plaited stock-whip held in her clenched right fist. Instead of the customary four-letter imprecation, the one suggested by this 'liberated woman' —and remember that was *Nova*'s original market—appeared to be 'Flog you!'

As I pointed out in my book *Hollywood, England*, the fashion photographer was the trend hero of the 1960s whose impact 'on journalism, on pop culture and on mid-1960s cinema proved to be far more potent, enduring (and ultimately more corrupting) than that of the satire movement. . . .Photography had the power constantly to create new fantasies, not simply to shatter ancient prejudices . . . this made it altogether more seductive, resilient and commercially viable as it created the "swinging scene" of the village-capital (which) it then sold to the world, so that by reproduction and repetition in tens of thousands of international magazines and newspapers the reputation of London as the place where "it's all happening" was given a fantasy perspective both sharper and more alluring than reality.' What was local swiftly became universal as more and more startling liberties were taken with convention with the aim of selling material goods but frequently with the effect of confirming a moral revolution.

A walk through London's Underground—the subway, not the drug-culture—in the late 1960s revealed to even the most casual eye how the urges and desires of permissive man (and, shortly, liberated woman) were reflected in the posters on the walls as well as the advertisements in the periodicals and papers on the counters of bookstalls. One needed to armour oneself with a kind of disabused double-think—the kind that came easily to that sophisticated generation of teenagers and the younger middle-aged—if one was not to see the advertising slogans and pictures as depicting a churning orgy of behaviour worthy of the erotic imagination of Hieronymus Bosch.

Here was the Duke of Wellington who, we were told, 'liked to get his hands on Ruby after dinner'—'ruby', though, was a port. Here was the warning to the wife whose husband may be 'in another man's arms'—though closer inspection showed it was no homosexual love affair, but simply shirt-sleeves that didn't fit properly. Here was something for the man contemplating his 'next casual affair'—it turned out to be suede loafers. And here was the lady teacher who, according to the time-honoured phrase, 'wants to meet students of either sex'—though the purpose was not flagellation or bondage, simply language courses. The slogan 'Does she? Doesn't she?' also proved to have nothing to do with copulation; the answer was, Yes—she does smoke. Right into the 1970s we had to live with the advertisements for a brand of vodka which boasted of its potency through its 'degenerate' after-effects on formerly humdrum nobodies who had become Instant Bohemians—it wasn't till 1976 that some discreetly tendered advice was taken from the advertising standards people and the drink was sold for itself alone.

It was the escalation of such sexual candour (or innuendo

integrated with laconic wit) that Marshall McLuhan's phrase 'accelerated transience' so aptly described: it was a world 'in which we are no sooner in a condition to look at one kind of event than it is obliterated by another'.

Advertisements and fashion lay-outs don't, however, make trends unless they are exceptionally striking and timely. They follow trends once they become apparent in the way people are acting generally. When women began to feel emancipated, or began to feel *the obligation* to feel emancipated, which is not at all the same thing but can often be just as potent in its effects, they became emancipators themselves in the kinds of advertisement or commercial appeal they thought acceptable. It was in the higher-priced range of women's magazines that the nude bosom first appeared on a fashion model; that a totally nude young Frenchman first advertised a brand of underpants by not wearing them himself; and that the transparent range of fashion-wear at the end of the 1960s made acceptable the 'now you see it, now you don't' line hitherto confined to strip-clubs for men or the earlier range of teasing poses in erotic magazines for the same sex. It was obvious that what one can call 'main-line cinema', to distinguish it from the back-street 'blue movies' of the period, was soon going to capitalise on stimulating the same kind of responses through fantasies of altogether greater vividness and suggestiveness. The interesting part of a trend like this is just before it becomes a veritable plague—before the desire to break old taboos turns into a desperation to find new taboos to break, which is the age that I believe we have now reached in the mid-1970s when we have run out of eroticism and are consequently witnessing an attempted restoration of guilt and constraint which in turn will permit some new transgression to be attempted years from now.

One of the early fruits of emancipation was the introduction of the lesbian love affair into films—I mean the *physical* act of homosexual love between women. For though the old notion of the 'love that dare not speak its name' was loosening its tongue quite rapidly in the early 1960s with the two Oscar Wilde films, with *The Leather Boys* and *Victim*, to name just four, the words weren't usually to be seen associated with the deed—and when they were, the lovers were women. This was partly because female homosexuality was more protected by public ignorance of what it was that women actually did together; partly because it could be depicted more decoratively on the screen without loss of audacity because of the biological fact that men's sexuality hangs out while women's is tucked in; and partly, too, because a more romantic and lyrical approach was possible which would commend itself to women who might have been put off by the crasser male techniques.

The photography from the very beginning became the audience's 'go-between', making the titillation acceptable by giving it the gloss of fashion rather than dealing too specifically with the glass of form which might have caused unease among the patrons. The trick was to wrap up the eroticism in impeccable lighting, adding music that plucked at the heart-strings, and interior decor or, even better, exterior settings in parts of the world that were beyond the means of most viewers to reach except in such fantasies. Such a trend has reached its profitable peak in films like *The Story of O*, which resembles a fashion model's daydream of sex, and *Emmanuelle*, which simply transports the daydream to a travelogue setting. Both films, I am afraid, were merely a series of fashion textures as far as I was concerned—and it is entirely appropriate that they should have been directed by a man who was formerly a fashion photographer for the glossies. I found rather more fun, if no more success, in some of the earlier essays in this *genre*, before the liberation became an inundation.

BATH NIGHT/*Les Amants*

It is not really important that *Les Amants* has had a running battle with the English censor lasting over a year. Nor is it fatal to it to have lost a moment or two's footage. If you wish to know, chiefly the moment when a man and a woman share a bath-tub together. These are incidental to Louis Malle's film. Some even think the excisions improve it. I do.

In spite of the scene being there and rousing violent criticism at the Venice Festival last year, the film took a prize. In Paris, at the box-office, it took a fortune. Some called it pornographic. Its defenders called it chaste. And there were those again who called it naïve. When a film does all these things, it usually has something notable. It is best that there should be no doubt that the word is 'notable' and not 'notorious'. And I think that is the case now.

Of course there is still a lot to shock, if nothing to titillate, in Louis Malle's modern adaptation of an eighteenth-century *conte libertin*. Quite simply, it is the story of one night of love. It happens in the moon-whitened grounds of a château, on a lake, in a bedroom while the house-party is asleep, and on the morning afterwards, or, rather, later the same day when the guests assembled for a fishing expedition see their host's wife drive off with the man she has slept with. Jeanne Moreau plays the woman, her ever-so-slightly cruel mouth and globe of a forehead more expressive of sex than any display of her body. The young man is played by Jean-Marc Bory. As an actor, he is not well-known here: after this, he should be.

The moment when the two meet on the terrace, after the lights in all the rooms have gone out, signals the start of an extraordinary passage. All that has gone before is a glancing, sophisticated series of sketches— bored life in the provinces, visits to Paris and the polo matches, flirtation with a diplomat, the week-end party, a chance encounter after a car breakdown with the youth who answers the news that he's the first man with an amused, slightly cynical but flattering, 'Oh, surely not the first, madame.' In the garden, at night, love transfigures the two of them. As they stand on a bridge, the glasses they have been holding accidentally meet. The bell-like note thrills like no sound I have heard in pictures. Passion made audible. The mood is classical, yet overpoweringly romantic. The camerawork of Henri Decae ex- udes sympathy with it. Earlier, a coil of pearls, a lamp-shade, some opalescent tone has prepared the way into the half-lights, physical and emotional, of passion.

But striking as these scenes are, Malle's great moment comes with morning, when both realise that they never again will enjoy each other so fully. Yet they don't part. They leave together, feeling neither sin, nor shame, nor regret. In the driving mirror, her unprepared face reflects a little disquiet for the future—but this is all. They drive on. . . . Malle has wished it to be so clear that they don't turn back that he has cut out of the film the husband's half-voiced thought, 'They won't get far.'

Of course it is an amoral ending, in the sense that the pair are never judged, never condemned by the filmmaker. He uses at points the woman's thoughts to insulate himself from deep involvement. And it is this absence of moral judgement which shocks, though Louis Malle would not agree, I feel. Malle worked with Captain Cousteau on the underwater film, *The World of Silence*, and probably the influence of the ascetic captain and the underwater world explain a certain monastic feeling about his style. He is young—27—rich, well-born, talented, a rejecter of labels which tie him in with the 'new wave' of French directors—and with this film he has set the critics at each other's throat.

The Birmingham Post, 3 May 1959

I was being too cautious. I didn't really think any such excision 'improved' *Les Amants*, though like most examples of such 'tokenism' on the censor's part, it didn't actually harm it, either. But opinion in those days—so newspapers believed, anyhow—wasn't prepared for news that two people shared a bath-tub when they weren't married to each other (or, I suspect, even when they *were* husband and wife). One staid executive on the newspaper viewed my praise for the film with disapproval: though nothing was said, the pressure was felt, and showed up in the wary balance of my opening paragraphs. Nothing was altered in what I wrote, but the still I used, a three-and-a-half inch single-column picture of a bare-shouldered Moreau with her back to the camera being embraced by Bory, vanished from the film column between editions. It was a 'once only' experience, viewable now as an interesting example of the public morality to which most newspapers in those days felt it was prudent to subscribe. The shift to an essentially youthful and permissive culture in the mid-1960s wasn't only good for newspaper circulation: it freed film critics, who were reviewing the art that was forcing the pace, from many of the irksome though hardly debilitating euphemisms and conventions maintained in those earlier days out of respect for readers' hypocrisies.

Maybe a word on 'pressures' in general is appropriate here. Most film critics worth their salt are able to withstand the promotional blandishments of receptions, luncheons and the like, the quantity of which has in any case severely dropped off (along with cinema receipts) in the past few years. It has never worried me to write a bad notice after lunching with the film-maker: one develops the same technique of evasiveness at the table which is practised as part of the job by those who brought one to the table in the first place. It interests me as a pheno-menon, and stretches me in a minor way as a polite dissimu-lator, for I have found very little of value is actually gained unless one has liked the film enormously or is prepared to voice one's dislike of it with exceptional force.

Very rarely do filmmakers like meeting critics: still fewer, I think, actually read the reviews, or indeed read much else, since so much of the business is conducted by talk not literacy. There are exceptions, but they are so few as to confirm the rule. Power is what interests them, either translated into money or ego, and critics are generally excluded from many revealing glimpses into either the dementia or the aspiration that contribute to the deal-making. I would sooner talk to producers or producer-directors: when I do, I am often surprised at the way one's own artistic judgment on a film coincides with theirs, whatever they maintain in public. Only one has ever tried offering me a bribe in return for golden words, and I had to admire the coolness of his enquiry, as we sat down to lunch in a restaurant, about how much per inch advertising cost on my paper—and then how many inches there were to the film column. After which, what could one say except, 'Shall we order?' He let me pay.

THREE'S COMPANY/*The Fox*

The Fox is one of those self-consciously daring films about the varieties of sexual attraction that three people—two women, one man—can experience when left to themselves in a snowbound farm.

There are at least four love affairs going on, sometimes concurrently, in the old chicken farm up in D. H. Lawrence country which has been transposed to the wastes of Canada. The first is between Anne Heywood and herself in front of the bathroom mirror, so as to prove that a woman who does a man's work about the farm hasn't lost what I believe romantic novelists call her 'essential femininity'. The mirror gets appropriately steamed up—few filmgoers will, though, as it is all so prettily antiseptic. The second affair is between Miss Heywood and Sandy Dennis, as a girl who had one of those 'bad experiences' with a boy in the woods on college graduation day and, as a result, has turned into a good cook without passing through the intervening stage of becoming some man's good housewife.

The two women are actually seen in each other's arms, which is some kind of cinema 'first'. But an arty montage of Miss Heywood's last heterosexual affair is superimposed upon the current lesbian one, thereby both confusing the sentiments and reducing the visibility.

Sex of the normally lustful kind comes knocking at the door in the person of Keir Dullea, a sailor home from sea, who disregards the shyly beckoning Miss Dennis in order to lay the butch Miss Heywood —the film's only stroke of unexpected irony which, unfortunately, is never satisfactorily explored.

But the fourth love affair is the one that's consummated with the most oppressive passion. It's the one between director Mark Rydell and his too, too beautiful photography. D. H. Lawrence's nature symbolism is already so overstrung—the male-ness of the intruding fox, the mid-winter bleakness of lesbian love—that the last thing it needs is underlining by a camera that adds its own self-entranced vision of the outside landscape to the lingering stares that pass between the trio indoors, and make it all an exercise in exquisite tedium. The film has the look of literature, not life—especially in the last scene where Miss Dennis simply stands by while the other two partners in the *ménage* chop down a tree on top of her—a barren tree, of course. You might just get by with the symbolism of the scene in print. On the screen, it simply looks like murder by deforestation.

Evening Standard, 23 May 1968

Language in the cinema is a study in itself—or should be. We are so used to thinking that the revolution in screen candour is something that meets the eye—which it is, of course—that we have forgotten how much of it was concerned with words that hit the ear. Once the verbal barriers erected by production codes were bent, it was inevitable that they would be breached: the sound tracks of movies from the mid-1960s on testify to the ways that the trickle of so-called verbal vulgarities was swiftly in spate as films grew bolder and bolder in their dialogue. The 'damn' uttered by Rhett Butler as he quit Scarlett O'Hara in *Gone With the Wind*, in 1939—'Frankly, my dear, I don't give a damn'—was the first use of a cuss-word in a major American movie since the Motion Picture Production Code had clamped the stars' lips shut on the awesome possibilities inherent in the aptly named 'talkies'. Even then, David O. Selznick had to pay a 5,000 dollar fine, like slipping money as an earnest of regret and apology into some 'swear box', and Gable took care to put the emphasis on the 'give' rather than the 'damn'. The word hardly seems epochal compared with what can be heard today.

In *Who's Afraid of Virginia Woolf?* for example it's been calculated that there are eleven 'God-damns', seven 'bastards', five 'sons of bitches', and various phrases like 'screw you', 'up yours', and so on. To protect themselves in advance, the director and screen-writer (Ernest Lehman) of the film inserted euphemisms in the first, laundered version of the film script: then they decided verbal dishonesty was damaging the play's artistic integrity and restored (most of) the originals, omitting only swear words like 'Jesus Christ!' when it was felt 'My God!' was a strong enough substitute. 'My God,' said a Warner Brothers executive when the final print was screened, 'we've got a $7,500,000 dirty movie on our hands.'

Fortunately for Warners, the old Roman Catholic Legion of Decency had suffered a number of embarrassing reverses over certain controversial films at this time and was in the process of 'modernising' itself, recruiting younger, better-educated priests (*'cinéaste*-priests', I suppose one could call them, on the analogy of 'worker-priests') and adopting less restrictive postures over what they called 'think films'. *Virginia Woolf* benefited from an 'A-4' rating, judged to be 'morally unobjectionable for adults, with reservations', which is three steps down from the elevated purity of a *Mary Poppins*, but permits the devout to patronise the box-office—which they did. It is when a 'revolution' of this nature is seen to be profitable—and when the extent of the profit is calculable to the degree this was—that it becomes a trend, a test of whether Americans accepted contemporary change in their films as well as their society. We know the answer to that now—practically anything goes. A society that had lost its consensus on what were once regarded as crucial issues like marriage, divorce and the like was clearly not of a mind to protest in the presence of the swear word.

These occurred more and more in films made by independent producers, not film studios: the independents had usually a quicker ear, and a readier tongue, for what the mass public was thinking—and saying. Buck Henry, Woody Allen, Jules Feiffer, Lenny Bruce had taken positions in their cartoon strips or cabaret acts that depended first and foremost on words, and they became leaders and sometimes martyrs of the new candour. In the screenplays some of them wrote, the word was more important than the image. The redoubts of orthodoxy must really have felt overrun by the enemy when even gentle, white-haired Spencer Tracy in *Guess Who's Coming to Dinner* in 1967, used a word like 'screw'.

Words as titillating factors appear more and more often in movies that sell themselves on their language rather than on any lubricious features of their photography. This is particularly true of best-sellers when brought to the screen: the object here is to shock without antagonising, or, rather, embarrassing, since a large part of the audience for, say, a Harold Robbins or a Jacqueline Susann story will consist of the middle-class and the 'square-ish' who wish to savour the sensation of modernity without feeling any contaminating fall-out. But it is no accident that it was in this 'late sensate period', as the sociologists would term it, that the movie version of a classic like *Ulysses* appeared.

The film's American release pattern in March 1967, made a big point of linking the established legal right to inviolability of Joyce's novel with the film that Joseph Strick had made of it: and to make caution doubly sure, the film was shown for three days only in 65 synchronised U.S. engagements, so that by the time the local moralists had been alerted and got to the cinemas, the screen would be blank and the box-office bare. By associating the raw language of the sound track with the book's classic status and then moving out of town quickly, *Ulysses* kept a jump ahead of legal action until it could safely come to rest or even come back for return engagements. In its *three-day* engagement, it grossed 800,000 dollars, more than it had cost to make, proving that people would rush to *listen* to a film in which there was otherwise little to startle the eye. The lustful thoughts uttered by Molly Bloom for over 30 uncensored minutes of sound-track were unmatched in cinema history for randy candour, beside which the language of *Virginia Woolf* was as mere vanilla flavouring, and even though only one four-letter word, 'fuck', had been admitted from the book into the film. Editing Joyce for the screen had obviously concentrated the libidinous tang of words in print. And there was also the vocal virtuosity of Barbara Jefford, as Molly, starting her great soliloquy with matter-of-fact earthiness, rising like a bird on a current of warm, sensual excitement and bringing the film to an amazing close on a note of pure aural orgasm—'and his heart was going like mad and yes I said yes I will yes.' Too bad one could have listened with one's eyes closed, without sense of loss, for all that was added to her performance by the mundane images that Joseph Strick matched to her words.

The use of linguistics as a tool to change films has been a story of profit and loss. The 'new vulgarity' has marched step by step with the 'new freedom'—and I am not sure that words don't prove the more powerful 'trace elements' in the continuing enquiry into social change. They hit the unconscious at a deeper level than images and resonate through the collective consciousness of society with more legal and moral shudders. In a later note, I have a few words to say about the risks that *Last Tango in Paris* was exposed to just by virtue of the words in it. But if the clockwork vulgarities of *The Carpetbaggers* are the price we have to pay for the painful use of language rubbed raw by self-revelation in *Last Tango in Paris*, it must be considered a bargain worth striking.

A PALER SHADE OF BLUE/*Therese and Isabelle*

Pornography has recently been going in for some 'upward trading'. Like all goods, hard and soft, it can be made to appeal to a better class of buyer by being given a more attractive kind of finish. American cinemas have been finding there are sizeable profits to be gleaned from the type of product called 'a class sin picture', which is the cleaned up version of the old blue movie that would have caused middle-class patrons to pass by on the other side of the street with a shudder. But now that permissiveness has softened up their resistance, they can go into the cinema openly—and even talk about the experience at the dinner table as if it were the latest contemporary art exhibition. Which, in a way, it is.

Audubon Films are American distributors who have pioneered the blue-movie breakthrough into middle-class respectability. Now one of their films, *Therese and Isabelle*, reaches the British screen. The event is worth commenting on in detail, even if the film is not, as showing how far social custom now tolerates in films what only a year or two ago it would have felt constrained to refer to in undertones. The cynically minded will also derive some amusement from the compromises that the filmmakers have worked out with the film censor even in advance of his seeing the film.

Therese and Isabelle is French-speaking, though it stars Essy Persson who is a graduate of Swedish sex films, and Anna Gael who has recently graduated, too, by marriage into the English aristocracy. They play schoolgirls who have a lesbian affair at a French finishing school. It should be said at once that neither actually *looks* like a schoolgirl of the age stated in the film; but then the film's first line of defence is that its heroines are supposedly innocent—at least Miss Persson is—of the vices which audiences might not find so pardonable in girls who are no longer, well, schoolgirls. However erotic the scene is, both of them are kept scrupulously well-groomed and impeccably photographed on the same principle that permits perfectly respectable magazines to print pages of nudes—a glowing skin tones down the thoughts of sin. The story is told in flashbacks by Miss Persson, as a (naturally well-groomed) adult revisiting her old school. They are very slowly-paced flashbacks. Again the lack of haste in getting to the picture's point provides an artistic alibi. So does the direction, which uses the fashionable 'time juggling' technique in which a character in an empty room turns her head and—*cut*—the room is filled with girls from the times gone by. It all looks like Antonioni mated with Alain Resnais—if that's not too incestuous a mating—and applies the patina of 'art' to scenes that might otherwise be thought unacceptably lewd. The technique succeeds up to a point only where the British censor has been concerned.

One scene of auto-eroticism, to judge from the telltale 'click' of a censorship cut, has been terminated prematurely. Another features both girls behind the chapel pews—they are unseen, nevertheless censorship precautions have been taken. For at this point all English sub-titles vanish from the screen for well over a minute, while Miss Persson indulges in some over-ripe French prose about her sensations. The theory here is that if you don't know French, you won't be depraved or corrupted by it. It follows, I assume, that if your French is up to standard, you'll have the wit and intelligence to resist depravity and corruption. One law for the 'O' levels, another for the 'A'.

The last of these scenes, give or take a heterosexual grapple with the local Romeo which is inconclusive, depicts what I take to be an act of cunnilingus. Sub-titles again cease, words take over, in French as before. American reports suggest it was considerably more explicit in that country—it is still surprising enough here, though possibly not for very much longer at the pace our screen is setting. *Therese and Isabelle* carries not the slightest conviction that it is all happening in a believable girls' school. Supervision is nil, teachers' suspicion is short-lived, every girl is a beauty. If I don't sound aroused by it, the short answer is that I was not. Necessarily excluded by my sex from such a relationship, I only entered into it professionally, but in fact the film carries a high charge of tedium, it is all so sanitised and un-lifelike. To be curious and bored, both at the same time is perhaps the virtue of this kind of film: it allows one to satisfy one's curiosity without any guilty after-feeling that one had actually enjoyed oneself.

Evening Standard, 2 August 1970

DIRTY TALK/*The Carpetbaggers*

It is not what you see in *The Carpetbaggers*, but what you hear. It is a film in which the sex, *all* the sex is strictly for the ear.

People don't make love in it, they imply lust. But they do so in words. Up-end producer Joe Levine's carpetbag and what tumbles out is a choice bundle of soiled dialogue: 'What do you want to see on your honeymoon, darling?'—'Lots and lots of lovely ceilings.' 'For once the hero is going to let the heroine show herself properly grateful.' —'Properly?' 'My pictures add dignity and culture to the movie industry'—'And three starlets a week to your bed.' 'What's the wildest thing you've ever done?'—'I was hoping I hadn't done it yet.' 'The fans write in for her autograph'—'If only they knew they could get everything just by pressing her doorbell.' The coy innuendo, the promise without the performance, the indiscreet fade-out, the fleeting shot of nudity so fast that the eye—even the *trained* eye of the film critic—can hardly catch it: there's not even the feeling of clockwork sex, of having it every hour on the hour, of characters being wound up before they can couple. What fills the day for most of the folk in *The Carpetbaggers* is not active sex, but inordinate money-making.

It is a perfect example of the work of filmmakers for whom story options, script budgets, collateral financing, box-office grosses and net returns have more fascination and more meaning than sex, which is merely a commodity that they package for sale to the customers, the end-link in the financial chain of manipulated sensation.

George Peppard is a surly young tycoon who has only to call his father 'impotent' for the old man to drop dead on the spot and leave Junior in control of his business and his stepmother—that's Carroll Baker. 'Do it now, mistreat me,' she is panting in her lacy widow's weeds even before the funeral. 'No,' he snarls—the sadist! Instead, he sets about pyramiding his investments and gaining his kinky pleasures by painting his name on the roofs of factories he buys up. Step-mama goes off to Paris and in two quick dissolves becomes 'a living legend' of the Twenties. Back home, Peppard, now a multi-millionaire, is still scorning the women who wrinkle his shirt-front with a passion that would give a launderer nightmares. 'Get a divorce,' he rasps at Elizabeth Ashley, playing his wife and asking how she'll pass the time till he comes home—and off he rushes to more business deals in fast cars and jet planes. Actors in *The Carpetbaggers* for ever seem to be either in transit or in conference. Even Peppard proposing marriage to blonde Martha Hyer, promoted from whoredom to stardom in the film empire he's bought, is still the businessman: 'All I want is your beauty and sex—you'll never make a better sale.'

It's impossible to believe in Alan Ladd as Nevada Smith, cowboy star of the silent screen, when the actor presents him as a tired old man who has hung up his saddle years ago. And on this showing Carroll Baker is not the new sex goddess who will render the screen combustible when she plays Jean Harlow: it's hardly a good omen that bleaching her hair merely cheapens her appeal. She is out-acted by Elizabeth Ashley, whose bright, vital and touching Twenties girl, who can laugh at herself one minute and turn sharply serious the next, is the only gleam of hope for the future at the bottom of this bag. Not surprisingly, however, the characters who are best acted are the ones who are best at juggling figures: Martin Balsam's film tycoon, Lew Ayres's company lawyer and Bob Cummings' agent with the 90 per cent smile and the ten per cent conscience. The people who made *The*

Carpetbaggers know these characters well enough to get them dead right. They are their own types.

Evening Standard, 22 October 1964

THE TRIUMPH OF THE SHREW/*Who's Afraid of Virginia Woolf?*

Very rarely does a film deserve to make the jump from the review columns to the news columns. But such a one is this week's arrival from Warner Brothers, *Who's Afraid of Virginia Woolf?* It is news because it proves conclusively and memorably that Elizabeth Taylor, long established as a star, is now also an actress at the very top of her powers. It is news, too, because the censors of two countries, Britain and America, have let it extend the frontier of frank dialogue further than some of us thought possible, and a few still think permissible. And again it is news because it gives the lie to the old and all too often well-founded belief that when a big Hollywood studio buys up a distinguished stage play with an audacious theme, it must emerge on the screen as vulgarised, eviscerated and pasteurised for the pop public.

In all these respects, *Who's Afraid of Virginia Woolf?* is a film of exciting consequence for the future—and riveting entertainment for the here and now. Albee's play takes to the screen like a transplanted poltergeist, not one whit tamed by its new setting. It is still a tragicomedy of married vindictiveness, a demonstration bout of love-hatred set in (and now around) the home of a failed faculty member (Richard Burton) and his man-eating wife (Elizabeth Taylor) which lasts from brawling midnight to whimpering daybreak. The night's fun and games are of the psychologically wounding kind that host and hostess inflict on each other with sadistic relish and then turn them on the young marrieds (George Segal, Sandy Dennis) who drop in for a nightcap and get caught up in a bloody game of mixed doubles.

Elizabeth Taylor's performance can be called the triumph of the shrew. Gone is every defence that a beautiful woman might have relied on to give her an easy ride over the heaving sea of Albee's verbal violence. She enters with a fatted face, slip strap showing, a braying voice, a greying wig that at moments of temper lashes around like a bundle of snakes, and a body that looks hard enough to take every knock and rubbery enough to bounce them back. With unerring, intuitive strokes, she builds up Martha's sluttishness with physical details like the casual drag at a cigarette filched from her husband's lips or verbal minutiae like the messy demonstration of wifely affection —'I want a big sloppy kiss'—that turns into bitchy harassment. She is the blazing equal of those big scenes of humiliation which are the play's heavyweight contests, when she taunts Burton with his ineffectualness till he literally chokes her off; yet she is incredibly touching at the end when her termagant's trumpeting is muted, and she blows a lament for the child she never had.

With heavy spectacles and hair flattened into a baldish effect, Burton ages himself as expertly as his real wife coarsens herself and gives his best screen performance ever, caustic, pain-ridden, sadistic, self-reproachful. For the first time the Burtons show their potential to be as great an acting partnership as the Oliviers were.

Opinion will divide over the wisdom of setting part of this four-wall hell in an empty roadhouse at dead of night, but Mike Nichols, making his debut as a film director, concentrates so inflexibly on his characters indoors and out that this brief shift of location did not worry me unduly. I admired the way he pursues the retching rhythms of the play, with only an occasional flurry of showy photography, like the one extraordinary interpolated shot of Elizabeth Taylor's arm reaching out for a cigarette like a striking snake. Most of all, I admire his insistence that nearly all Albee's raunchy dialogue should stand. For the people in the film are more than usually revealed by what they say: their 'goddams', their 'chrissakes', and so forth are their primal cries. The film censor was absolutely right not to smother them and to pass the film uncut. After this, how long will it be before the other forbidden words follow—what then will be left to be 'afraid' of?

Evening Standard, 7 July 1966

ICH BIN EIN BERLINER/*The Graduate*

No one, as far as I know, has yet put his finger on what gives *The Graduate* its degree of difference.

It's not simply its sexual candour, the directness with which people talk and act in and out of bed. Nor is it what the director, Mike Nichols, actually shows of the physical affair between a married woman (Anne Bancroft) and a college boy (Dustin Hoffman). Nudity is in fact more cleverly suggested than illustrated—by the use of flash-by-flash shots of the mistress stripping. What the eye can't focus on, the mind can't take offence at. And the technique wonderfully well expresses the scared boy's alarm without calling down on itself the alarm of the film censor.

But what makes *The Graduate* such a refreshing, stimulating and funny experience lies in the whole conception, not the selected parts. It is scripted, acted and directed largely as an extended satirical sketch for two performers (I don't think it has more than a couple of scenes shared by three people). The tone and tempo of the two principals' beautifully sharp and mutually revealing conversations are not those of real life, but of life being selected and satirised in the manner of night-club cabaret being performed for an audience of sophisticated grown-ups alive to every nuance of the sexual and social comedy.

You'll grasp the secret of the film, taste its peculiarly tart flavour if you remember that before he became a power on Broadway and now in Hollywood, Mike Nichols used to partner Elaine May in precisely this kind of dialogue in cellar revues and on LP discs. Remember, too, that Nichols is a Berliner by birth, and it's in Germany that the art of cellar cabaret flourished before Hitler. He must have carried it over to America in his artistic genes.

No boy, however gauche in real life, would call his mistress 'Mrs Robinson' throughout the entire affair. But this satirical touch is perfectly apposite to cabaret dialogue—and in fact the Bancroft–Hoffman scenes could be played with the lights out (and in one bedroom scene they are!) and still be scathingly funny to the alert ear of film-goers. Of course, they are even funnier with the lights on; for this kind of act calls for a closeness between the players that's almost symbiotic. May and Nichols had it: so have Bancroft and Hoffman.

Bancroft, from the word go, has the in-heat imperiousness of the man-destroying woman with whom Mike Nichols obviously finds some aghast fascination. She's not concerned with love, only sex. The way she orders the affair—almost literally so—is as unforgettable as it's un-American. Her bitch-in-the-manger rage when Hoffman falls for her daughter (Katharine Ross) is magnificent. Under her paw, he seems like some small, struggling puppy. But his very weakness is his strength. He earns sympathy and wins laughter as the awkward innocent, making every false step when he books a hotel room for the affair, uttering odd *whimpers* even when alone and floating in the swimming pool that he uses as an isolation tank from his impossible parents, and interrupting these sessions with libidinous leaps of his imagination on to his mistress. It is not Hoffman's fault that towards the end, Mike Nichols loses control of the film's satiric discipline and it takes a comic header into surrealism with Hoffman turning into someone who looks uneasily like the anarchic misfit played by David Warner in *Morgan, A Suitable Case for Treatment*, and the film sucking up to the teenager audience like an adult condescending to the kids. Hoffman is still funny, but he belongs to another film. I prefer him in his earlier moments as A Suitable Case for Seduction.

Evening Standard, 8 August 1968

Revolutions in the cinema seldom come from the Underground. Andy Warhol hasn't overthrown the main-line cinema, for all the sensation his movies created. One would hardly expect them to do so, given the commercial terms by which the main-line movies live (or die); but it is disquieting not to find even his influence apparent in any of the major film-makers work. The more 'commercial' his partner Paul Morrissey has become, the nearer he has moved to orthodoxy, not subversion; perhaps the Warhol 'Superstars' will feel transcended only when they are accepted on the same footing as the common-or-Hollywood genre of 'Superstars'.

I don't even think all the full-frontals or freakish sexuality demonstrated so flamboyantly in the Warhol movies had very much effect on censorship—though the effect on the police was demonstrated in at least one well-publicised but fatally misguided raid on a London cinema in February 1970, where *Flesh* was being shown. The two co-directors of the place pleaded 'Guilty' to not observing club-cinema regulations and were fined £100 each, a sum Warhol himself settled, and the film eventually got an 'X' Certificate later in the year. But this was the only *cause célèbre* arising out of the Underground, unless one includes the protest made at the end of 1971 in a letter to *The Times* signed by 13 film critics who thought it unfair that Peckinpah's *Straw Dogs* should be certificated and Warhol's *Trash* be refused one. (This is referred to elsewhere.) Nor did the existence of club cinemas in London, where films could be shown without censorship certificates, do much to incite the so-called commercial cinema into the arcane displays that were supposed to be featured for the delectation of club members. The reason was immediately obvious to anyone who, in those days of non-decimal coinage, paid his pound sterling for what he hoped would be his pound of erotic flesh. The two pieces reprinted here catch the atmosphere in London 'arts labs' and 'club cinemas' at a particular moment in time; and for this reason I have included them. But they also illustrate the fact that there is more to be gained from the increasing candour of the commercial cinema, in the sense of opening up areas of human behaviour to inspection, than there ever was from the Warhol vogue or the pitiful erotomania suggested by London's rash of club cinemas in the permissive 1960s.

The old idea of filmgoing was that you looked at the picture on the screen. The new one is to have 'a total experience'—you take in the cinema audience as well. It won't be enough soon for film critics to use their eyes: we must get used to turning our necks. The New Arts Laboratory in Robert Street, NW1, is offering orientation courses in this. They're also showing Andy Warhol's camp Western, *Lonesome Cowboys*. I decided to take in both experiences.

Someone at the box-office shows good psychology and takes 12s. 6d. off me. All my critical impressions of the place sharpen at once. I go upstairs to the 'People Section', which is also called the restaurant. A young man there whose job it is to bring the people and the food into a creative relationship tells me he likes the column I write. So far, a successful evening. Downstairs to the cinema where a screen hangs from the ceiling. A yellow mo-ped is being dismantled in the conversation pit. Two Japanese sit silently together. I hog the remaining chair. Nothing happens for five minutes, then we're told we're in the wrong place. (The trouble with arts labs, I reflect, is that even when nothing happens, you can still mistake it for 'a happening'.) The Japanese and I find the right cinema, roasting hot on one side, dead cold on the other. On *my* side, I am intrigued to observe, I can actually see my breath in the air—the way Huxley used to see rainbows in his trouser creases when he took mescalin. Is this the start of something? I wonder.

The lights are on but a film about unloading cattle from a boat is flickering palely on the screen. Even allowing for an occasional friskiness, it looks tame Warhol. Then the lights go out and I find it wasn't Warhol at all. Warhol is the copulation scene that springs instantly on to the screen. 'On second thoughts,' says the girl in it, 'if I don't do it now, I'll never do it.' She does it. She has a very white bottom that could do with make-up in a film where this feature of the cast soon becomes as familiar as their faces. Andy's boys are on screen now, making like cowpunchers and doing things that frighten the horses. The sound isn't too good. Occasionally one thinks one hears a four-letter word that one thinks one recognises. That's how bad the sound is. But sometimes one can hear a witty line. 'Who's talking about castration?' says someone. 'You've been reading too much Zane Grey.' 'Shall I have a perm?' muses one beautiful badhat while his buddy uses the hitching post for ballet exercise.

Viva, the girl I've already observed, soon comes over as the hit of the film. Everything she says comes in a deadpan twang from Cloud Nine and she looks like a thin, angular Margaret Dumont who is always suffering indignities—usually stripping—from the camp Marx Brothers. 'They're from France,' she says, to excuse them, 'they're voy-yours.' And in a line worthy of Hermione Gingold, she prompts the cowboy who wants to be an altar boy to yield to her seductions with the reminder, 'Would God have left *his* pants on?'

One needs to follow Warhol's casts the way one follows strip-cartoon characters: then a lot of the film becomes funny in an in-joke way. Unfortunately they don't come in such small doses as Peanuts or L'il Abner, but at 100 minutes a stretch of narcotic mumbling and repetitive horseplay. The best place to view the films is in the company of the converted. Even so, as we filed out of the New Arts Laboratory, a young man bawled at us, so as to encourage the waiting queue, 'Were you disturbed, were you *deeply* disturbed?' I'd have had to say no. I'd have said that in fact we were all slightly bored.

Evening Standard, 22 January 1970

POUND OF FLESH/*Blue Movie*

There's one kind of cinema that hardly ever invites the critics to look in and review what's on the screen. Which is very odd. For what's on the screen in London's new rash of cinema clubs is obviously of considerable public interest. For one thing, it is advertised as being 'completely uncensored'. Having occasionally had my eyebrows raised by what goes on today in films that are 'completely censored', I felt a pressing need to investigate a couple of the cinema clubs, spurred to my researches by the recent interest the police took in Andy Warhol's *Flesh*. Did the other clubs, I wondered, have anything that could match *Flesh*, pound for pound?

So first to Cineclub 24, Tottenham Court Road. It was showing *The Secret Sex Lives of Romeo and Juliet*. I put down 6s. for membership—and then I waited 60 minutes. The law apparently requires you to wait 60 minutes before you're eligible to see 'completely uncensored' movies. You must also be 18. And if you've come from overseas to see *The Secret Sex Lives of Romeo and Juliet*, you must put down your passport number. While you wait, an election committee of the club considers your application. 'Do you think I'll be elected?' I asked the lady at the box-office. The lady thought so. I thought so, too. I don't think cinema clubs blackball many candidates. One hour later I put down another 10s. ('first three rows') and became Member 28768. I got in just in time to verify that bald-headed men in macs actually do exist. Then the programme began. At which point I got a surprise almost unequalled by any other I've had in 15 years of professional filmgoing.

The show opened with a documentary on pig breeding. A totally straight-faced, fact-packed advertisement for the Pig Industry Development Authority. It must have lasted over 20 minutes. It told us all, but *all*, about pigs—the white collared peccaries, the black pigs of Vietnam, the ferocious Malayan barbarossa, the gentle Essex saddleback. . . . 'And so to one of five progeny-testing stations,' droned the narrator, John Slater. And so indeed! There we learned that the good pig clears its trough in 20 minutes, that 11 million pigs are born (or was it devoured?) annually, that radar is used to gauge the depth of fat on the pig's back. 'How well do you know your joints?' cried Mr Slater accusingly. The club members, who no doubt had had different cuts and joints in mind when they came in, looked blank and bored. But I'll say this for the film: it was 'completely uncensored'.

It was followed by a nice little 10-minute film in experimental colours about horses. It was made by the National Film Board of Canada and children's matinées would love it. Then came a trailer for Cineclub 24's next presentation, *Rhythm of Love*. And *then* came a trailer for *The Insatiables*. You can see *The Insatiables* at Cineclub 24's across-town cinema, Cinecenta, where you *don't* need to be a member. They don't make an issue of this, though. And then came the work of director A. P. Stootsberry, the one we'd all come to see—*The Secret Sex Lives of Romeo and Juliet*.

It turned out to be a corny parody of *Laugh-In*. I forget how many times they crack the joke about 'beautiful downtown Verona'—six or seven at least. Yes, bosoms are bared and so are buttocks, but not much of the in-between areas. Instead there's heavy reliance on comics who pop up, *Laugh-In* style, with innuendoes like, 'This is going to be a *hard* film to sell, folks,' and two-liners like 'What did Joan of Arc say at the stake?'—'Damn all these faggots.' I am afraid much of the audience seemed let down: it may have been all too American for them.

Down the road next to the Compton Cinema Club in Old Compton Street. And 60 minutes later, poorer by 15s., for six-months membership, and 12s. 6d. for a ticket, transparently disguised as Member 262420, I was admitted to their 'completely uncensored' show. I'd asked in advance if any films about pigs were being shown—you never know, pig-breeders are a pushy lot. The title *Temple of Love* and *Free Love Confidential* seemed reassuring. But the first turned out to be a sober travelogue on 2,000-year-old Hindu temples and their intertwined carvings. As for the main feature, a story of two bored wives who pose for a photographer and then get blackmailed, its free love was kept so confidential that it was not even to be seen. All parties keep their pants on and what's visible is not so fetching anyhow that one misses the rest.

Club films seem to be aimed at the type of person who doesn't know what the ordinary cinema offers nowadays. 'Completely uncensored' is a statement that's factually accurate, but, on the basis of what I saw, sadly disappointing. I don't think the clubs have much to fear from the police. But I think they've everything to fear if film censorship were abolished for the rest of us—for what they'd advertise then in place of the furtive promise of forbidden delights is something I find hard to imagine. Maybe the Pig Industry Development Authority has the answer.

Evening Standard, 5 March 1970

TRIANGLE/*Sunday, Bloody Sunday*

In appearance, John Schlesinger's new film is the opposite of *Midnight Cowboy*. *Sunday, Bloody Sunday* is a London film where the other was a New York one. Mood and nuances are its flavour, not events and climaxes. Yet what links the male hustler of the one film to the sophisticated trio in this one is Schlesinger's view of life as something to bear with rather than manage, to live through and survive rather than dig into and enjoy. How much will you settle for? This has been his theme since his first feature *A Kind of Loving*. The title is reminiscently apt in this case, a triangle story in which only two angles ever meet at any one time.

Penelope Gilliatt's screenplay sets the film in a London that's in a state of change. Society is getting devalued, like the sterling currency in the 'economic crisis' bulletins that filter in by press and radio throughout the film. Some people can hedge their share bets. For the rest, it's hard enough getting through to the values in life without fighting the value of money. As someone says, leafing through a picture-book of Church martyrs, you have to be bludgeoned into feeling anything today. The sheer complexity of life is siphoning the vital energy out of people. It's no accident that the three people in *Sunday*,

Bloody Sunday are forever having to go through the channels of a telephone-answering service, just to maintain contact with each other.

One of them is a doctor played by Peter Finch. He's successful in his practice, but the patients we see him with show us the limitation of medicine in healing the soul. He's Jewish, but he's uprooted himself from his faith, so that the film's *barmitzvah* party at the Café Royal returns him to a nation of strangers. And he's homosexual in his affections—the incompleteness of his life perfectly caught in a home that's silting up with those pricey bric-à-brac that are consolation toys to the lonely. He is also unable to hold his boyfriend, one of those cool young mutants of the hip generation played by Murray Head. A kinetic sculptor, the boy's latest lighted marvel shines like a beacon in the doctor's garden, a sad substitute for the warm body in bed. The scenes between the men are as nonchalant as those between any married couple—the first time I've experienced *this* in a film.

Though fundamentally homo-, the boy is functionally bi-: his other contact is a divorced woman played by Glenda Jackson. Too educated for her own emotional good, it's typical of her that what she took first from her husband's house were the books in the library. ('They left spaces,' he complained: which tells all that's needed about *that* marriage.) She's the kind who has to work to occupy her mind—again, typically, it's work in management consultancy, a job that mends broken careers or fosters ambitions without salving people's pride or enhancing their lives. The metaphor of wrong connections is everywhere in the film. What swings the triangle affair is not sexual jealousy: the man and woman are almost maddeningly well adjusted to sharing the boy. It's the deeper discontent of living—of asking 'What does it all mean?' and, even worse, of crying 'Is this all there is?'

Gradually the two older people have to come to terms with life, with the admission that the 'options' are diminishing. They are stuck with what they have, or have not. The boy, because of his youth, his generation's attitude to living, is the one who can still choose—and he does. 'Be satisfied with what you've got,' says Schlesinger, 'it may be better than nothing at all.' It's a moment that put a catch in my throat when, at the very end of the film, Schlesinger directs the camera of Billy Williams so that it catches a deserted but stoic Finch in such a way that the doctor becomes the patient and talks directly to us the audience. A bold stroke muted by its very touchingness, it succeeds exactly in its intention. A connection has been made at last. Finch and Glenda Jackson give performances you couldn't better: I doubt if *they* ever will, either. Murray Head perhaps lacks the boy's allure to let you know why he's so bisexually appealing: but he's a character of lesser weight, the catalyst who forces a reaction without entering into it. In this aim, he's just right.

The film has a vast variety of moods. Some are infinitely sad, like the slow, opiate feel of the all-night chemist's where addicts wait for their National Health drug fix. Some are hilariously sharp and satirical, like the weekend that heroine and boyfriend spend babysitting for a household of freethinking trendies who have Oxfam posters above a laden fridge, keep pot behind the *Tristan and Isolde* LP and collect peasant rugs and coloured intellectuals in an attempt to get back to basics. Peggy Ashcroft (as the heroine's mother), Maurice Denham (her father), Tony Britton (a sacked executive), Bessie Love (a gimlet-eyed switchboard concierge) and Vivian Pickles and Frank Windsor (the trendies) show Schlesinger's skill at picking only the best for even the smallest parts. Luciana Arrighi's overall design, Norman Dorme's art design, and Harry Cordwell's furnishings extend the characters so solidly into their everyday environment that you can see how each of them will go on living after the film ends. Joseph Janni's superbly detailed production does something more: it catches the insecure, self-questioning essence of the 1970s as acutely as his film *Darling* embodied the mood of aggressive self-advancement back in the 1960s.

Evening Standard, 1 July 1971

One's age and sex do make a difference to the review one writes, though one wishes they didn't. I suppose there are other examples of this truth in the present book that readers will recognise more readily than I, but Schlesinger's film brought it home to me when my highly adulatory review was answered by a shoal of letters and telephone calls from Gay groups—then coming out into the open in London—all taking me to task (seemingly without pre-arrangement) for devaluing the Murray Head character to the status of a catalyst. To be fair to myself, they didn't blame my view as an inaccurate one: they blamed Schlesinger and Penelope Gilliatt for refusing to explore the dilemma more deeply and me for refusing to recognise that the boy was the most 'progressive' character in the film, the only one who could 'make it' with both sexes. As a middle-ageing heterosexual, I had awarded the palm for bravery to the other two. I can see now there's a lot to be said in support of the other view: but we are still waiting for the film that will explore its implications with the insight and sophistication of *Sunday, Bloody Sunday*. Making much the same point some five years later, Robin Wood, a self-acknowledged Gay, remarked that 'at least the audience was being encouraged to feel sympathy for Gays. And just having two men kiss was a breakthrough.'

Joseph Janni added a lugubrious little postscript in 1975 which had nothing to do with sex, but did bear out the opinion I put in the last few lines. Schlesinger, he said, put such value on getting things right—a legacy from his days as a television news-magazine reporter—and over the few days he was shooting the scene between the Glenda Jackson character and her financier father, he would telephone Janni before breakfast and demand fresh supplies of 'facts' about the way the international stock markets were behaving. Janni would go down to the apartment below his where an obliging City broker would feed him facts, figures and forecasts that were then relayed to Schlesinger at the studio to be added to the script in time for the day's first take. Looking back some five years later, when the British economy was flat on its back, Janni lamented that the accuracy of such professional advice had only gone into the dialogue and not been acted on by those who were making the film!

CAVIAR TO THE GENITAL/*Last Tango in Paris*

Although we've never seen a film like *Last Tango in Paris* before, the film industry being what it is—not a creative industry at all, but an imitative one in which only a few creative people are tolerated—we shall certainly be seeing plenty like it in future. That's the first thought I have on paying it a second visit. The second thought is how well it survives, and indeed exceeds, one's reactions which are inevitably directed to seeing the standard content of many a nameless blue movie done here with a concern for what is going on beneath the skin that transcends the material and turns it into irreproachably non-porno-graphic art. And the third thought, which surprises me more than I thought possible, is how funny much of the film is. Genuinely, humanly amusing is the interchange of thoughts, words and relationships between the consenting parties—and also between the people they rub up against in the world outside the Paris apartment where they are locked into their purely physical sex-relationship.

Bertolucci has said he's re-made *Love Story*. More accurately, he's re-made almost any story of Ernest Hemingway's you care to nominate. It's the old Ernest that beats through the Brando–Schneider affair. The very deal they make, to know each other by feel alone, has the flavour of a Hemingway wager. The apartment is the 'great good place' where it all happens, or should happen. Brando playing the American ex-journalist, ex-boxer, ex-globetrotter and ex-flophouse proprietor whose wife has killed herself in the moments before the film opens, is a Hemingway character if ever there was one. 'Look death in the eye,' he tells the girl, 'and only then will you be free.' Which is a Hemingway maxim *par excellence* by a writer who found *his* freedom in just that way, looking down the barrel-eye of a hunting rifle. The dialogue, too, has the randy sand-papered wit of Hemingway which he might have put on paper if he'd lived on into the age of permissive publishing. The fact that Brando keeps his clothes on—save for one brief, softly-lit and totally passive scene—gives him a paternal relation-ship, a kind of 'Papa' status, towards the girl whose trim, unfettered nudity adds to her child-like—dare I say Shirley Temple-like?—ingenuousness. ('Come on the Good Ship Lollipop,' cracks the prone Brando at one point.)

The man's self-hatred, his masochism, that's Hemingway, as well. Resentful of his wife, who's found escape from the world with his 35-cent cut-throat razor, he communicates by self-degradation in the way a Hemingway hero might have likewise over-compensated by going after big game. He tries to get back to base-camp so as to make a fresh start by forcing the girl to humiliate him, or else to suffer his humiliating attacks on her. I think this is why it's a non-erotic film, in the sense of never arousing a cinema audience: there's too much pain going on in the characters for that. It only begins to be a touching film when Brando discovers love, ironically by way of debauchery, and is rejected by the girl who, for her part, has discovered that a liaison with a man is one thing, but a lifetime with him is quite another.

'The tango's a rite,' says Brando. When the dance is finished, the music starts up again. 'Not for me,' says the girl in effect, high-tailing it back to her *fiancé*, a deliciously funny sketch of a callow youth by Jean-Pierre Léaud, a telly director making a pretentious film about 'first love', whose every rose-coloured tint is contradicted by the dark side of the girl's sexual tastes back in the secret flat with Brando.

Brando has brought his co-star up to an acting pitch that works like a perfect duet. The dialogue is as snappy as a Tracy–Hepburn exchange was in *its* day. When the girl mispronounces the word 'whore'—'a leetle waar,' she calls herself—Brando pounces on her error and jestingly plays with it like a kitten with a wool-ball. 'Who are you?' she asks, and slyly, teasingly, he replies, 'If you look real close you'll find me hiding behind my zipper.' Brando is better than I ever remember him. That dimension Norman Mailer detected of autobiography in his monologues—'I've been called by a million names all my life: I'm better off with a grunt or a groan than a name'—adds to the way the man strips layer after layer off himself. Curled on the floor mattress, caught in a pool of that amber, late winter sunshine light with which Bertolucci suffuses his film, the character melts into Brando the way butter melts into its dish—if I dare risk that kind of simile in this kind of film.

What about that now infamous 'butter scene'? The censor's ten-second cut has done nothing to impair it and has only underlined the sheer ludicrous uselessness of a system of film censorship that aims to protect people by 'seconds' and 'inches' from what was in the first place a totally unexploitive scene. Shocking, yes: but wholly justified in terms of context and execution. My final impression is of a film that's audacious, original and unique. What, then, has the controversy over it proved? Several things.

First, that without those of us who defended the film's right to be seen by the public, it might have suffered greater depredations, even total banning. Secondly, that people can now never see it with the fresh eyes of the first encounter, but will be constantly matching its screen reality with the intolerant accusations made against it and its maker. Against this, of course, must be set the numbers who might never have gone to see it at all and now, going perhaps for the wrong reasons, may possibly enjoy it for the right ones. Thirdly, the argument showed the ugly natures of people who want to ban what they have had no acquaintance of themselves—the freedom of the media was extended to bigots who hadn't laid eyes on a frame of the film but nevertheless seized the indulgence they were granted to impugn, decry, abuse and condemn the film, as well as those who made it *and* those critics who *had* taken the trouble to see it. The cinema is today the most vulnerable of the arts. Its freedom is under relentless attack. It's hard to think of another area of human endeavour where basic ignorance, not to say ingrained malice, would be regarded as an exalted quality among the enemies of tolerance forever eager to attack it—as was undoubtedly the case with *Last Tango in Paris*. That's the disquieting thought we carry into the future.

Evening Standard, 15 March 1973

The 'disquiet' proved justified. Barely a year after I'd written this, I was locked into seemingly endless colloquies and briefing sessions with solicitors and lawyers who were defending United Artists Corporation Ltd against a private prosecution launched against Bertolucci's film under the Obscene Publications Act of 1959—the first time action under the Act had been taken against a movie then playing in a public cinema with a censorship certificate. As it turned out, a bold judge at the Old Bailey decided the Act did not apply to films in commercial distribution—or, at least, that conviction would be hard to obtain when the film had only been 'published' to the manager of the cinema that was profitably exhibiting it. So the trial closed almost as soon as it had opened, with no Defence witnesses being called. But it was a revealing experience for me.

What it proved to me was the total futility of trying to pass moral judgments on aesthetic works, and particularly when the visual image was bound to be judged by words on the printed page, i.e., the screenplay that most jurymen and jurists would have had to rely on to refresh their memories and reach their conclusions. As everyone knows who has seen it, the dialogue in *Last Tango in Paris*, while raw and shocking, is also sparse and intermittent: much of it is in French (not a language in which British juries are generally fluent); and, in any case, so much depends on looks, lighting, camera-angles, rhythm and order of shots and so on, in deciding whether an audacious desire is turned into an illuminating insight, or simply remains vulgarly obscene. It would be asking much of lay people to recall the inflection in Brando's voice, the expression on Maria Schneider's face, or the impressionistic dimension added to physical detail: yet all these were demonstrably more to the point in defending *Last Tango in Paris* than the continuity script which would have been the main basis of question, cross-examination and juryroom reference. It is a question we shall have to consider with the utmost seriousness if—as I confidently anticipate— films are shortly brought inside the scope of the Obscene Publications Act in its revised form, which will permit 'expert witnesses' to be called for the defence, allow the work to be considered 'as a whole' for redeeming artistic or social worth, and (one must hope) inhibit private prosecutions of this nature. Short of providing cassettes of the allegedly obscene film and installing videotape playbacks, I cannot see an acceptable solution to the problem of bringing a film to judgment.

Even then, my experiences in this case reinforce my fears that the Law will tend to treat cinema fiction as if it were a matter of legally determinable fact—since the characters of Paul and Jeanne in *Last Tango in Paris* came to seem, even to me, more life-like than the actual film corporation which was the defendant. It was *their* deeds, or misdeeds, that QCs, solicitors and others were discussing well into the late hours of the night at the Inns of Court, as if the couple had actually existed and were even then awaiting trial in some suitable confinement, or preparing to surrender to the court officials and be led into the dock, having already surrendered their passports. We were discussing their sex, love and morality with a hair-splitting thoroughness that may have been welcome in whiling away tedium in medieval courts of love, but which appeared ghastly in the extreme misuse of time and talent when it took place in twentieth-century courts of law. Till my dying day, I shall remember the probing and the quizzing, the supposition and the speculation, surrounding the act of buggery in the film, when Brando compels Schneider to repeat after him a string of denunciations that include the term 'Holy Family'. Wait a moment! Was he speaking in lower-case? Did he merely mean 'holy family', the bourgeois institution of the family regarded as a hallowed part of crippling convention?

It was important to know. If he meant Jesus, Mary and Joseph, then a charge of blasphemy might well be added to the accusation of buggery in which the character stood in peril. Which did I think he meant? Did I? Did I *really*? Was I *sure*? Could I be relied on, under cross-examination, not to waver and weaken and capitulate? After an hour or so's extensive examination in this vein, I was certain that film criticism however poor the haul that the average week brought, was a soft option indeed.

I had a pang of envy, however, at the legalisms employed to describe, in shorthand form, several of the most hotly contentious moments in Bertolucci's film. Some of them seemed so much more *suggestive*, just by virtue of their very euphemistic character, than anything one could possibly be permitted to print in a newspaper film column. The one that stands out in my memory referred to the humiliation that the Brando character seeks when he forces the girl to humiliate him with her specially sharpened finger-nail. 'Digital buggery' was the callous phrase devised to refer to it: my own suggestion of *doigt du seigneur*, offered in an almost hysterical mood of exasperation with the unreality of it all, was judged much too flippant. As it happened, 'digital buggery' later fell into disfavour, since it was judged much too inflammatory to be used by the Defence. We compromised: and the terrible and terrifying moment of truth in the film was henceforth known as 'the bathroom scene'. As the other, even more notorious moment, had already been dubbed by the Press as 'the butter scene', I could only wonder at the awesome way discretion was turning one of the most tragic and humane films of our time into a list of larder provisions and domestic offices.

HABEAS CORPUS

In an earlier *Encounter* article, I referred to the vision of the 'disintegrating man', citing John F. Kennedy's assassination in Dallas as an image that has run through the movies of the last decade with iconographic vividness. But the medical materialism that the cinema added to its view of death hasn't stopped there. It has affected the other bodily functions in ways that, while not so mortal, are probably less mentionable and until fairly recent times were certainly not viewable in the commercial movies. Once you burst open the envelope of skin that contains a man's identity, you are in duty bound to continue your investigation—and goodness knows where you may come out. The memory of Nathanael West's young hero, Balso Snell, springs irresistibly to mind; appropriately enough (in the context of this article) he chose to approach the Trojan Horse of Western civilisation through its posterior opening. Significantly, he was compelled to forget his dignity, and at the end of his intestinal journey found that he had lost much else, too.

What must strike any persistent filmgoer—and here critics are the worst offenders—is the screen's growing involvement with the capacity of man to define himself and his society through his own degradation. The heroic personality has been dismantled years ago—indeed it would have been surprising had it survived all of a piece in an age so violently at war with itself. But the anatomy lesson isn't nearly over yet: in fact, it's hardly begun. Once flesh and blood proved materially and commercially malleable to make a moral point (sometimes, anyhow) involving the slow-motion depiction of bloody slaughter, then other precious bodily essences and fluids are open to inspection and exploitation. They are ones—and they reside in places—that are appropriate to the unheroic postures in which modern man so frequently fixes his identity, on the screen at any rate. All life, it's been said, is a return to the womb. Really? one replies politely, concluding that, if so, then life must have missed the turning, since it is so clearly headed for less salubrious regions of the psyche and physique. The stools of kings used to be examined for the omens they held: in a more democratic age, at least one film has constructed itself with the same material issue in mind, and indeed in view.

The involuted indignity and savagery of much mass entertainment which feeds on the theme of degradation has much in common with Nathanael West's infinitely more rarefied view of mass contamination and individual ineffectualness. One would wager that West, to judge from the films I shall presently examine, is all set for the Great Rediscovery treatment lately lavished on F. Scott Fitzgerald, significantly a contemporary labourer of his on the Hollywood 'dream dump'. Professor Alan Ross, in his introduction to the 1957 edition of West's collected works, found the writer's slightness of reputation at that time not easy to understand, and he put it down to the possibility that West's ruthlessness was 'too near the bone for an American audience with a mass neurosis and a guilty conscience'. He had made society 'undisguisedly repulsive and meaningless'. Well, no one can say that society today is unready, or even unwilling, to have such evidence presented to it for self-recognition. If Scott Fitzgerald wanted to be the historian of the heedless affluence of the kind we have recently been passing through, then Nathanael West clearly appears to be the soothsayer of the desperation that has sprung, with the suddeness of Present Shock, out of the same illusion of security and endless plenty. One wonders what West would have felt, had he been spared his fatal car crash, to see (or even collaborate on, for he would be only in his early 60s today) some of the cinema's visions of disintegration that have extended his own perceptions of what Professor Ross called 'those "X" qualities that, midway between germs and tremors, lurk anonymously, feeding on individual frustration. . . .'

Like *The Dream Life of Balso Snell*, the film *Last Tango in Paris* is a journey through the anatomy of illusion. Though in this case the 'material man' enters a natural landscape of his own neuroses and perversions—'perversions' one should recall here, were once defined as things one hadn't done oneself, yet—at least he enters it, like West's hero, through the anal regions. He confirms the baseness of his own identity in order to exorcise it, and he does so through a couple of fundamentally anal acts that push the moral crisis of the character, played by Marlon Brando, to the outermost limits of physical abasement. Brando is an actor who has done some of his best work along this frontier. The business of being a film star in America is so profoundly dissatisfying that some natures substitute masochism-in-performance for the satisfactions that elude them off-screen. Brando is one of these natures. But appropriately enough, he has had to wait for his first truly European film in order to 'go the whole hog', as his character in *Last Tango* would encourage the compliant flatmate played by Maria Schneider to do. Interestingly, the act of fellatio never figures in the movie. (It's hard to imagine its omission if the film had been a made-in-America production.) It might have connoted the woman's worship of the man's 'maleness', whereas the intention is not to sustain the male's ego, but to vastate him and it—and the moment when he compels the girl to accompany the act of buggery with a stream of associate obscenities surrenders language to the Id with a power of Dada-like intensity.

One recalls that the first edition of West's *Balso Snell* bore Schwitters' manifesto—'Everything The Artist Spits Is Art'—as its epigraph. Bertolucci's emphasis on everything that the genteel viewer might consider obscene could lay him open to the same charge of disdainful mockery as the Dada-ists incurred, were the integrity of his film not so soundly lodged in Brando's performance. In other ways the film has neat Dada-ist allusions—Bertolucci is pre-eminently a literary and painterly talent—and especially in the marvellously imbecile 'clockwork' tango where Brando's impetuous baring of his buttocks on the dance floor is the pure gesture of scandal that the Dada-ists championed. Bertolucci may have directed that moment, but I doubt if he inspired it. Brando's signature is all over the film.

Last Tango in Paris has the character of a voyeuristic autobiography on Brando's part. Not of course in the act—but in the thought. As Norman Mailer has pointed out, all the allusions the character runs through in the extemporised soliloquy when he is lying recumbent beside the girl refer to the multitude of roles that Brando has played in earlier films. But whereas he assumed an identity when he put on the mask of character in those films, in *Last Tango* he strips himself fictionally naked in a way that makes it immaterial whether or not he ought to have laid himself physically naked—a point that seems to have irritated female chauvinists. The aim is the same in word and deed: self-degradation, Brando's view of the world, is summed up when he shows his arse to it.

To understand how deep *Last Tango* goes in its legitimate exploration of man's sense of his own indignity, you have only to compare it with Liliana Cavani's new film *The Night Porter*.

The Night Porter shows that ideas walk—or, in this case, crawl—where the simultaneous appearance of similar themes is concerned. It begins in a semi-grand Viennese hotel, circa 1957, when the night concierge, an ex-SS man played by Dirk Bogarde, is recognised by—and himself recognises—a guest, a former concentration camp inmate played by Charlotte Rampling, whom he had taken pleasure in torturing physically and mentally during the war. In the end they come down to a closed-room relationship reminiscent of *Last Tango* in which the two people push each other to extremes of sado-masochism involving his chaining her to the wash-hand stand lest his ex-Nazi affiliates kidnap her, and her making him walk over broken perfume bottles on his bare feet in the bathroom. The notorious 'butter sequence' from *Last Tango* is echoed in the climactic tussle between the two—by now besieged in his apartment by his cronies—in which Miss Rampling, transfixed by the pains of night starvation, makes a lunge for the remaining jar of strawberry jam, and she and her lover roll over and over, fighting for possession of the spreading stickiness, until, with her assistance, he at last achieves what can only be, given their relative positions, a cathartic ejaculation. After which, all that remains is for him to don his old SS uniform—handily, perhaps thoughtfully, stashed away in the closet—and for both of them to be gunned down on one of those long bridges that *Last Tango* made fashionable for doomed lovers' meetings.

Maybe *The Night Porter* requires a feminist response; some women certainly find it more persuasive than I did; it probably subtly flatters the female resentment of being 'put upon' by the male by pushing it to such extremes. Otherwise, the taste for each partner's perversions is so under explained that one suspects the director felt that listing them, depicting them, and working through them would be sufficient. It is possible, of course, to see it in Jesuit terms, rather than in those of De Sade—'Give me a girl at a tender age and she is mine for life.' But such explanations, sceptical or not, flatter the film's own short-term aims which, I suspect, were to depict a relationship solely in terms of its abnormalities, particularly its physical and bodily aberrations, without really examining it. Where *Last Tango*'s abiding impression is that Bertolucci knew exactly what to leave out, the makers of *The Night Porter* were intent on calculating what to put in. It would be hard to know what could be taken out of Bertolucci's film without harming it irreparably: very easy to guess what could be removed from Cavani's film without anyone missing it, if the law or censorship in any country so insisted.

The same theme of degradation, stripped of any of Bertolucci's compassion, is what animates the current trade in 'pop porn' in the United States; and given time, it would be instructive to study the interchangeability of art and pornography as represented by, say, *Last Tango* as against *Deep Throat*, or *Behind the Green Door*, or *Inside Miss Jones*. I doubt, though, if it will be given time, as the judgment of the U.S. Supreme Court on what constitutes pornography has already been handed down and appeals against the law enforcement officers of the local communities who have the say-so are already beginning to work their way up the judicial system again. Another 18 months or two years seems likely as a limit to the so-called 'permissiveness' that at present shows few signs of abatement in the United States, to judge from the brazen ubiquitousness of the 'pop porn' movies even in what were once the 'best neighbourhoods'. Charles Reich's 'greening' of America would appear to have been indelibly succeeded, for the moment anyhow, by the 'blue-ing' of America. The *Los Angeles Times* applies a tone of its own to the advertisements its pages carry for the 'pussycat' and other theatrical chains where the hard-porn stuff comes to rest, often for many months before the police act, though it is now moving out of town into the drive-ins and motels where one price is made for rooms with movies and another (and higher) one for rooms with movies *and a waterbed*. The newspaper prints the porn advertisements in a lighter shade of type than the legitimate cinemas which retain their jet-black respectability. (Presumably only the masturbators' eyesight is at risk in this perfect compromise between morality and commerce.)

What the porn movies have in common, besides their anatomical freakishness, is the explicitness of sexual ejaculation, now visibly portrayed and indeed regarded as an earnest of authenticity—the trade calls such demonstrations 'come' or sometimes simply 'cum' shots. Where pelvic thrusts and erect members were deemed sufficient only a few years ago, visceral evidence is now wanted as a guarantee that the act is not being simulated. The 'candour' of such shots is frequently lauded by the manufacturers of such movies. All of those I spoke to in a recent visit to Los Angeles deplored the absence of similar candour from *Last Tango*, despite my argument that the mental, not the visceral emphasis in the film ensured it had got its priorities right. (I am bound to say, though, they would have had a point had they reproached *The Night Porter* with similar coyness.)

Such films are more interesting for what they are not than for what they pretend to be. They are not fetishistic, in spite of unrivalled opportunities. They go straight to the act, more or less. Perhaps the almost universal absence of underwear on male and female bodies robs the fetishist impulse of at least one starting point. The major examples in the field are not homosexual, either. The reason seems to be that hard-porn movies are dictated by the audiences' tastes—not *vice versa*—and the audiences for them are generally young, rarely black, mostly married and overwhelmingly heterosexual. (Ironically, this means that overtly homosexual movies suffer less from police interference than those which are believed to have a more disturbing and inflammatory appeal to stable communities.) I have found none of them erotically stimulating in the slightest degree. They only serve to remind us, sadly perhaps, how limited are the number of ways of achieving sexual pleasure: after the umpty-umph repetition of the few standardised if perverse acts, even curiosity droops. (I have observed more interesting variations on the cabin wallpaper of one Asian commercial airline, inspired by the traditional couplings and triplings of indigenously erotic philosophy, than I have ever seen in a movie picture at ground level.) Perhaps what the porn pictures have added, small though it be, is the release of wit in their genre as well as the release of semen. One is grateful for the temporary relief of the gag line (no pun intended) in an otherwise unvarying cartoon of human lasciviousness like *Deep Throat*—for example the latecomer (still no pun intended) who surveys the post-coital sprawl at the orgy and, distinguishing a familiar feature among the participants, asks, 'What's a joint like you doing in a nice girl like this?'

246

The illusion of 'living cartoons' is paradoxically stronger in most of these porn films than any plausible representation of reality. Here again the anatomy is relied on for the exaggeration that must be put into cinematic animation as well as sexual exhibition if the customers' thirst, which is fortunately periodic not satiational, is to be slaked. In the case of Linda Lovelace, the best-known star of the genre, being the heroine of *Deep Throat*, the exaggeration consists of a misplaced clitoris which isn't sited in the usual position, but somewhat south of her epiglottis, so that for poor Linda to find fulfilment as a woman, so the argument runs, the sex act must be oral. This is not just a tawdry excuse for depicting fellatio—though it is that, *too*—but a necessary variation on an act that's now so commonplace in publicly exhibited movies that it has only a residual medical interest—namely in the state of 'unnatural' relaxation required by Miss Lovelace's larynx in this case in order to obviate 'gagging'.

More and more the functions of the body are standing in for the performance of the sex act that was once supposed to represent the breath-taking ultimate in cinema. As the porn movies trade upwards—a reaction to the legal situation threatening them from the body politic as it comes slowly and indignantly into conflict with the body phallic—the commercial movies (or, rather, the 'legitimate' cinema, since porn is highly 'commercial') are steadily plumbing new areas of the bowels and intestines to define *their* attitude to life and maybe hit new riches.

La Grande Bouffe (or *Blow-Out* as it is titled in Britain) postulates its view of man entirely on the breaking point of his bladder and bowels. It is the non-sexual functions of the four male friends slowly gorging themselves to death in a Paris mansion which dominate Marco Ferreri's film. Where food was used as a means of lubrication in *Last Tango*, it here becomes an instrument of self-immolation. After a rough passage at a Cannes Film Festival press conference in 1973, Ferreri has become notably more reticent about speaking of the 'meaning' of his film. But he claimed then, and I see no reason to improve on his claim now, that the gourmandising is an allegory of bloated Western capitalism, contrasted with the ascetic Marxist (or, more probably, Maoist) East, represented by an Oriental visitor who offers the guests a flask of quick poison to save themselves the trouble of a slow death by gluttony. It need only be observed that as allegories go, this is a banal one; and Ferreri's degree of imaginative dexterity is no match for what is really required, namely the horrible deftness of a Luis Bunuel. Ferreri is a man, to use his own metaphor, who ties a bib round his neck and calls for elbow room as he squares up to what's on his plate.

Although sex takes place between and even during courses, the accent of interest is not put on 'Come and spend it', but on 'Come and get it'. Constipation, not fornication, is what affronts the eye. (Predictably, the women guests at the feast hold out better than the men.) As the men sink into pools of their own excrement, expire in hurricanes of farting, or grope their way through the fall-out from an overloaded lavatory, the view of man in society, defining his role in the system, obstinately refuses to refine itself out of Ferreri's point-blank view of four guzzlers. One critic has perceptively recognised the resemblances between the plot's ingredients and De Sade's *120 Days in Sodom*— food being substituted for humanity and the indignities being inflicted on it rather than practised upon each other. But the overpowering feeling of *La Grande Bouffe* isn't the exploration of every kind of sexual experience, which De Sade details, so much as the harping upon one type of very infantile gratification. All the men to some degree revert to infantilism. Marcello Mastroianni attempts to insinuate the manifold of his Bugatti (sic) sports car into his mistress the way small children often embarrassingly fiddle with unfamiliar toys. Philippe Noiret's judge appears to have a housekeeper who indulges his need to be breast-fed and he collapses at the end to a proffered pair of warm human breasts after failing to make any headway with the simulacra in pink blancmange. Even the Michel Piccoli character, embarrassed by his convulsive anal detonations, attributes his shame to the childhood admonitions of his mother. In short, the competitive cramming of food into tummies, the fixation with dirt, the flushing and the farting, all recall the polymorphous perversions that Freud detected into the infant child. The outrage in *La Grande Bouffe* isn't inflicted on a compliant girl, but on the domestic larder; yet the oral gratifications are remarkably similar and it is this aspect of that film that is sensed and resented by people who otherwise see it simply in terms of vulgarity and indecency. It reminds me of Maurice Sendak's infinitely superior fable of Mickey, the little boy who got baked in batter ('Stir it! Scrape it! Make it! Bake it!') and was almost popped into the oven until he escaped in the nick of time to fetch some nourishing milk 'so we can have cake in the morn'. The oral eroticism is more artfully—and artistically—sublimated in the Sendak illustrations, but *La Grande Bouffe* might appositely be re-titled *In the Night Kitchen*.

It can only be a matter of time before this trend reaches its logical conclusion. Indeed I am not sure if it hasn't done so already. Bodily functions—urinating, vomiting—play a large part in the shock values of *The Exorcist*. The Devil had previously only sought a tenancy in the womb, as in *Rosemary's Baby*. How predictable and inevitable that evil should now be manifested through the less mentionable orifices of the human body. But we still await the film on cannibalism which Polanski seemed to be bracing himself to give us a few years ago in *Donner Pass*, a project about pioneers entombed in winter snows and forced to eat each other in order to survive. He has still to get round to it. Meanwhile *Soylent Green*, an underrated film as far as the accuracy of its prophecies goes, has constructed a world, increasingly like our own in the present apocalyptic energy crisis, in which cadavers are briskly recycled into 'people's pabulum'—an idea that Nathanael West would have relished for its neat reversal of the Christian belief that bread becomes the Host in the mouths of the faithful. In this case, the faithful become the bread.

'The Body and Its Uses' is a title we might give to the increasing materialism of a cinema that has little or no faith in the spiritual and is increasingly feeling the exhaustion of its own sexual permissiveness. A feeling of collapse is emerging even here as more and more *outré* stimuli are applied to audiences to evoke a response from them. Maybe the screwing down again of sexual taboos by legal censorship in various lands is needed to invigorate audiences who have been jaded by the turbulent permissiveness of recent years: compulsive opposition to such measures as those lately proposed in the Cinematograph and Indecent Displays Bill, for instance, is better than phlegmatic *ennui* at having 'seen it all'. Even so, the metaphor which art makes for society has a baleful significance as one watches the exhaustion or perversion of so many of man's physical functions. The logical end of it all is his reduction to be merely a function of someone else's direction; and even here the cinema has given us the distant early warning in the movie *Westworld* which postulates a parallel and man-made universe within our own into which tired mortals can escape, like holiday-makers on a package tour, to refresh themselves with artificially created sex and violence. 'Westworld' in the film is architecturally built along the most traditional lines of Hollywood Westerns, though of course the title lends itself to being interpreted as *the* 'Western World' in the geo-political sense. Its inhabitants are programmed robots, androids of impeccably human appearance, except that they tend to have computerised vision, on whom the last indignities of flesh and blood may be inflicted by the visiting humans with the comforting knowledge that such programmed automata can't fight back. Apart from their computerised, non-lethal natures they have all the bodily functions, including the sexual, that humans have; and if mortally injured in a gun battle, or by an impulsive human rapist, a spell on the lab bench while scientists repair their audio-animatronic innards puts them to rights again, ready for the next day's fray. Man's splendid capacities for transcending and reproducing himself have thus been shrunk into a console-controlled world of transmission systems and *doppelgangers*.

The theme of a society in which people are manipulated for other people's gratifications and rewards is a reversal of the microcosmic world of *Last Tango* where two people made a compact to explore themselves for their own physical satisfactions: but the one follows from the other. As *Westworld* discovers, however, no system is perfect. Just as carnal knowledge ironically promoted real love in *Last Tango*, so a flaw in the system frustrates the manipulative perfection of *Westworld*'s set-up. At this point at least obsession with the self gives way to necessarily enforced concern for the surrounding world: which is some kind of comfort.

It is more than can be said for most of these films. With the dazzling exception of *Last Tango*—the only one to have got the mutual exploration of mind and matter in revealing and nourishing adjustment— what they represent, indeed what they flaunt, is an increasingly opportunistic displacement of interest from human relationships to bodily functions, from intangible emotions to the all-too-physically present viscera and fluids and tissues. We are given a vast amount of information about the characters' innards, but a decreasing amount about their inner lives. The truth is that in most of the cases I have mentioned they have none. Which is why their conduct in films like *The Night Porter* and *La Grande Bouffe* and *Deep Throat* throws us back on ambiguities, narrative obscurities and sheer guesswork which don't seem to be so much the intention of the filmmakers as the consequences of their lack of concern for the psychology as opposed to the physiology of their films. In overtly porn pieces like *Deep Throat*, etc., this is probably all that is to be expected; for, after all, porn has historically turned human beings into sex objects. But the example is an infectious one today, when the screen can show almost anything it likes before the local DA and the police move in on it—and even then afterwards, too. What we are increasingly discovering is that even in the 'big commercial' picture, the characters are merely the functions of physical organisms and therefore without much sense of mystery. The spiritual interest of *The Exorcist*, say, has become simply a minor dimension of the film's major metamorphosis of the child's body.

In this and other films, one is even deprived of the satisfaction that comes from the primacy of the senses. For the senses are no longer the prime movers of events. They are acted upon, rather than acting upon. They are residual to the reflexes. They are mere appendages to the much flashier things that the anatomy can get up to on its own. The people in such films are akin to 'Action Dolls', those internationally popular simulacra of human beings whose powers of plastic mimetism primarily enable them to do the things that human beings do, and do them particularly well. At first it was merely smiling and crying and squeaking; then voices were added; then the sexes were specifically identified by the addition of their respective organs; and now the accent has been well and truly put on simulating the functions of urinating and even defecating. Now the 'Dolls' excel in areas of intentional or involuntary behaviour that most human beings would prefer not to acknowledge publicly, or, at least, socially. The screen simply shows us larger sizes of 'Dolls' in action. The body is given a licence to do its own things—and the waste products of the body have become the prime material of the drama.

Encounter, May 1974

Index

McKern, Leo, 61
McLuhan, Marshall, 213
McQueen, Steve, 169
Mechanic, The, 164–5, 177
Mele, Fino, 94
Melvin, Murray, 82, 123
Mercer, David, 193
'Method' style, 4
Metro–Goldyn–Mayer Co., 3, 96, 127, 129, 130, 142
Meyer, Russ, 62, 63
Michener, Charles, 172
Middlemas, Frank, 123
Midnight Cowboy, 233
Mikael, Ludmilla, 33
Miles, Sarah, 47, 52, 60, 190, 195–6
Milland, Ray, 104
Miller, Jason, 87
Miller, Jonathan, 38, 155
Mills, Sir John, 61
Milton, John, 138; Works, *Paradise Lost*, 138q.
Minnelli, Liza, 114
Miranda, Carmen, 101
Misfits, The, 31
Mishima, Yukio, 175
Missouri Breaks, The, 178
Mitchell, John, 115, 118
Mitchum, Robert, 60
Mitford, Nancy, 18, 21–2: Works, *The Changeling*, 18q.; *Count Your Blessings*, 21q.
Moby Dick, 31
Monroe, Marilyn, 3
Montague, Lee, 28
Montand, Yves, 19
Morant, Richard, 65
More, Henry, 73
Moreau, Jeanne, 215–16
Morgan, A Suitable Case for Treatment, 103, 228
Morgenstern, Joseph, 158
Morocco, 56
Morrissey, Paul, 160, 162, 229
Mortimer, Caroline, 58
Moses, 71
Mother Joan of the Angels, 83
Moulin Rouge, 31
Mr. Deeds Goes to Town, 187
Murdoch, Iris, 10; Works, *Flight from the Enchanter*, 10q.
Murphy, Stephen, 159–60
Mutiny on the Bounty, 26, 130, 183–4
Myra Breckinridge, 62

Nabokov, Vladimir, 35; Works, *Laughter in the Dark*, 35q.
Neame, Ronald, 35
Negulesco, Jean, 18, 21
Neville, John, 28
New Arts Laboratory, 230–1
Newman, David, 156
Newman, Joanne, 121

Newman, Nanette, 29
Newman, Paul, 4, 121
Newsweek, 172
Nichols, Mike, 178, 226–7
Nicholson, Jack, 96, 97, 169, 176, 178–81
Nickelodeon, 131
Night Flight, 113
Night Moves, 154
Night Porter, The 42, 244–6, 250
Night They Raided Minsky's, The, 47, 50–1
Night Watch, 65–7
Nightingale, Howard, 120
Nine Hours to Rama, 5
Niven, David, 20, 203
Nixon, Richard M., 38, 114–16, 117–19, 206
Noiret, Philippe, 248
Nolan, Lloyd, 110
Notte, La (The Night), 94
Nova, 211
Now Voyager, 192
Nureyev, Rudolf, 131

Oates, Warren, 100
O'Brien, Edna, 101
Obscene Publications Act, 239–40
Occult: interest in, 81; spread of, 78
Oedipus Rex, 113
Olivier, Baron, 25, 51
O, Lucky Man!, 107, 108–10
Oman, Julia Trevelyan, 35
Omen, The, 80
On the Waterfront, 98,183
Once Upon a Time in the West, 177
Ondricek, Miroslav, 109
One-Eyed Jacks, 183
One Flew Over the Cuckoo's Nest, 189
O'Neal, Ryan, 103–4, 105, 122
One Hundred and Twenty (120) *Days in Sodom*, 248
Orsini, Umberto, 94
Orton, Stanley, 40
O'Sullivan, Arthur, 122
Outlaw Josey Wales, 188

Pacino, Al, 143, 145, 164, 169
Pakula, Alan J., 118, 153, 173
Palestine Liberation Organisation, 193
Paper Chase, The, 151
Parallax View, The 153
Paramount Pictures Corporation, 119, 164
Parker, Charles, 83
Parker, Dorothy, 192
Parker, Suzy, 21
Parks, Gordon, 142
Parsons, Estelle, 99
Pasolini, Pier Paolo, 74–5
Pearson, John, 40
Peau Douce, La, 47, 48–9
Peck, Gregory, 11, 80
Peckinpah, Sam, 31, 100, 157–8, 160–2, 229
Penn, Arthur, 99, 154, 156–7
Penthouse, 211
Peppard, George, 224